Macromedia **Flash MX** MAY 2005

Kristian Besley
Hoss Gifford
Todd Marks
Brian Monnone

friendsof

DESIGNER TO DESIGNER™

Flash MX Video

© 2002 friends of ED

First printed June 2002

Trademark Acknowledgements

Published by **friends of ED**
30 – 32 Lincoln Road, Olton, Birmingham,
B27 6PA, UK.

Printed in USA.

ISBN 1-903450-85-3

Flash MX Video

Credits

Authors
Kristian Besley
Hoss Gifford
Todd Marks
Brian Monnone

Technical Reviewers
Steve Parker
Leon Cych
Todd S. Darling
Vibha Roy
Michael Walston

Proof Reader
Pam Brand

Managing Editor
Ben Huczek

Commissioning Editor
Matthew Knight

Technical Editors
Jon Bounds
Gavin Wray

Author Agent
Chris Matterface

Project Manager
Simon Brand

Graphic Editors
Matt Clark
Katy Freer
Chantal Hepworth
Deb Murray

Indexer
Fiona Murray

Cover Design
Jon Bounds
Katy Freer

Kristian Besley   www.graphci.com

Kristian Besley was born in Wales, grew up in the same street as Catherine Zeta Jones, and read Media Arts following interests in film and design. In his little spare time, you'll most likely find him creating random stuff which will eventually appear online at graphci or somewhere else, or laughing at personalised number plates. One day he vows to reform seminal band Ken.

Special thanks to Mark Rees and Adrian Davies for music stuff; Richard Collins - the inspirational archipelago; Cath and Pete for equipment, Ben for processor-time; and Matt the imagineer..

Contrary to the screenshots in his chapters, Kristian Besley uses only hardware branded with the Apple logo.

RIP Freshfroot.com and Pilipala.co.uk.

Music credits
Dance tracks by and © Adrian Davies (ade@deedesigns.com). www.deedesigns.com
"Shooting Star" and "No...We Won" by Ch'p Run Roadkill. © Mark Rees. www.tarmark.com
"Records Back" by The Groundnuts & Independents. © The Groundnuts & Independents.
"Show Your Colours" and "Dunno" by Nozzle. Copyright 2000-2001 Koncrete Kite Records, p. Townhill Music 2000-2001. www.mp3.com/nozzle

Footage
BMX footage shot at Backyard Jam (www.backyardjam.com) at the Telford International Centre, UK. Special thanks to Seventies (www.seventies.co.uk).

Hoss Gifford   www.h69.net

Hoss was the founder of agency Flammable Jam back in the summer of 2000, and is also curator of his personal site www.h69.net. He regularly sponges his way around the world, getting free flights in exchange for talking at new media seminars. His inspirations include the number 69, Paul Daniels and Ron Jeremy. Hoss is passionate about the abstraction and simplification of process, allowing creativity to blossom in the absence of clutter. Don't worry if that sounds a bit pretentious – he also reckons we should all take this stuff a bit less seriously, and be happy with making 'quite nice things that entertain people for a wee while'.

Todd Marks

In 2000 Todd moved from teaching Mathematics and Computer Science in the public sector to VP of Research and Development at digitalorganism (www.digitalorganism.com). Since then Todd has worked extensively with ActionScript, PHP, Lingo, and numerous other development languages, placing cutting edge code in projects including digitalorganism's showcase site. With Todd's contributions, digitalorganism has received three Flash Film Festival nominations, Macromedia Site of the Day, and two Addy Awards, He also helped start the digitalorganism's educational site, www.doeducate.com.Todd is a Macromedia Certified Subject Matter Expert, a doeducate instructor, and has been a technical editor, contributor and author for several books about Flash.

Brian Monnone   www.monnone.com

Brian is the Senior Multimedia Producer for Tocquigny Advertising in Austin, Texas. He has been computing for over 17 years and has found himself doing what he loves to do, "making really cool stuff". Brian works on projects with AMD, Dell, HP, USAA and a host of other companies creating Flash content, websites, video, and other types of multimedia for them. Brian has won awards for his works and accolades for his personal site. He finds inspiration for his work and plenty to do with his wife and children nestled in the hills. He enjoys his job and couldn't think of anything else he would rather do professionally than multimedia design.

Welcome

Let's make movies! Interactive movies, totally integrated into your Flash interface! With Macromedia Flash MX you have the power to import digital video and sound, and manipulate them just like any other media object. That's a whole world of design possibilities, whether you intend to output on the Internet, on CD-ROM, or just make a bizarre video toy to play around with on your own machine.

This book hopes to take you through all you'll need to know about producing such wonderful toys. The first section will give you a thorough grounding in how best to import your video and sound into Flash and the many different ways that you can manipulate it once it's in there. Then, in the second section, we'll go through a complete real-world case study from pre-production on the video to final output on the web and CD-ROM. Finally, we'll delve into the murky world of advanced ActionScripting, and create a fully object-orientated sound and video playing Flash component.

But we're really getting ahead of ourselves, there are a few things that you'll need to know to get the most from this book.

Code and video downloads

There is a wealth of code, video, and sound support files available for this book. They aren't essential to use this book to the full, as everything in the book can be built from scratch using your own MPGs, MOVs, and your own mouse-clicking, ActionScripting fingers. But, if you'd like to see exactly what the authors have done, or use exactly the same clips as they have, then they are organized by chapter at www.friendsofED.com/flashmxvideo.

By the way, if you haven't yet got your dirty paws on Macromedia Flash MX you can download a fully-functional 30-day trial from www.macromedia.com.

Layout conventions

We want this book to be as clear and easy to use as possible, so we've introduced a number of layout styles that we've used throughout.

- We'll use different styles to emphasize things that appear on the screen, KEYSTROKES OR SHORTCUTS and also hyperlinks.

- If we introduce a new **important term** then these will be in bold.

> *If there's something you shouldn't miss, it will be highlighted like this! When you see the bubble, pay attention!*

- When we want you to click on a menu, and then through subsequent sub-menus we will tell you like so: File > Import . This would translate to:

- If there's something you should type in then it'll be 'in single quotes'.

- If there's a practical exercise for you to follow then it'll be headed

Like this, in a bubble

1. Then the steps that you have to follow will be numbered.

2. Follow them through, checking the screenshots and diagrams for more hints.

   Further explanation of the steps may appear indented like so.

3. When you get to the end, you can stop.

Support – we're here to help

All books from friends of ED aim to be easy to follow and error-free. However, if you do run into problems, don't hesitate to get in touch – our support is fast, friendly, and free.

You can reach us at support@friendsofED.com, quoting the last four digits of the ISBN in the subject of the e-mail (that's 0853), and even if our dedicated support team are unable to solve your problem immediately, your queries will be passed onto the people who put the book together, the editors and authors, to solve. All foED authors help with the support on their books, and will either directly mail people with answers, or (more usually) send their response to an editor to pass on.

We'd love to hear from you, even if it's just to request future books, ask about friends of ED, or tell us how much you loved *Macromedia Flash MX Video!*

> *To tell us a bit about yourself and make comments about the book, why not fill out the reply card at the back and send it to us!*

If your enquiry concerns an issue not directly concerned with book content, then the best place for these types of questions is our message board lists at http://friendsofed.infopop.net/2/OpenTopic. Here, you'll find a variety of designers talking about what they do, who should be able to provide some ideas and solutions.

For news, more books, sample chapters, downloads, author interviews and more, send your browser to www.friendsofED.com. To take a look at the brand new friends of ED Flash MX bookshelf from which this book comes, take a look at www.flashmxlibrary.com.

section 1
Core Concepts

Introducing Video

What we'll cover in this chapter:

- *A variety of current applications of video on the web.*

- *Current technology's **limits** on delivering video content across the web.*

- *How **embedding video** using Macromedia Flash MX can break these limits.*

- *Examples of how **video**, **interactivity**, and **vector graphics** can be combined creatively using Macromedia Flash MX to produce stunning web experiences.*

This book doesn't just aim to show you the dry technical details of how to use video with Macromedia Flash MX; it aims to illustrate some of the creative possibilities opened up by the inclusion of support for video in Flash MX. In short, we hope to inspire and explain in equal measure.

This means that before we jump into the practicalities of using video with Flash MX, we're going to take a quick step back and ask ourselves what video is used for on the web at the moment. People have been proclaiming the emergence of video on the web for a while now, so we need to understand where it has been successful, what's holding it back, and how Flash MX offers some answers to these problems.

What is video currently used for on the web?

Video is used on the web in a number of different areas at the moment. We're going to take a quick look at its main uses: music promos, movie trailers, product displays, educational content, and television/webcasts.

Music promos

Since the MTV boom, the promotional music video has become as important as the actual single itself. Millions of dollars are spent on making a promo that receives more airplay than the next single, hoping to guarantee a greater volume of sales.

This has forced directors to incorporate much more into the videos to make them stand out. A recent trend is the elongated promo video, where narrative and dance sections are added to the start, middle, and/or end sections of the promo. The video for Daft Punk's *Da Funk*, for example, includes sections where the music completely cuts out and returns from a ghetto blaster. It's becoming harder and harder to be innovative, and directors are continuing to borrow techniques from other areas in order to try and create something fresh.

Pop videos have successfully proven their suitability for television, but how do they translate onto the web? Well, every major artist has a web site where the emphasis is on giving as much to the consumer as possible, and the promo video can form an essential part of this. An online promo video can both reward the devoted fan with some content, and show the potential new fans much more than simple static images of their heroes in mid-air power-chord riffage (not to say that you can't use these as well, though...). For prime examples of promo video use, take a look at www.mtv.com/music/video.

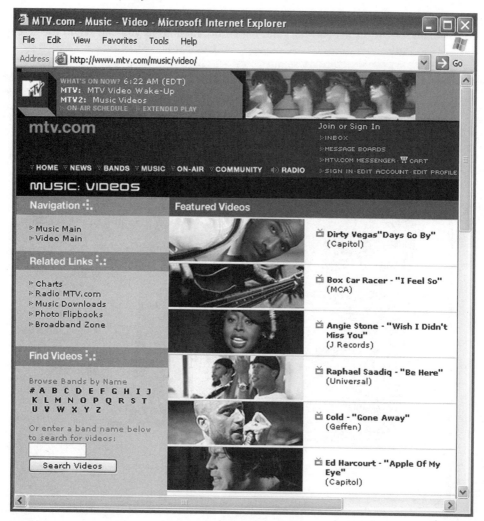

Movie trailers

When a movie is being marketed, a number of trailers are created specifically for use with the different media available. An example is the promotional material for *Star Wars Episode II: Attack of the Clones*, where there are a total of four completely different trailers! Usually, the cinema trailer is a lengthy affair, while the trailers made for television are trimmed down in length. The trailers released on the web are usually of greater substance than the TV versions, allowing the web user a degree of selective control before parting with their money at the box office.

The QuickTime site (www.apple.com/quicktime) is a success because it contains a large number of trailers, and also because it takes the user's bandwidth into consideration when streaming them. The different trailers are defined by the physical size and quality of the video.

For example, the trailer for the film *Amelie* is available in three different bandwidth categories (low – up to 56k; medium – ISDN, cable, and DSL; and high – broadband) as you can see in the screenshot:

Product display

Advertising on television has become a commonplace intrusion to the movie premiere and other television programs. Streamed broadcasts on the web (such as that provided by Real Networks) have recently started to include 10-15 second advertisements breaking up the broadcasts.

However, displaying a product doesn't always have to be straight advertising. In certain cases, video can help to show a product's dimensions and can open up a whole environment, tasks that are often limited by still images. The hardware gallery on www.apple.com takes a different approach to displaying an item, giving the user the ability to rotate around and zoom in to the product at impossible angles.

This capability gives an incredible sense of scale and context to the products, as you can see here with Apple's PowerBook G4:

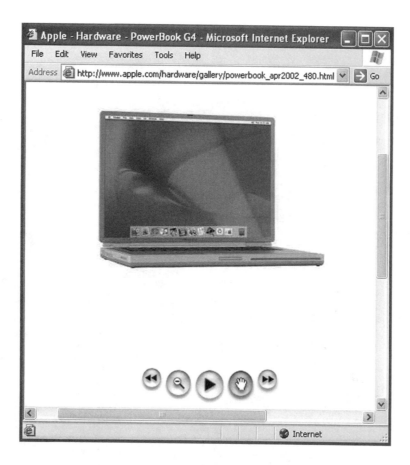

Educational

Video on the web is often used as a medium for learning, in a variety of formats – from recorded video to 3D animations. Away from the classroom, video is obviously a fantastic educational tool, keeping kids stimulated and subconsciously educated.

Educational content on the web doesn't stop at the primary school level. Video has long been used as a visual aid for scientific ideas and is an essential part of sites such as NASA's Glenn Research Center (http://microgravity.grc.nasa.gov), where it is used to demonstrate complex theories in the most efficient way. Try explaining how particles move in Brownian motion without a video aid!

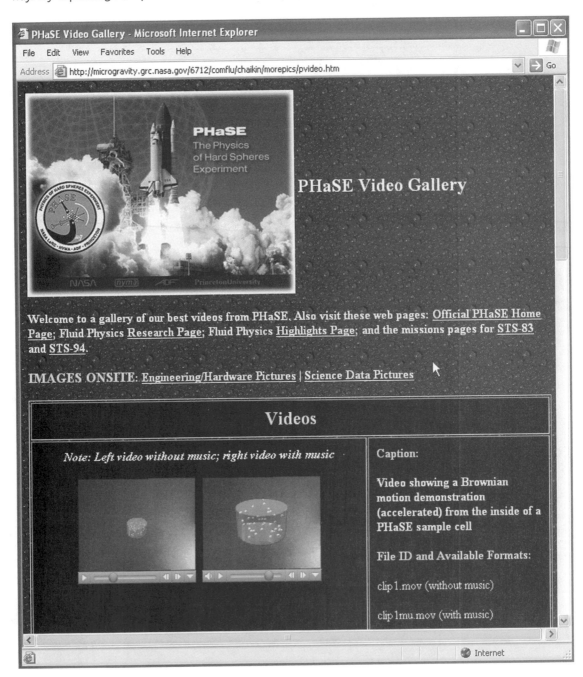

Television and webcasts

Seeing as you may still have trouble programming the VCR, wouldn't it be good if you could watch missed TV programs online? Well, it probably won't surprise you to discover that watching a television program on the web is already a reality. Many TV programs are specially prepared for the web, and are broadcast using streaming applications such as the RealOne Player and QuickTime.

www.bbc.co.uk is a good example of a site that allows the user to view certain television content on demand:

The content is streamed and takes the user's bandwidth into consideration before displaying it. Even though this sounds appealing, the broadcast is sometimes physically small on screen, and can be of very low quality on slower connections.

It is also now common to webcast events. Live music concerts, significant world events, conference keynotes, and demonstrations are broadcast live on the web or pre-recorded for future webcasts.

These webcasts are intended for those people who aren't able to physically attend the events (and which may be invitation only).

The bad news: why the WWW is not the new TV

For many years now, the idea that the web will become closer and closer to television has been promised. So, why hasn't video and multimedia taken off on the web?

Not enough users have broadband web connections

Broadband connections allow over 512kbps (kilobytes per second) loading speeds in comparison to the common modem speed of 56kbps. Even though broadband technology has been available since 1995, the take-up of the technology has not been as fast as expected in most areas of the world. The UK is a prime example of this fact – in the US, 22% of all web users have broadband connections, compared to a meager 5% in the UK.

It's worth knowing that certain demographic bands are more likely to have broadband connections than others (companies and business institutions, for instance) so, if you have done your research properly, you can justify designing for a broadband audience in certain circumstances. Sites such as www.bmwfilms.com have clearly done their homework...

The average Mac or PC isn't powerful enough

Many desktop machines aren't powerful enough to run high-quality, high frame rate video, or highly compressed video files. File compression is the process of squeezing a file so that it becomes smaller in file size and is therefore quicker to download. Certain forms of compression require more work from the processor than others in order to display video content. So, if the user's hardware is unable to keep up with the compressed video, frames will be skipped making the video play back jerkily.

You may well think that this is a considerable problem. If we assume that the user has a modem connecting at 56kbps, then we can also assume that they haven't got the fastest computer on the market. Compressing clips to make them small enough to download might also make the video clip harder to display on their low spec machine.

There are no easy answers to this problem, but machines are gradually increasing in power – the minimum specs for the Flash Player 6 are Win 95/NT or Mac OS 8.6. Well-used compression options can do a lot to help, as can loading solutions. Supplying different options for different connection speeds, as with the *Amelie* trailer we talked about earlier, is also a good idea.

There isn't a standard delivery method

Video content on the web is usually served up through one of the main plug-ins: QuickTime, RealOne Player, or Windows Media Player. Each has their pros and cons (refer to the appendix on video plug-ins for more details), but each plug-in fundamentally provides the same service by delivering video content across the web to the user from the user's browser.

QuickTime is installed as standard on a Mac and Windows Media Player as standard on a PC running Windows, but there is no standard cross-platform installation. So, it's simply not possible to assume that a large proportion of your audience have the correct plug-in, whichever one you use.

The good news: why Flash MX has the answer

If you're learning Flash for the first time with the MX version, then you're pretty lucky. The ability to embed video in Flash MX has taken away the pain and skill needed to incorporate video in previous versions of Flash.

That said, a few top Flash designers used previous versions to create some great Flash pieces, such as Brendan Dawes' renowned application that lets you edit the famous shower scene from Hitchcock's *Pyscho* (you can find it at www.saulbass.net/psychostudio):

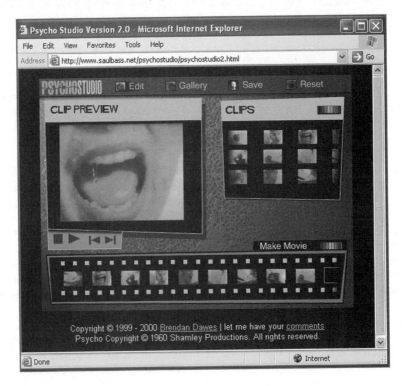

We've said that the ability to embed video straight into Flash saves a lot of the pain that people went through previously but that's not what matters, is it? What are the people who view the fruits of our long and painful web design labors going to notice?

A widespread video plug-in at last

Because the Flash Player can provide the web site and video content in one complete package, the user is also saved a potential plug-in download from any of the other players (RealOne, QuickTime, and Windows Media). It may seem a small fact, but it's a very important one: the Flash Player 6 is a considerably smaller download (400k for the PC, and around 800k for the Mac) than any of the dedicated video players mentioned above – RealOne Player weighs in at a 8.52MB download, for example.

According to Macromedia's own statistics, the Flash Player is widely distributed, with 98.3% of all online users (totaling 436 million worldwide) possessing a version. At the last count (taken in March 2002), approximately 90% of all online users had up to and including version 5 of the player. These figures alone suggest that Flash is now a giant on the web. When compared with statistics for the three main video players, it is obvious that Flash is the most popular and widely distributed browser plug-in available today. In other words, people are more likely to see web video provided via the Flash Player than in any other form.

The other problem that Flash MX overcomes is the issue of video and web page integration, because Flash embeds video directly into the SWF file. Therefore, it enables easy integration, unlike the clunky business of starting up RealOne or Windows Media Player every time you want to view video content. This may not sound significant, but it enhances the user experience immensely. The average user doesn't want to worry about conflicting player technologies or pop-up windows; information should be served up to them in the easiest way possible and Flash MX allows this to happen.

A better solution to dealing with file size and processor constraints

If you're still not convinced by Flash's new video capabilities, then remember why the application is already well known – vector graphics and interactivity. Flash MX enables you to create multimedia environments and interfaces, combining kbs-heavy video and ultra-light vector graphics. It also heralds a new medium on the web where both media converge, enabling interactivity and multi-layered media composition.

Combining different elements not only offers new creative possibilities, but also offers new ways to address file size and processor constraints: if you're only showing video some of the time, then you can optimize other movie elements around this to work with bandwidth constraints.

The days of static media on the web are numbered. With Flash MX you can now create a TV program that waits for you before proceeding, or video that allows you to take the narrative in a number of different ways based on the user's decisions. The only limit is your imagination!

The inclusion of video with Flash MX also opens up a few other avenues, and we're going to take a quick look at three of these before we finish.

Animation

If you've never had the pleasure (and some of the pain) of using a 16mm or Cine/Super 8 camera, then don't start thinking about doing it now! As much as working with film is a truly fantastic and physical experience, being cooped up alone editing in a dark room with no windows for four days is not!

So what has all this got to do with Flash and the web? All film and analog content has to be digitized first in order to appear on the web, and because there are still a huge number of stop-frame animators working with film, it has to be converted to a file suitable for the web (such as a MOV or MPEG) before it can be shown. Hotwired Animation Express (www.animationexpress.com) is one site with many digitized animations alongside Shockwave and Flash movies:

The great thing about Flash MX is that, because it can import this digitized content, you can also animate over it within the Flash authoring environment, so that remake of *Who Framed Roger Rabbit?* is achievable at last!

Educational

Flash MX enables us to include interactive elements along with our videos, so it's a perfect application for authoring online learning aids. Flash is now able to create complete CD-ROMs, so you don't always have to use Director to embed video anymore. Flash has the added bonus of being able to create projector files for both platforms without having to own a separate copy of the application for each platform, as you do with Director.

Movie

Flash 5 has already provided some refreshingly creative takes on movie promotion. Take a look at the web sites for the movies *Requiem For A Dream* (www.requiemforadream.com) or *American Beauty* (www.dreamworks.com/ab/) shown here:

Besides being embedded within a Flash movie and easily integrated into a web site, trailers or movies can now be interactive in Flash. You could let the user choose the ending, or you could make a *Timecodesque* split screen movie and only play the sound from the user selected pane at that time – giving the user a totally non-linear experience where interaction is as important as the narrative. Flash could also make quick work of multi-lingual subtitles, storing the information in variables or a database and laying them over the main movie.

Conclusion

Macromedia Flash MX is now the real deal, a multimedia application capable of embedding video content. As you can see from this chapter, video is already rife on the web, and Flash can be used to deliver it in a much better way. It gives the web designer the ability to work on multimedia web site design, without worrying about pop-up windows, plug-in and cross-platform issues, or other external factors. Embedded video in Flash MX allows the user to sit back and enjoy the content without the hassle of plug-in downloads and disorientating redirections. We're both happy!

If that's not enough, just think about the creative possibilities brought to us by Flash MX. Unlike standard web video players, Flash MX can do more than just serve up video content in isolation. Throughout the book, we'll be looking at some of the ways that you can imaginatively use video content in Flash MX. We'll also be learning some practical skills: how to create compact Flash and video movies; how to cater for different audiences and bandwidths; how to work with and manipulate video frames; how to import Flash videos on demand; and much more.

As you'll have worked out by now, this book is organized into three sections. Part 1 will teach you the skills you need to harness the potential of video in Flash MX with the help of some cool examples. Part 2 will take you through a real-life case study to show you the inside line on developing a Flash MX video project from start to finish. Then, Part 3 will delve into some of the more advanced video techniques opened up by the power of ActionScript, showing you how to build a fully customizable video and sound player component:

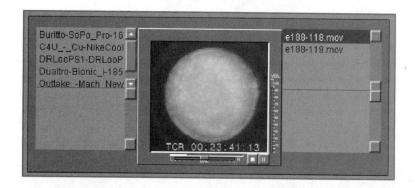

We'll start by introducing you to video editing using some (free) applications available for both Mac and PC platforms in the next chapter. Hi ho and away...

Editing Video for Flash

What we'll cover in this chapter:

- **Capturing** video onto your hard drive

- **Editing** clips in **Movie Maker** and **iMovie**

- **Exporting** your video ready for Flash MX

Before we dive into Flash, we need some video content to use there. You could try saving your video, taking it straight into Flash, and working out which bits of it you want to use there, but I wouldn't recommend that – Flash isn't designed for this, and it's an easy way to create extra work for yourself and land yourself with a Flash file size bigger than you want.

The alternative is to use an editing program of some kind to prepare your video. Now, you're probably quite scared of these editing programs – there are some powerful, expensive, and complex editing programs (like Premiere, Final Cut Pro, or Avid) out there, with entire books devoted to them. You may already know something about these, or you may want to go and take a look at them when you've finished the book, but the truth is that what we need to do here isn't that complex at all. In this chapter, we're going to use the simple, and – more importantly – free editing packages that come as standard with Windows XP and Mac OS.

For the benefit of both platforms we've included a separate tutorial for each of the relevant editing applications – Movie Maker for Windows XP and iMovie 2 for Macintosh. We don't usually recommend skipping exercises, but here we recommend that you choose the exercise for your platform of choice and ignore the other one. In both cases, the process that we'll show you goes something like this:

The footage that I've used for this chapter was recorded on miniDV format at an indoor, street style BMX competition in the UK. I turned up at the competition with no tripod, no idea of layout, and only a little idea of what would actually be on show. I'd not normally recommend this, but you can't plan everything all of the time!

Before we start, a quick bit of background.

Non-linear editing

If you've ever had the pleasure of editing on an analog system, then the non-linear approach to video will come as a welcome surprise. Unlike analog editing, video arranged in **non-linear editing** is not automatically written to tape or rendered.

With analog video systems, video is copied from the source tape (or master) to the destination tape, and new segments are added to the end of the tape. This means that adding an extra segment anywhere but at the end of the tape requires a lot of horsing around, and some time to re-edit.

Non-linear systems enable video content to be stored on a hard drive in digital form and the order of the final edit changed by simply moving clips around in the timeline. Once the order of the final edit is determined, it can be rendered to tape or disk. Because the order of the edit can be changed at any time, it gives great flexibility for easily changing a section later on in the project.

Not only have non-linear editing (or NLE for short) applications made editing easier, but applications like Final Cut Pro and Premiere have allowed people to make movies without having to hire huge editing rigs at enormous cost. Now anyone with a DV camera and a computer can make a movie.

FireWire and DV

The creation of Apple's **FireWire** technology (also known as IEEE-1394, iLink, and DV In/Out!) has added to more successes outside the studios. FireWire is a port that allows 400Mb/s of digital transfer, making it suitable for capturing high-quality digital video at a steady rate.

Before FireWire and DV, video needed to be converted from analog videotape formats such as VHS, to digital via a capture card. Not only is DV considerably higher quality, but there are many annoying problems with digitizing analog video – frequently dropped signals during conversion for example.

The DV format is high quality, robust, and unlike film, is suitable for any conditions because it is so manageable (no more crews and metal tins!). This is all without even mentioning that you can edit straight with it, and you don't need to get it developed to view the rushes.

Before we start working, a little bit on something generic to all editing applications: transitions.

Transitions

A transition is a visual crossover between two clips, as opposed to a straight cut from one shot to the next. Let's see how they look in a simple example compared to a straight edit:

Imagine that we have two 1.5-second clips in a straight cut. We have spliced them both together so that our edit looks something like this (each frame represents 1/2 a second of video):

1   2   3   A   B   C

... the whole sequence lasts 3 seconds, the first clip plays, and then the second clip plays.

Here's the same edit with a cross dissolve transition – where the opacity of the first clip is lowering, whilst the second clip is becoming more pronounced:

1   2   3
        A   B   C

Because both clips are overlaid, the second sequence is shorter than the first (two rather than three seconds in total), but shifts the focus over nicely by fading the second clip in slowly.

Transitions can break up a predictable straight cut, but shouldn't be used unless you are creating a particular effect. For example, a number of slow transitions between country landscapes can create a mood, atmosphere, and thoughtfulness that straight cuts just can't match.

You can also use transitions to cover up some blemishes here and there. In my BMX edit, I had a clip that just wouldn't participate as a straight edit – the flying biker I was following with the camera, went out of my view because someone was standing in the way!

Here's a segment of the original clip (this segment lasts just over 3 seconds):

As you can see, midway through someone turned out the lights and I missed the landing... arrrgghhh!

Because I liked the first half of this clip before the dreaded darkness sets in, I decided to use it. Unfortunately, cutting this clip mid-air didn't work that well, so I decided to use a transition to ease into the next clip.

The result is viewable as `dissolve.mov` or as part of the final edit, `bmx_stylee.mov` (or `bmx_stylee.avi` for Windows).

Both of our basic applications allow you to add transitions, and it's time to get stuck in. We'll start with Movie Maker – Mac readers can skip a fair few pages until they reach the 'iMovie for the Mac' heading.

> *By the way, I'm using a PAL system, hence the 25fps you might see in the exercises. Note that NTSC systems run at 30fps. This doesn't make any difference to the exercises, but it might when we come to working with Flash – but we'll cover that when we come to it in the next chapter.*

Movie Maker for Windows XP

Movie Maker is a basic non-linear editing application that comes installed with Windows XP. Advanced users may find it a little limited, but it contains all of the essential components required to import, manage, edit, and export a mini movie.

If you have a DV camera then you can select or film some footage to use, but don't worry if you haven't – Movie Maker allows us to work with many Windows video formats.

Starting up

The traditional location for Movie Maker is in **Start > Program Files > Movie Maker**. If you cannot locate it, install it from the XP System disk before we begin.

Once you have it installed, open the application and we will begin. You'll be presented with a window looking like this:

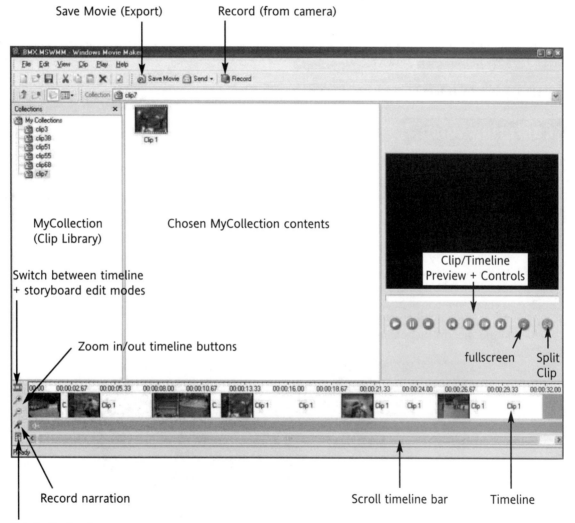

As you can see, there's not too many elements to grapple with – the emphasis here is to allow an easy and potentially rapid working environment. Rather than go through all of these options out of context, I'll explain what you need to use as we go through this exercise.

Movie Maker works with a number of key elements – the clip library, the timeline, and the preview pane. The clip library is a store for all of the media used in a project, and clips are pulled from it into the timeline – the edited sequence. The preview pane is used to review clips and the edit created in the main timeline.

There are a couple of ways to bring video into Movie Maker:

- Capturing video from a source: this involves plugging in a video or DV camera, and bringing the footage from it onto your computer's hard drive.

- Importing a file: this simply involves locating a video file on your hard drive, and bringing it into your Movie Maker project.

Let's take a look at these options and bring in some content to play around with.

Capturing video

Capturing video through FireWire into Movie Maker couldn't be much easier. Due to FireWire having the ability to control DV cameras, all reviewing and cueing of footage can be controlled from your PC. If you haven't got a camera and are simply going to use some video footage that you already have saved, then you *can* skip to the next exercise, but this isn't going to take long, and you might need to know how to do it one day...

1.   Switch your DV camera on, insert a tape with the footage you want, and plug the FireWire lead from your camera into your PC's FireWire port.

2.   If your camera is all hooked up, click on the Record button in the toolbar or choose File > Record.

3.   In the window that opens, click on the play button:

The gentle whirring that ensues means that your PC is controlling the camera and is prompting it to play our DV tape. If nothing tangible appears in the **preview pane**, then there are a number of possible reasons for this. The main causes are:

- The camera has not been recognized by Windows XP. Check the top left of the window to see if it has found it.

- The tape has come to an end or has run out of footage. In this eventuality Movie Maker will behave pretty strangely, sometimes showing gibberish in the preview pane and other times refusing to do anything. Click on the rewind button to send the tape back a little before attempting to play again.

4. If all has gone well and you are watching footage of, well, whatever..., cue the tape to some footage that looks good (or, at least, can show to others without shame) and pause it there.

Movie Maker has a number of different import options:

- **Record**: Allows you to specify the tracks for import – Video and Audio, Video only, or Audio only. Stripping out any unwanted elements at this early stage will save you some work later.

- **Change Device...**: If you have a number of input devices recognized by Movie Maker, then you can specify which to import from here. This is only relevant to those with more than one camera or device on their system – a webcam and video capture card, for example.

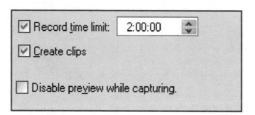

- **Record time limit**: This allows you to place a limit on the length of import. This might be useful if you are working on a project where all of your clips need to be the same length, or if you have to import a large amount of video and pop off to work on something else while you're waiting. (Movie Maker has a neat way of showing you how much video your hard drive can store at the bottom left of this window.)

- **Create clips**: This setting allows you a little control over how Movie Maker works with the DV camera during import. If this is switched on, Movie Maker will make a new clip each time it gets a signal from the camera. A signal could be a cut in recording sessions, an error or a mark placed on the video by the camera. If this isn't ticked, Movie Maker will ignore all of these factors and record one big clip.

- **Disable preview while capturing**: Ticking this will allow your PC more processor power when importing the clip, which will help minimize the possibility of skipped frames. The video will stop playing but the sound will continue, giving you an idea of how far the video has gone and helping you know when to halt it.

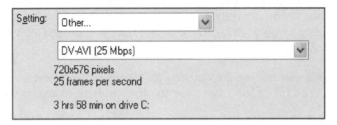

- **Setting**: This allows you to specify the import quality when the clips are captured. The top drop-down menu has four options: Low, Medium, High and Other. The first three of these are presets, whilst the Other option allows you to create a custom setting.

In most cases, I would recommend importing at the best possible quality and choosing a setting with no compression on the sound or video. The simple reason for this is that footage should be kept in pristine condition while you are working with it – it's only when you come to export video that you should think about compressing it.

In the above screenshot, and for my video, I used the Microsoft DV-AVI setting as I was importing from a DV camera. This setting keeps the quality as near to tape format as possible.

The number expressed in the brackets (25 Mbps in the screenshot) is the speed required to capture the format efficiently. As we mentioned earlier, because FireWire passes 400Mbps, you are not likely to lose or skip any frames. If you are using a slower capture system – such as a webcam through USB, you might need to choose a lower setting if you lose frames during import.

Importing a file

Even though Movie Maker allows you to capture video, the chances are that you will find yourself using footage from elsewhere now and again – off your hard drive, the web, e-mail or enhanced CDs for example. Movie Maker also allows you to import audio and image files. These could be a pre-recorded soundtrack for your movie, or images for a title sequence.

Files are imported into Movie Maker with **File > Import**. Movie Maker is able to import the following file types:

When a file is selected and imported, it is placed in the **My Collections** clip library:

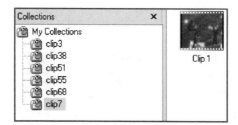

From here, the clip can be dragged into the timeline, previewed, or just admired. Clips saved in the My Collections folder are permanently stored there, meaning that you can make a library of movie clips.

Even if you have captured some video, let's see how importing works in practice.

1. Search your hard drive for some video clips, or download the clips for this chapter from the friends of ED web site.

2. Once you have found some, choose File > Import, locate the required clips and select them. To choose a number of clips, hold down the CTRL key when selecting them. Try and select 4 or 5 clips if possible to give you something to work with.

3. Once you have selected your clip or clips to import, press Import. The clips will now appear in the My Collections library. When a collection is clicked on in this pane, the clip(s) will appear in the central pane on screen.

4. Once you are happy with your clips, save the project (File > Save Project) somewhere safe and we'll proceed to get on with some editing.

Working with the clip library

There are a few things that we can do to our clips before bringing them into the edit to make our job a little easier. Movie Maker lets you split and combine clips.

Splitting a clip into two

When you have a clip that has two key areas of interest, it's best managed as two clips. Doing this is simple: click on a clip in the library, move the playhead in the preview pane to the split point, and click on the Split Clip button.

When you do this, you'll then have two clips in the library with similar names:

Clip 1   Clip 1 (1)

Easy. Now, you've gone and split the clip accidentally, how do you stick the parts back together?

Combining a number of clips

Select the clips that you wish to combine and right-click to get the context-menu, select Combine from the menu, and you're done.

Both methods allow you to manage your clips a little and make our next step a little easier.

Editing modes in Movie Maker

Editing in Movie Maker is mainly controlled by the simple drag 'n' drop process that you're all used to from a thousand other Windows operations. A clip is picked up in the clip pane and dropped in place.

The actual arrangement and ordering of clips in Movie Maker comes in two flavors – timeline and storyboard. Even though they are vastly different, they are both incredibly useful for your Movie Maker workflow. You can switch between the two modes at any time during your project, using the switch to the top left of the timeline:

Storyboard mode

Storyboard mode enables you to layout clips in order of their chronological position – the movie will run in order from left to right.

Storyboard mode is great for getting a quick edit together with no fuss. It's a simple case of dragging and dropping the clips from the clip pane, releasing them into the film frames below, and then pressing play to see if the sequence fits.

This mode comes unstuck when it comes to precisely treating, trimming and timing clips. This is where timeline mode comes to the rescue.

Timeline mode

This mode allows far more precise editing than is available in storyboard mode, allowing you to trim clips, add some basic transitions, and to have control over the timing of the project. Timeline mode is a little more complex to look at, but that's only because of the way that the length of a clip is displayed:

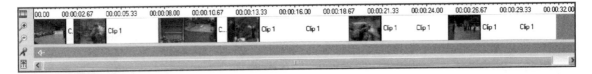

As with storyboard mode, clips are dropped on the timeline. Movie Maker will show a little intelligence when it comes to dropping a clip and will offer to place it before or after another clip in the timeline. The timeline positions of the clips can then be fine tuned by dragging them around in the timeline area. The zoom buttons are useful here, as they will enable you to fine tune your editing and transitions.

Timeline mode also allows us to trim our clips a little by moving the start and end points of the clips and also allows us to add some basic transitions.

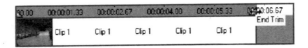

Now that we've had a look at both modes, let's get some editing done (at last).

Arranging our clips

At this stage you should have a number of clips ready to work with, and create our masterpiece. We should also have a clean timeline – if not, click on the clips there, and press the delete key to erase them.

What we're going to do is to use four or five clips to make a quick edit. Don't worry too much about the potential order of the clips – the emphasis here is on working with Movie Maker. If your clips work in a narrative manner, then you won't have to think too much about their order anyway.

1.   Select your first clip from the clip library and the My Collections pane.

2.   Set the editing mode to storyboard mode, and drag a clip from the library into the first frame of the storyboard, as shown on the next page:

3. Return to the clip library, and drag another clip down to the storyboard. Drag it into position next to the previous clip and you should see a marker appear indicating where it will be placed:

4. Drag a few more clips from the library until you have five or so clips in a sequence:

So far, we've been working blind, but now we'll get to see how our sequence looks. It's worth pointing out that there is no limit to the amount that you can preview your movie, and there's no time delay before preview, it's an instant thing.

5. Select Play > Play Entire Storyboard / Timeline to preview the movie. You will now see a preview of the storyboard sequence, probably a little imperfect, but not to worry – we'll tidy it up in a moment.

The chances are that the current sequence (especially if you used clips from many different sources) is badly paced as a whole, and the individual clips need trimming. If you have sound on your clips you will also find that it emphasizes the hurried and unplanned nature of your first movie. You can blame me if you like!

Unfortunately, Movie Maker is a little limited when it comes to detaching sound from video clips. For now, you'll just have to put up with this until you can kill the sound during export in the next chapter... if it helps, try unplugging your speakers!

6. So what do we have at the moment? We have five or so clips in a loose order in the storyboard. Let's change the order a little. Change to storyboard mode and then click and drag the first clip in the storyboard past the last clip and release it.

Our first segment is now our final segment. Neat huh? This just shows us how easy non-linear editing applications are, and how their flexibility can save us a lot of hassle. Now preview the movie and you'll still notice those small bits that need trimming and shortening.

7.   Switch into timeline mode. Here, we'll trim the clips a little and add some transitions to break up the straight cut monotony.

> *When you are working in Movie Maker you are able to switch between the two modes at any time – and there is no penalty for doing this.*

8.   Decide on which of the clips needs a trim and select it in the timeline.

9.   Place the cursor to the far right-hand side of the clip and up high with the time signifier. The cursor should change into a double-headed arrow, suggesting that you can increase or decrease the length of the clip:

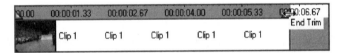

10.   Click and drag the double-headed arrow. As you do this, you'll notice that the preview pane shows you the point that you've moved the trimming playhead to.

11.   Select an end trim point and a start trim point. Movie Maker will then shift up the other clips around the trimmed clip so that there are no gaps. Shortened clips also show the full length of the clip in the time signifier bar when selected. Look for the five o'clock shadow – the gray bar that comes up in the timeline:

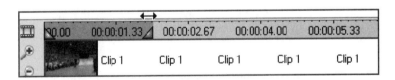

> *If you want to reset the length of a clip automatically, select it in the timeline and choose* Clip > Clear Trim Points.

12.   Go ahead and trim/rearrange your clips. Don't be scared to leave a little extra at the start or end of them, as we'll add some transitions in a moment and can use these extra bits. Preview the movie and keep your eye on the edits. Make some mental notes of places where there could be extra trimming or the edit could benefit from a transition.

13. Now we'll add the basic cross dissolve transition to any places that require it. To add a cross dissolve transition, simply click and drag one clip to the left in the timeline (remember that transitions occur at the end of one clip and the start of the next) so that it overlaps another clip:

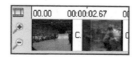

Remember to use the zoom here to be a little more precise with the timing of the transition, and when you are finished, preview your movie to see how the cross dissolve looks.

14. Finish editing the movie, using transitions and trimming where necessary.

If you think you are done, press the **Fullscreen** button to view it. If you want to add some titles to your project, remember that you can import image files into Movie Maker and use them.

Exporting

When you're happy with your movie, we can export it.

1. Click on Save Movie in the toolbar. You'll get the following dialog:

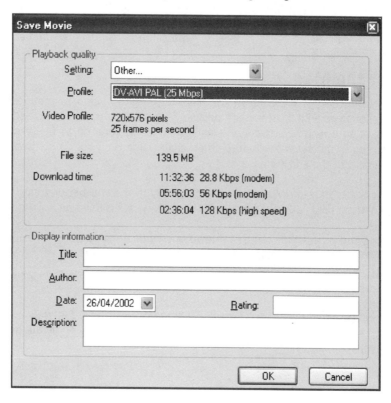

As we saw when we imported a file, Movie Maker gives us a number of standard settings and a custom setting labeled Other. Movie Maker also helpfully gives you an idea of how big the exported movie will be, and how long it will take to download on a few different bandwidths.

If we were intending our exported content to be used in Flash, I would suggest that you export at the best possible quality (as shown in the screenshot), but we'll export our movie at the medium preset so we can show it off to others this time.

2. Change the Setting to Medium using the drop-down menu. You'll notice that the physical (pixel) size of the movie has been reduced and the file size is a little smaller than before.

3. Before exporting we can place a watermark on this movie, so that people know that you made it. This is usually done if a movie is to be distributed or placed on the web. Fill in the info boxes in the Display information section to do this.

4. Now click on OK and sit back for a moment while the movie is exported.

5. Once it has finished, you'll be prompted to view it. Click OK and enjoy all your hard (or not so hard) work.

And that's it for Movie Maker. If you play with the application, there are a couple of extra bits that we've not covered here, but we've covered the majority of it. You are now a Movie Maker master and have the power to create some web classics. The rest of this chapter is taken up showing you how to do pretty much the same with iMovie for the Mac, so – unless you want to experience a strange feeling of déjà vu, and throw away your fierce platform loyalty – you can now skip to the summary, and the next chapter.

iMovie for the Mac

Since the introduction of FireWire on the Mac, the desktop video revolution has really taken off and iMovie has a lot to do with it. As you are probably aware, iMovie was the first editing application to come free as part of an operating system, and since then it has gone on to be used by design professionals, pupils, and used in the occasional competition challenging Hollywood directors to see a project through from the camera to the edit suite.

A little after the release of iMovie came iMovie 2. With it came better transitions, titles, digital effects (coloring, contrast, etc.), speed control, and the novelty reverse clip direction!

To be current, and to show off some of iMovie's new functionality we will be using iMovie 2, but most of the actual editing we will be doing will be applicable to iMovie if that's what you are using.

Starting up

If you are running a Classic OS, then iMovie 2 is traditionally installed in your Macintosh HD. For those of you running Mac OS X, you'll find iMovie in Macintosh HD > Applications folder. If you have an uninstalled copy, go ahead and install it now before we begin.

If you are all ready, open iMovie 2 and you'll be presented with this:

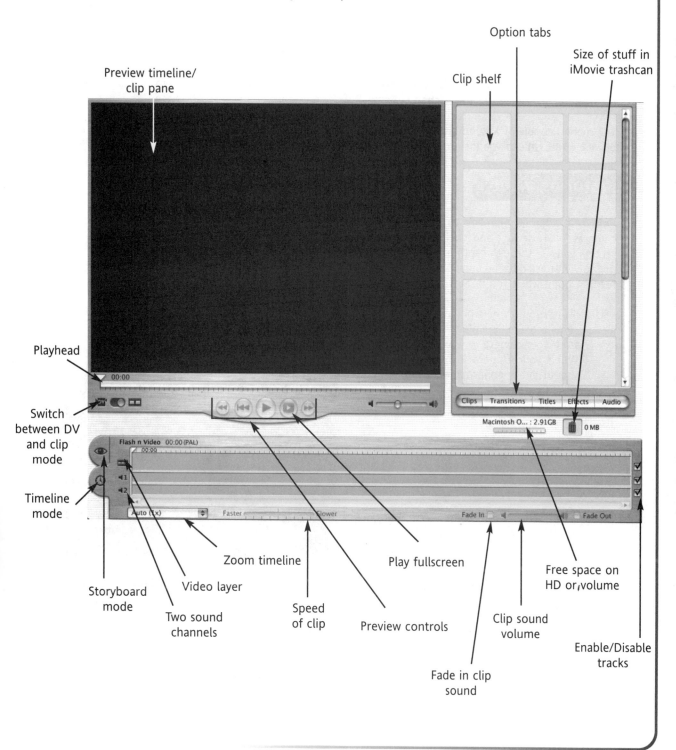

Option tabs

Size of stuff in iMovie trashcan

Clip shelf

Preview timeline/ clip pane

Playhead

Switch between DV and clip mode

Timeline mode

Storyboard mode

Video layer

Two sound channels

Zoom timeline

Speed of clip

Play fullscreen

Preview controls

Free space on HD or volume

Clip sound volume

Enable/Disable tracks

Fade in clip sound

The interface might look a little bewildering right now, but later on it will seem like the easiest application that you've had the pleasure to use! Rather than go through all of these options out of context, I'll explain them as we go through this exercise – that way, you can see them being used at the same time as finding out what they do.

iMovie is a drag and drop application that can be used for a speedy edit, or for something a little more advanced. We won't go through all of iMovie's options, but we will be able to manipulate content comfortably by the end of this section.

There are a couple of ways to bring video into iMovie – capturing video from a source, or importing a DV or image file. Let's take a look at these options and bring in some content to play around with.

Capturing video

Capturing video through FireWire into iMovie is amazingly easy. As FireWire has the ability to control DV cameras, all reviewing and cueing of footage can be controlled from your Mac through iMovie. This section will run through capturing some footage from a DV camera. If you haven't got one of these, you might want to skip to the import section below... or you might want to stick around and see what happens for that point when you do finally get your hands on a DV camera.

1. Switch your camera on, insert a tape with some footage, and plug the FireWire lead from your camera to your FireWire port. When your camera is hooked up, you should get a confirmation from iMovie like this:

    If not, check that the switch at the bottom left of the preview pane is set to DV – the camera icon. If you've checked this and still don't get anywhere, check your FireWire connection at both ends, and make sure that the camera is on and set to VCR mode, ready to review footage.

2. Once you have the confirmation, press play below the preview pane. The gentle whirring that follows means that your Mac is controlling the camera and is prompting it to play your DV tape. If nothing tangible appears in the preview pane, then the likelihood is that the tape has run out of footage. In this case, click on the rewind button to send the tape back a little before attempting to play it again. Those of you running versions of Mac OS older than OS9 might also want to search http://kbase.info.apple.com for the latest Firewire extensions.

> *If you want to record some live footage from your camera, switch it to record mode (sometimes known as camera mode), and smile!*

3. Importing into iMovie is easy – just press the massive Import button below the preview pane. So, when you find a piece of footage you like, press the Import button just before it begins. iMovie will then begin to import the video into a clip in the clip pane on the right of the screen. The time of the clip will grow as you continue importing.

4. To stop importing, click the Import button again. You will now have a clip in the clip shelf:

> *By default, if iMovie senses a new recording session on your tape, it will create a new clip in the clip pane and continue importing.*

Believe it or not – that's it for capturing with iMovie!

Importing into iMovie

If you don't have a DV camera, then you have a bit of a problem with iMovie as it can only import DV video files, and isn't able to import MOV, MPEG, or any traditional QuickTime supported formats. Here is a partial list of the formats that iMovie does support:

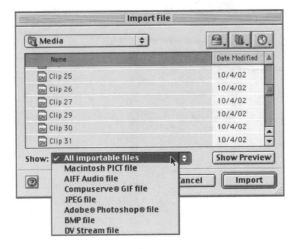

iMovie will also import certain other types of files, such as MP3s. This means that the full import capabilities of iMovie are not shown in this list. If you are unsure about whether a certain file format is supported, give it a try. There are ways around the limited import options. If you are working exclusively from found files, then you can just use DV files.

You can also convert files to DV format first. This will involve a small investment in QuickTime Pro. QuickTime Pro comes as part of the QuickTime plug-in and player installation (a version of which comes pre-installed on all Macs), and needs to be unlocked with a registration number purchased from Apple. It is priced at $29.99 at the time of printing.

> *If you would like to know more about QT Pro, DVision from friends of ED have released Revolutionary QuickTime Pro 5 & 6 (ISBN: 1903450527), which goes into detail about its considerable potential.*

QuickTime Pro can then act as a conversion utility between file formats, and is able to export in DV format, enabling you to import video files in all of the QuickTime supported formats and send files out in an iMovie friendly format. It is a worthy addition to your DV toolkit.

Here, we're just going to use some DV files that come with iMovie.

1.   iMovie comes with a tutorial project inventively called iMovie Tutorial, which is located in the iMovie application folder. Choose File > Import, navigate to the tutorial folder and find the Media folder within it.

2.   Even though the files in this folder do not have the DV extension, they are all DV files. Use SHIFT-select to select the six files and click Import. The files will then be placed in the clip panel on the right.

The six DV files in the tutorial are fairly long clips of two kids washing their very hairy dog in a tub on the drive. Even though the subject matter might not be to your taste, the clips are long, of high quality, and the sound is very clear – perfect footage for experimentation.

Working with clips

Now that we have some clips to work with, let's prepare them before editing... no, stop right there. Always name your clips! It might seem like an extra thing to do right now, but you will appreciate it if you're working with a lot of clips, or just when you return to your project files after a while away. You can rename a clip by clicking on its name in the library and typing over the original name.

This BMX project was a perfect example of the former – I had 71 imported clips to work with. The first thing I did was to categorize all the clips by the following criteria:

■   Location – e.g. halfpipe, quarterpipe, floor, rail

■   Action/Type – e.g. fall, air, lineup, jump, static camera

Of course, some of the clips of don't play by my rules and can be filed under a number of categories, but the concept is pretty tight and it makes working a lot quicker. I sorted the clips by these criteria because the video should be paced and diverse, and these labels help me to edit quicker and concentrate on composition, rather than hunting for a static clip or a moving clip or whatever. After naming the clips, I then bunched some of these clips together where possible and moved them to the bottom when they had been used.

After that diversion, let's get down to preparing our clips for editing.

1. Click on a clip in the clip pane. This will take iMovie into clip mode (if it was previously in DV capture mode), and will show the imported clip in the preview pane:

From the preview pane you can do a number of things:

■   Play / review the clip.

■   Play the clip full-screen.

■   Trim the clip.

The last of these is the most important as it enables us to cut off the fat, and leave only the tasty and lean bits. Let's give it a go.

2. Get an approximate idea of how you would like to trim your clip using the review buttons, and place the cursor where you would like start the trimming. To advance frame by frame, use the arrow keys on your keyboard.

3. Place the cursor just below the preview pane timeline, hold down the mouse button, and drag. You'll notice that two white arrows appear and that the timeline between the two arrows has turned yellow. This indicates a selection:

The time of the selection is indicated above the selection, as you can see.

4. Click and drag the white arrows to the correct start and end points for your trim.

5. Now select Edit > Crop to crop the clip to the selected area. You'll notice that your clip is shorter in the clip pane. If you view it in the preview window, it only shows the trimmed content.

> *A word of warning here – because iMovie is working with our imported clips, it is always a good idea to keep a back up of the originals. The best way to do this is to make a duplicate of the project folder, but this is not always an option if your project is too big. Another way to keep originals is to make a copy of the clips in iMovie. This is done by holding down the OPTION/ALT key and dragging a new copy of the clip out from the original.*

Besides this standard trimming, there is another way to manage our clips – by splitting them into two. Let's see how this works before starting our edit.

6. Select one of the clips in the clip pane. The clips content will now appear in the preview pane.

7. In the preview pane, move the playhead to the required split point.

8. Select Edit > Split Video Clip at Playhead, and our single clip is now two clips in the clip pane with similar names for easy reference:

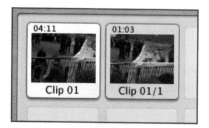

> *If you ever want to restore a clip back to its original state past an Undo, then choose* Advanced > Restore Clip Media.

At this point, we've seen quite a few ways to work with our raw footage, so let's get onto that editing that I promised you.

Editing modes in iMovie

As we said earlier, editing in iMovie is mainly controlled by the simple process of drag and drop. A clip is picked up in the clip pane and dropped in place.

The actual arrangement and ordering of clips in iMovie comes in two flavors – timeline and storyboard. Even though they are vastly different, they are both incredibly useful to your workflow. You can switch between the two modes at any time during your project, using the two tabs to the left of the timeline:

Storyboard mode

Storyboard mode enables you to layout clips in order of their chronological position (the movie will run in order from left to right):

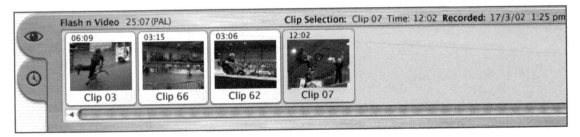

As you can see in the screenshot, iMovie displays some useful information about a chosen clip (in either edit mode) just above the sequence of clips. You might find this info handy when it comes to remembering details on long-term projects.

Storyboard mode is great for getting a quick edit together with no fuss. Simply drag and drop the clips from the clip pane, release them into the film frames below, and then press play to see if the sequence fits.

This mode comes unstuck when it comes to precisely treating, trimming, and timing clips. This is where timeline mode comes to the rescue.

Timeline mode

This mode allows far more precise editing than available in storyboard mode, allowing you to trim clips, add some basic transitions, and to have control over the timing of the project. Timeline mode is a little more complex to look at, but only because of the way that the length of a clip is displayed.

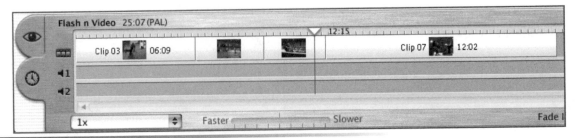

As with storyboard mode, clips are dropped onto the timeline. iMovie will show a little intelligence when it comes to dropping a clip and will offer to place it before or after another clip in the timeline. The timeline positions of the clips can then be fine-tuned by dragging them around in the timeline area. The zoom menu below the timeline is useful, as it will allows you to fine tune your editing and transitions.

> *Both editing modes in iMovie allow you to add transitions.*

Now that we've had a look at the editing modes, let's get some editing done (at last).

Arranging our clips

At this stage you should have a number of clips ready to work with, and create our masterpiece. You should also have a clean timeline – if not, click on the clips in there and press the DELETE key to erase them.

What we are going to do is to use four or five clips to make a quick edit. Don't worry too much about the potential order of the clips at the moment. If your clips work in a narrative manner like the iMovie tutorial files then you won't have to think too much about their order, but the key thing here is to be confident with the way that iMovie works.

1. Switch into storyboard editing mode. We'll get a basic composition of clips here, before fine tuning them in timeline mode and adding some transitions.

2. The first thing to do is to trim your clips. (Remember to copy them first, and save the originals.) Leave a couple of clips with a little too much slack at the start and end, so that we can use them for transitions.

3. Select a clip from the clip pane and drag it into the storyboard. The storyboard highlights where you are going to place the clip before you release it.

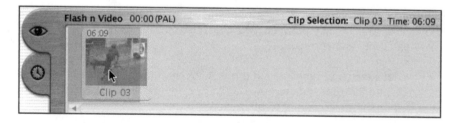

> *You might have noticed that the clip disappeared from the library when it was placed in the storyboard. To keep a clip in the library when you move it to the storyboard or timeline, hold down the OPTION/ALT key. This will make sure that you keep the original in place. If you have lost your first clip in this way, select* Edit > Undo *and go again.*

4.   Repeat step 3 a few times so that we have a sequence of clips:

Now we get to see how our sequence looks. It's worth pointing out that there's no limit to the amount of your movie that you can preview, and there's also no time delay before preview – it's instant.

5.   Deselect any of the clips and press the play button to preview the movie. You'll see a preview of the storyboard sequence. This will probably look a little shabby, but not to worry – we'll tidy it up in a moment.

6.   Let's shift a few of the clips around and change the sequence a little. Select the first clip on the storyboard and drag it to the gap inbetween the third and fourth clips:

A ghostly clip scares the other two clips into moving aside!

7.   Deselect all of the clips, and play the whole movie. Even if your trimming was amazingly good you'll find that a straight edit between two clips just doesn't work at certain points. This is where transitions come to the rescue.

8.   For now, let's switch to timeline edit mode. Click on the clock icon to the right of the storyboard to switch into timeline mode. You should see the same clips as before, except that they're elongated or shrunk according to their length:

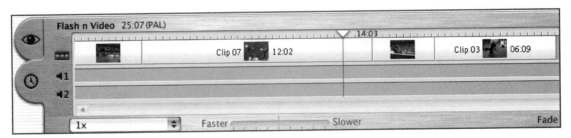

The first thing we need to do is to relieve our ears by removing that skipping racket. The sound from the clips also makes it harder for us to visualize how our edit looks, so it's time to strip the sound from the clips in the timeline.

9. Select all of the clips in the timeline by pressing APPLE+A or SHIFT-clicking on them.

10. Choose Advanced > Extract Audio to remove the audio tracks from the clips and place them in the audio layer of the timeline:

11. With the audio clips still selected, press the BACKSPACE key to delete them.

12. Play the whole movie again, and it should be easier to concentrate on the sequence.

13. Now, let's be having those transitions! Select two clips next to each other in the timeline and click on the transitions button. A small list of available transitions is revealed, along with a Speed slider and a preview pane:

14. I'll leave you to experiment with the different transitions. For now, I'm going to use a basic cross dissolve transition. With both clips still selected, click on Cross Dissolve transition. You should get a small preview, but if you blinked you might have missed it.

15. We can also get a preview from the preview pane. Click on the Preview button, and a large size preview will be shown. This loses a lot of frames but is only meant as a preview.

16. Change the Speed slider and try a few variations. The figure shown is the length of time of the cross dissolve transition.

17. If you are happy with your timing and if the preview looks good, you need to get iMovie to render the transition. Click and drag the Cross Dissolve transition down onto the timeline.

18. Release it in between the two clips and a strange link symbol appears in our timeline:

The black/red bar is a progress bar shown while iMovie renders the transition. Once this has finished, click Play and watch the beauty of your transition.

Now I'll leave it up to you - finish editing the movie with the skills you have learnt here, and when you're done - watch it back in full-screen mode. In a while we'll see how to add some sound to it to finish it off.

Exporting your movie

Once you have something that you're happy with, you can publish it so that it can be imported into Flash (or put straight onto a CD, DVD, or the web). iMovie exports in QuickTime format so you end up with a MOV file, compatible with most plug-ins and systems.

When it comes to exporting to QuickTime, there are a number of presets available:

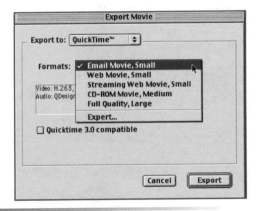

And also a custom mode, labeled here as Expert. The presets apply compression and use smaller physical sizes than the project movie.

If you are importing your video into Flash, I would recommend keeping your video in the best possible quality format, so wherever possible use Full Quality, Large. This keeps the file in DV format, with no compression and maintains the original frame rate and size.

If you want to send your movie back to the DV camera, you can do this by selecting File > Export Movie *and setting* Export to Camera. *This is useful if you wish to distribute the video in other formats such as VHS.*

However, you might find that this gives you a pretty hefty wait when importing it into Flash. If you find this, use Expert mode in iMovie, reduce the export physical size, and use DV-NTSC or DV-PAL (depending on your system) as the compressor. This will maintain quality but will be will be a smaller file due to the reduced physical size – you should then get a quicker import into Flash. In this export, I've halved the physical size:

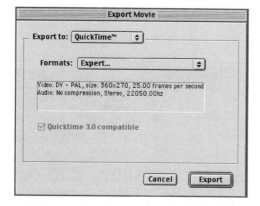

For now though, choose one of the moderate presets – say CD-Rom Movie Medium – click Export, and save it somewhere. After a little wait, locate the file and open it to watch it. If it's good, keep it somewhere ready for the next chapter, otherwise trash it and start again. We'll be working with footage in the next chapter, so you might like to use footage that you won't easily get bored of.

If you'd like to add some music, sound, or some other fancy work to your movie, read on – that comes next....

Other iMovie tricks and features

When iMovie 2 was released, it brought with it a number of new features to enhance the editing experience a little more. Let's take a look.

Clip direction

iMovie 2 has the ability to reverse the direction of a clip or sequence of clips – both video and audio are reversed. To do this, select a clip in the library or timeline and select Advanced > Reverse Clip Direction. When a clip has been reversed in the clip library, it will be signified by a backwards arrow in the top right:

To restore a clip so that it plays in the right direction, select Advanced > Restore Clip Media or simply re-reverse it.

Clip speed

Clips in the timeline can be stretched or shrunk up to 5 times length either way. Although I didn't use this effect for my BMX video (it would have been excellent for the air clips), it is great for dramatic speed scenes. Think action movie explosions or watch the video for Fatboy Slim's 'Gangsta Trippin'.

Select a clip in the timeline and use the speed slider below the timeline to increase or decrease its speed:

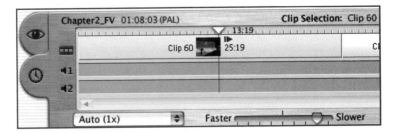

This is also great for getting those amazing slowed down voices and sounds (think of David Lynch slowing down and speeding up animal noises for screams in 'Eraserhead' and 'Blue Velvet'). Remember that you can also extract sound from a clip for it to perform independently of its video source (more on this in a moment).

Clip effects

If you have a particular style, or need to brighten up the color of your clips then the Effects tab is for you. There are a number of different ways to manipulate your clips, from the ever-useful Brightness/Contrast filter to the never useful Water Ripple effect:

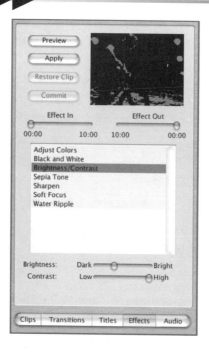

You can download more effects and filters in the iMovie 2 Plug in Pack (Mac OS X only) from www.apple.com/imovie/enhance.html.

To add an effect, select a clip (or clips) in the timeline, click on the Effects tab and choose an effect from the list. With most effects you can change the intensity of the filter and view a preview in the Effects preview pane above. Clicking on the Preview button allows you to watch a preview in the main window, and you can then change the timing accordingly (in the screenshot, my effect will last the whole length of the clip). Changing the timing will fade out the effect to normal gradually over the set time.

Go ahead and experiment with these effects to see if any of them suit you. You might find that subtlety becomes the order of the day after a while, but in the meantime, feel free to abuse them for a bit of fun.

Audio fading and volume

iMovie 2 lets you control the fading in and out of sounds, and the clip volume:

Select a clip in the timeline and the sound controls will be set to the clip's current settings. To stick in a fade, tick or un-tick the Fade checkboxes, and use the slider to control the volume. As you can see, it is possible to have a clip that fades in *and* fades out. The settings will automatically take effect. If you return to the clip later, then the settings will appear for you below the timeline.

CD track import

If you are musically challenged and would like to use some other music on your project, you can import songs from CD. Slide in a CD and it will appear in the Audio tab:

To import a portion of a track, click on the play button to listen, and the Record Music button to capture it. A growing purple bar will then appear in the audio layer of the timeline. To import a whole CD track, click and drag it into the audio layer of the timeline. You should then see a long purple bar.

> *If you intend to have sounds and music in your project, it is best to keep them separate to make them easier to manage and work with. Try and keep audio layer 1 for sounds and layer 2 for music. This way you will know what something is immediately and won't have to slow down your workflow by playing the guessing game.*

Mic import

Besides CD tracks, MP3s, and AIFFs, iMovie 2 can also import directly from the mic input of your Mac. If you don't have a sound editing application then this can be really handy, enabling you to record voice or any other input through your mic socket.

> *If you have a G3 iMac – that tiny hole at the top center of your monitor is a microphone. Maybe you should think about using it in iMovie?*

To record your mic input, select the Audio tab and click on the Record Voice button. You should see the audio levels bar twitching, and a growing orange bar in an audio layer of the timeline.

Titles

Once you've finished your masterpiece, you have to give yourself praise in opening titles and the end titles. It's common for people to give themselves a number of separate credits...

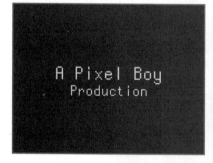

....the amount of self-praise you require is up to you!

Many titling options are available in the Titles tab. You'll see a number of different effects, options and a good old preview pane:

Titles can be placed over clips, over black or over an imported image file. The box at the bottom of the tab is the most important – it is where you enter your actual text. Above that are options for the font size, type and color. It might seem trivial, but a font must be correctly styled for your video to make the whole thing fit – 'Times' is a little bit classy for a down and dirty BMX video isn't it?

As well as styling your font correctly, the type of titling effect you use is also hugely important. Some of the titling types obviously conform to convention – such as the Scrolling Block for end titles, and Music Video for MTV-like information, but some of the others are quite different and punchy. Think about what you want the viewer to focus on before using a crazy titling effect overlaid on video.

If you're curious what the circle with compass points is, it controls the directional flow of your effects. Give it a whirl. It can subvert the conventional.

To place a title over black, deselect any clips in the timeline, choose a titling effect and enter your text. Change the options as appropriate, and preview it until you are happy with it. Then click and drag the title effect from the list onto the timeline. This will create a new clip in the timeline and will take a little while to render.

To place a title over a clip, select a clip in the timeline and sort out your titles. Once you have everything ready to go, drag the title effect down to the timeline and place it before the clip.

After rendering you should have something like this (I used the Music Video title here):

For a little more width for your titles, tick the QuickTime margins checkbox.

If you are looking to do something a little more sophisticated, it might be worth creating your titles specifically – in Flash for example – because the titles here are only intended for basic projects. Look to the titles from *North by Northwest* to *Seven* for inspiration.

Summary

Now that you've had a quick go at editing, go away and play around with it. See what you come up with and get familiar with the tools. In the next chapter we'll be importing our videos into Flash and getting down to work, so it might be more fun if you have your own footage to play with.

Bringing Video into Flash

What we'll cover in this chapter:

- ■ *Video formats* and those that can be imported into Flash MX.

- ■ Using the *Import Video Settings* when importing video into Flash.

- ■ The *review data rate* and *keyframe intervals*.

- ■ Exporting video using the *FLV* format.

- ■ Exporting video using *Sorenson Spark*.

- ■ Comparing *Sorenson Spark* and *Sorenson Squeeze*.

- ■ *Optimizing* your video.

You have some video, it's been edited, and is ready to import into Flash, right? Well... almost! Before we jump into importing the video there are several things we'll need to know about first. In this chapter, we'll look at how to get the most out of your video by optimizing the file size while retaining the best possible quality.

Optimization can be frustrating at times and joyful at others. A small adjustment here or there may mean the difference between a video with low file size and acceptable quality, and one that is too large with unacceptable quality in addition. Understanding why things like data rate, keyframes, and compression methods are important will help you achieve low file sizes and better quality video in the end.

Before importing

Macromedia Flash MX can only import video formats if you already have the appropriate players installed on your system, so you may need to go and install these if you find that things don't work as you expect.

QuickTime 4 (available from www.apple.com/quicktime) or higher must be installed to import the following video file formats on either Windows or Macintosh platforms:

- Audio Video Interleaved (**AVI**)

- Digital Video (**DV**)

- Motion Picture Experts Group (**MPG** or **MPEG**)

- QuickTime Movie (**MOV**)

For Windows users, DirectX 7 or higher must be installed to view these video file formats (you can download the latest version from www.microsoft.com/windows/directx):

- Audio Video Interleaved (**AVI**)

- Motion Picture Experts Group (**MPG** or **MPEG**)

- Windows Media File (**WMV** or **ASF**)

Importing video into Flash MX can seem daunting at first because of the various video and audio compression formats, but don't worry – we're here to take you through all the options.

The first thing to remember is to always use source video that's as **uncompressed** as you can get. Yes, you read that correctly! If you try to compress video beforehand, then you're getting in the way of Flash's built-in video compressor, Sorenson Spark, which does an excellent job of compressing the entire video. Sorenson Spark is what's known as a motion video **codec** (short for compressor-decompressor).

If you want even more control over the file size and quality of your imported video then you might want to take a look at a product called **Sorenson Squeeze**. You'll probably have seen Squeeze advertised on Macromedia's site; it's an application purposely designed to compress video for Flash MX. There'll be more on Squeeze later – for now, I'll take you through some of the many options available to you when you import video into Flash.

Importing a video: preparation

The original source video for our exercise is an Audio Video Interleaved video – an AVI for short. High-end video editing programs usually output to AVI or QuickTime's MOV format. The AVI is 10 seconds long with sound, and weighs in at 92 MB! This is without any compression, so for the purposes of this exercise, I've taken my 92 MB AVI and applied Motion JPEG A compression to render it as a QuickTime MOV file called `driver_final.mov`.

This flies in the face of what we've just said about compression, but in this case it has resulted in a file size of 4.6 MB, which might just allow you to download it from the code download area at www.friendsofed.com. If you haven't got the modem and/or patience to do that, or if you'd prefer to use your own video, simply substitute any video file for `driver_final.mov` in this exercise.

1. Inside Flash, we need to set the frame rate of our movie to the same as our video file. Open a new Flash movie and use the Property inspector (Ctrl+F3) to set the frame rate to the same as our source file – 30 fps. (If you're using a different source file and you don't know the fps rate, then pop ahead a couple of pages to the section headed Frame Rate to see how to find this out.)

2. Creating a new movie clip symbol in our Flash movie to import the video into allows us to manipulate the video more easily than if we import the video clip on to the main timeline itself. Select Insert > New Symbol (or use Ctrl+F8). In the Create New Symbol dialog box check the Movie Clip radio button, and give your movie clip a suitable name.

3. To import the video use File > Import... (Ctrl+R). Select a video file – `driver_final.mov` in our example – and then check Embed Video in Macromedia Flash Document in the Import Video dialog box:

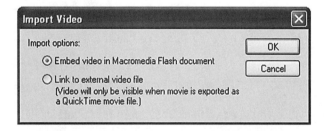

The other import option here is to Link to external video file. This option is only available when importing QuickTime videos. You could think about using this if you were presenting a video in its original form, such as a movie trailer or speech. This way the Flash file itself does not contain the video file, and the video is only loaded when called upon. This method is very limiting, though, as you have to export the Flash content to Flash 4.

Import settings

We're going to halt our little exercise for a minute while we look at some of the options. Don't worry though – we haven't abandoned it, and we'll be returning just as soon as we have the knowledge that we need to give the video the best possible settings.

For now, take a look at the Import Video Settings dialog box that displays the Sorenson Spark video settings:

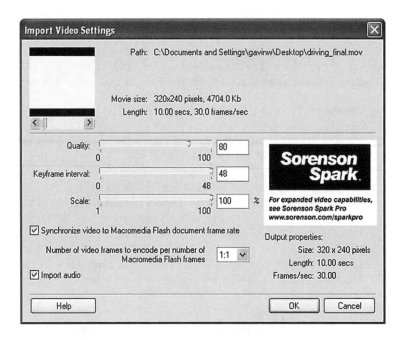

There are several settings to adjust here. You'll notice that the Movie Size and Length are shown, as well as a scrollable preview of the video itself.

Frame rate

Before importing your video you need to think about your frame rate in Flash. If, for example, your video is shot at 30 frames per second (fps) then you need to set the frame rate in Flash to 30 fps in order to get the best possible playback. You can see the fps setting of the video you're importing after the length of the video, to the right of the scrollable preview window.

The reason we want to adjust the frame rate inside Flash is because the audio portion of the video will *always* play back at the original video frame rate. The imported video will play back at the frame rate you specify in Flash but the sound will always play back at the frame rate of the original video file. It's obvious to see how this can be a problem. For example, if you are importing video of a person talking, such as a news anchor, the lip-syncing will be either too fast or too slow unless you specify the original fps setting. It is possible to compensate for different frame rates when you import the video, and we'll look at this later.

Quality

The first setting is the Quality slider. This slider adjusts the amount of compression that's applied to the video clip. It's not a good idea to set the Quality to 100%, because the video that results could actually be larger in file size than the original clip itself! It's best to lower the Quality setting a little, even if it means setting it to 95%.

For the web, a larger amount of compression is best, but a small amount of compression is ideal for CD-ROM presentations. CD-ROMs can have a much higher data rate than web-based video because the video is delivered locally and CD-ROM transfer rates are high. It's important to recognize that slower computers may *still* have problems viewing the video from a CD-ROM because of slower CPU processing speeds, so don't go overboard.

Keyframe interval

The next setting is the Keyframe interval. This slider adjusts the frequency of keyframes (frames with complete data) in the video clip. This setting could make or break your video in file size and playability! A keyframe is important because it stores a complete frame from the video clip. A setting of 30 will place a keyframe at every thirtieth frame. A lower setting, such as 5, will create a keyframe on every fifth frame. The extreme is setting the Keyframe interval to 1. I would *not* recommend this.

So why are keyframes so important? There are generally two types of compression. The kind that Sorenson Spark uses works by checking for areas in each video frame that do not move much from frame to frame. This type of compression is called **temporal** compression and is also known as **interframe** compression. It attempts to determine the areas in each frame that stay the same, and do not need to be redrawn from frame to frame.

This is one reason why clips with a lot of movement in, or clips shot using an unstable camera, can take up much more space and bandwidth – with everything moving, very little stays the same from frame to frame. Compare a clip of a person talking taken against a static blue background to one of an all action sports shot, both the same length, and you'll find that the first file is much smaller.

Here's an example of using too much interframe compression. This is a frame from this exercise's example video with very high compression applied:

The compression is trying to find bits in the frame that match previous frames and, with such a fast changing video, fails to do so. This high compression is not particularly desirable, so careful tweaking is in order.

The other type of compression is called **spatial** compression – also known as **intraframe** (that's *intra* and not *inter*) compression. The level of compression is applied to each and every frame regardless of the surrounding frames. The Sorenson Spark codec uses interframe or temporal compression, but also utilizes spatial or intraframe compression through the use of keyframes. As you can see, the Sorenson Spark codec is a powerful one! It uses interframe compression to try and compress the majority of the video *and* uses intraframe compression to maintain the quality of the video.

This means that the compression applied with the Quality setting will directly reflect on how well the keyframes setting will work. This is a balancing act and one that should be experimented with to get the best possible quality with the lowest file size. Increasing the compression means lowering the image quality, and adding keyframes means retaining image quality from frame to frame.

To give you an idea of how keyframes affect file size, I imported my video using different keyframes settings. Here are the two most important combinations in this case:

- A video imported at 90% Quality with a Keyframe interval of 1 produced a video that was 1.2 MB.

- The same video imported with a Keyframe interval of 48 produced a 712 KB file. The quality of this second video wasn't terribly different to that of the first!

It's important to remember this may *not* always apply to your video. My video has constant motion, meaning that it may not be able to utilize the Keyframe interval setting as you would be able to do with a video of an anchor newsman being filmed with little overall movement.

> *If you're not already maxed-out on technical data, then you might want to know that Sorenson Spark also saves space through color space reduction by storing information in 2x2 blocks of data: "For each 2x2 block of data, YUV 4:2:0 stores 4 luminance samples (Y), one for each pixel, but only two chrominance (U, V) samples." The human eye is far more sensitive to brightness or luminance than to color or chrominance, and this method greatly reduces the amount of information needed to reconstruct the image, which provides a much higher compression ratio. It's a little bit outside our remit here, but for more information about YUV 4:2:0 compression visit www.adamwilt.com/DV-FAQ-tech.html.*

Scale

This setting determines the dimensions of the video clip once it's imported into Flash MX, and is a bit simpler than the last two settings! If you scale the video down from the original size, it will be lower in file size, and will consequently play back better.

Synchronization

The next setting is the Synchronize video to Macromedia Flash document frame rate. Here we can compensate for the fps issue I talked about earlier, and adjust the playback to change the video's frame rate to equal the Flash movie frame rate.

For example, I like to set my frame rate for multimedia presentations to 60 fps (that's quite high, so be sure that your target audience can view presentations running at this speed). This frame rate obviously won't be ideal if I want to import a 30 fps video, as a 30 fps video imported into Flash's 60 fps movie will yield a five second video instead of the ten seconds of the original clip. The sound will also be out of sync.

By selecting Synchronize you can have the video make up or remove the difference in frame rate during the importing process. A video at 30 fps imported into a 15 fps Flash movie, with Synchronize on, will drop frames to make the video match, producing a choppier video but leaving the sound synced. Sorenson Spark will drop every other frame to make up the difference.

Sound

Finally, we have the option to import sound along with our video. It's important to note that not all sounds can be imported: you can only import sounds if the audio codec that was used to compress the sound in the original file is supported on your computer.

As with video, it's best to import sound into Flash with as little prior compression applied as possible. The best option, if it's available to you, is PCM that is essentially uncompressed audio. You can, however, import audio that's compressed if you wish. A good example would be a QuickTime movie with the audio compressed using 16-bit Little Endian Compression at 44.1 kHz or simply MPEG Layer 3 (MP3).

Do note that all audio compression formats may not import into Flash. If this is the case you'll receive the following error message when you try to import the video:

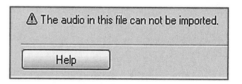

As mentioned earlier, your computer must support the audio codec used to originally encode the sound. Another thing to consider is that MPG or MPEG audio tracks may not import well. Trying to import an MPG video *with* its audio track may result in not importing the *entire video* at all! If you're having problems importing video with its sound then open the video in a video editor and try to recompress the video and sound with audio codecs and compressors that are supported by your computer.

> *A quick and inexpensive solution to recompress your MPEG, MPG, or any other non-compatible video or audio format is Apple's QuickTime Pro. This enables you to import lots of video formats and export them to another format such as MOV, for example. QuickTime Pro is available at* www.apple.com/quicktime/download.

Entering our import video settings

Now that we've got the lowdown on the power that the Import Video Settings options hold over the Flash video universe, let's get back to our exercise and enter the settings that we want for our video file. The settings mentioned here are obviously those for our sample `driver_final.mov` file. Each video file will be different, so if you're using other footage, then use your newfound knowledge (and some trial and error testing) to come up with the best solution for that particular piece of footage.

1. For the video in our example, set the Quality to '90' to try and retain a good to high quality, suitable for broadband distribution.

2. Set your Keyframe interval to '48', the highest inside Sorenson Spark, and leave the Scale setting at 100% – 320 x 240 pixels.

3. In this exercise we've set our Flash movie to 30 fps, which matches the video frame rate, so syncing is not necessary.

4. We need to select Number of video frames to encode per number of Macromedia Flash frames. For example, to play 1 frame of video for every Flash frame, we'd choose 1:1 from the drop-down menu. Dropping frames from the imported video doesn't slow down the motion of the video, but it displays fewer frames per second, so that the video may appear choppy during playback if you overdo things. Here, we'll choose to play every frame along with the Flash frame rate, leaving the setting as 1:1:

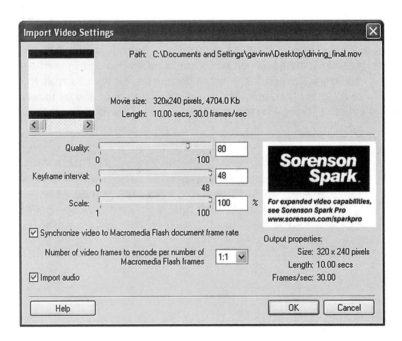

5.   Click OK and wait for the compression process to end – Flash compresses the video at this stage rather than compressing it during the exporting of the final movie. By doing it now, when you export your Flash movie the process will not be slowed down by the need to also compress the video, making the whole process smoother.

6.   When you are importing the video directly to the stage, a warning message (as shown below) appears if the imported clip contains more frames than the timeline in which you are placing it. Choose Yes to extend the frames, or the whole of the video will not be shown – the video will only play back if there are enough frames in the Flash movie to play them.

So there you have it! We've successfully imported our video into Flash and are ready to do some Flash-style editing with the video itself. This process isn't the most glamorous, but it's the foundation on which successful Flash video presentations are built. Some time spent getting these settings right is the key to making sure that you don't create unnecessarily large video assets, and this puts you in a position to go on and have some real fun.

Sorenson Squeeze

The compressor included with Flash MX, Sorenson Spark, is good but there's something even better. It's called Sorenson Squeeze. To get the lowest possible file size and retain the best possible quality you may want to investigate this program, as it's by far the best way to compress video for Flash. So, let's take a look at this powerful little piece of software and what it can do for your video. You can download a trial version at www.sorenson.com (5.5 MB for the PC and 10 MB for the Mac).

Sorenson Squeeze is a standalone program by Sorenson Media that encodes high quality video for Flash MX. The idea here is to bring the raw video into Sorenson Squeeze, compress it, and then import it into Flash *already* compressed.

With Sorenson Squeeze open, let's discuss what we can see:

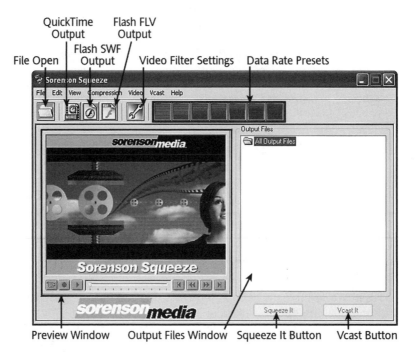

The seven Data Rate Presets buttons at the top of the interface are set up to give the best possible data rates depending on where the final video output will be viewed. The Preview Window on the left is where you can view the imported file. This, however, is not where you would view the *compressed* video. To the right of that window is the Output Files Window and it's here that you'll be able to see the settings that will be applied to your video for compression. At the bottom is the Squeeze It button, which will begin the compression process, and the Vcast button, which gives you the ability to publish your video online.

Another great feature of Sorenson Squeeze is the ability to capture video directly from a digital camera. The one drawback is that if you want to add sound to the video, then an external video editor must be used. You could also simply add those sounds along with the video and piece it all together in Flash itself, of course. In these situations, I normally add sounds or music in a non-linear editing (or NLE) program such as Adobe Premiere 6.0 or Sonic Foundry's Vegas Video 3.0.

Before we begin, let's compare two videos, one encoded with Flash MX's built-in Sorenson Spark codec and the same video encoded with Sorenson Squeeze. Both videos were tested to approximately retain the same sound and video quality.

The first video was compressed from 4.7 MB to 716 KB, impressive to say the least:

encoded using Sorenson Spark

The second video, however, was compressed from 4.7 MB to 430 KB!

encoded using Sorenson Squeeze

Take a close look at these two images. They both look a little compressed although the second image seems to look a little 'smoother'. The interesting thing is that the second image actually has a *higher* file size as a JPEG than the first. But wait a second – the second image is taken from a video clip that was *lower* in size than the first? What does this mean?

It's simple: the Sorenson Squeeze compressor managed to produce a video clip *smaller* than Sorenson Spark and maintain higher visual quality! Squeeze is extremely useful if you intend to work frequently with video and Flash MX, and need the smallest possible file sizes.

Squeezing the video

It's important to note here that we are using Sorenson Squeeze to get the best possible quality at the smallest possible file sizes, so using raw video is the best way to do this. If we import video that has already been compressed and then try to compress it even further, the image quality may suffer. Imagine this analogy: take a photograph and crunch it up in your hand into a ball, unwrap it flat, and then crunch it up again. Do this over and over and you'll begin to see the image quality fading away. The same applies to video. If you take raw uncompressed video and apply compression to it, then import that same video into another program and apply a different type of compression, and so on, the video will lose quality over time.

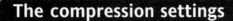

The compression settings

Let's start importing our video into Sorenson Squeeze.

1. Click the File Open button and choose a raw video file (`driving_final.mov` if you're following our example). You should now see the video in the Preview Window.

2. We need to choose a format to encode to. There are three options here: QuickTime Video, Flash SWF, and Flash FLV. To import the final compressed video into Flash MX we'll choose the Flash FLV format, so click on the Flash FLV format button:

   Flash FLV is a new file format that is native to Flash MX only. Although there are other video formats we can use in Flash MX, this file format is by far the best format to use for importing compressed video into Flash MX.

3. Next we need to choose a data rate to encode the video at. You'll notice that the data rate buttons are only highlighted after we have chosen a video format. The seven preset encode buttons should now be active. Let's choose the fourth setting Broadband:

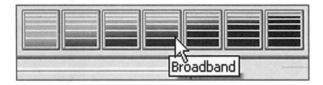

This setting will not be absolutely perfect for our output, but don't worry – we can adjust it to really tweak our video to perfection in a moment. Notice that our preset settings are now shown in the Output Files window:

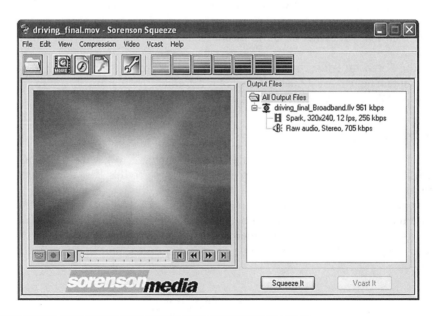

After experimenting, if we export using these predefined settings, the resulting total file size of the video and soundtrack combined will be just over 2 MB! Not good. I could have chosen a lower preset but I like this one because it will closely resemble the settings I want in the end. So let's dig in!

4. Look in the Output Files window and select the line that begins with Spark. Go to Edit > Output Compression Settings… to open the Compression Settings dialog box:

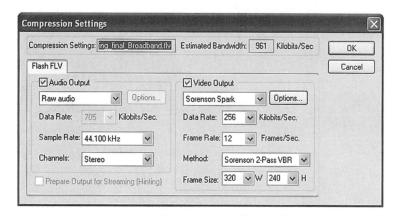

5. We want the audio to be good but not great; after all, we're still trying to deliver this video online. CD quality sound typically has a data rate of 48 Kilobits per second or higher, and a sample rate of 44 kHz or higher. We'll set these one or two steps lower to still maintain good quality sound but without the added file size, so select Fraunhofer MP3 at 32 Kilobits/Sec in the Audio Output section of the dialog.

6. Still in Audio Output, change the Sample Rate to 22.050 kHz and choose Mono from the Channels drop-down menu. Your audio settings should now match those in the screenshot:

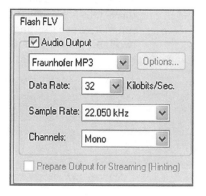

7. Let's move over to the Video Output side. Set the Data Rate to 350 Kilobits/Sec, and change the Frame Rate to 1:1 (you could also type '30' into this field). This means that the video will be compressed using the same frame rate of the original video, so in our case the frame rate will be 30 fps.

8.   Select Sorenson 2-Pass VBR from the Method drop-down menu. This is one of the more important features in Sorenson Squeeze, and is not available in Sorenson Spark. 2-Pass VBR (Variable Bit Rate) encoding is a special way of compressing a file that uses more data during high-action scenes and less data during low-action scenes. This means smaller file sizes and increased performance. Almost every DVD Video feature film available today uses variable bit rate encoding.

9.   Lastly, set the Frame Size to 320 x 240. Your final settings should now be the same as those shown here:

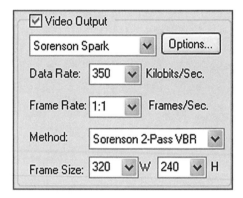

You should notice at the top of the Compression Settings dialog that the Estimated Bandwidth is now 382 Kilobits/Sec. I could be satisfied with these settings but I'm not, and neither should you! So let's keep digging.

10.   Click on Options... in the Video Output section. This opens up the Sorenson Spark Settings dialog box. There are three tabs here and the first one is a summary of the settings from the other two tabs. Click on the Encode tab:

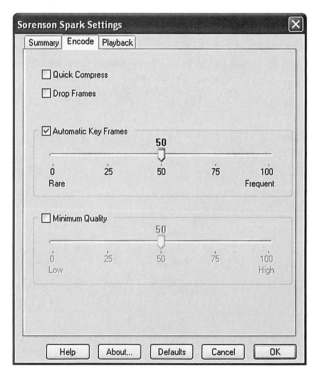

11. The first setting is Quick Compress. This option compresses video about 20% faster by sacrificing a little quality, but the quality loss is usually very minimal and hardly noticeable to the eye. Our video is only 10 seconds long and will take anywhere between 30 seconds to 2 or 3 minutes to compress, depending on your computer speed. No big time loss here, we've 30 seconds to spare, so leave this option unchecked.

12. The next checkbox is the Drop Frames option. This option is really only important if you select the last setting on this tab, the Minimum Quality slider. The Minimum Quality slider can be used to adjust the minimum image quality of the encoded video but there is always a sacrifice when adjusting a setting like this: there will be some frame rate loss, meaning lower image quality in each frame. For this exercise, leave this setting turned off.

13. The main setting in this tab is the Automatic Key Frames slider. This lets you specify the amount of change possible from one frame to the next before a new keyframe is added. Set this to 75. This will automatically create keyframes a little more frequently than the default 50 setting – our video has constant motion in it and requires a larger frequency of keyframes than a lower setting could provide.

14. Now click on the Playback tab, and check the first option, Image Smoothing. This helps reduce the 'blocking' effect that Sorenson may create from compressing.

15. Also check Playback Scalability. This option helps when playing the video across multiple computer platforms. If the video is played back on a slower computer, the video will drop frames by half in order to compensate for the computer not being able to keep up (so a 30 fps movie would become a 15 fps movie and so on).

16. Click OK and then click OK again to accept our Output Compression Settings.

Video Filter Settings

With Sorenson Squeeze we can also edit the video using the Video Filter Settings button located on the main interface.

Click on this button and let's take a look at some of the features in the filter editor:

At the top left is the preview window. At the top right are the Contrast, Brightness, Gamma, White Restore, and Black Restore controls. You can adjust these settings using the sliders while viewing the changes in the preview window on the fly.

Next is the Deinterlace option. This is another very useful feature in Sorenson Squeeze. The short explanation is this: in an **interlaced** video the frame is divided up into two fields. The two fields display every other horizontal line. The first field is drawn from top to bottom and then the second fills in the gaps. This usually happens in 1/60 of a second on a 30 (29.97 to be exact) fps video clip and is not noticeable to the naked eye.

Most televisions use interlacing. In the following images you can see the difference between the two fields by comparing the area inside the circle, the spare tire on the back of the Land Rover:

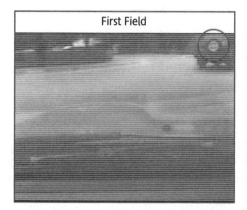

The reason televisions use this method is because older television sets had problems showing video correctly due to the phosphors used to display images. The images would fade at the top of the screen before the image could finish being shown at the bottom. Because of this problem in the past, interlacing has become today's standard.

> *It's worth noting the two most common video standards in use worldwide: NTSC and PAL. NTSC (National Television Standards Committee) is used mainly in North America, Japan, and Taiwan. PAL (Phase Alternate Lines) is the format used in Australia, New Zealand, Europe, and most other countries. The NTSC video frame rate is 29.97 or 30 fps, and PAL uses 25 fps.*

Computer screens, on the other hand, do not display video this way. They utilize non-interlaced or progressive scan displays. This simply draws the image from top to bottom in a solid field. More recent digital video cameras give the user options to shoot video in a deinterlaced, solid 30 fps mode, which is the standard for multimedia video. However, most video *will* be interlaced and at 29.97 or 25 fps.

Altering filter settings

Knowing this, we need to deinterlace our video to get the best possible visual quality with the applied compression.

1. Select Auto Remove Interlacing from the Deinterlace drop-down menu.

2. The next setting is Video Noise Reduction. This will try to remove 'grain' or 'unwanted noise' from the picture. Leave this alone this time.

3. Do the same with the Cropping and the Fade In and Out features. Cropping lets you actually *crop* the video, not simply adjust the height and width – if you chose the 16:9 ratio setting, for example, it will cut the appropriate amount away from your clip rather than resizing it. Fade In and Out allows you to add a white or black fade at the beginning or end of the video, and adjust the duration.

4. Finally there is the Normalize Audio option. This setting will analyze the video, look for the loudest sound, and adjust the rest of the track accordingly so that loud sections will not distort. Leave this alone, make sure that your settings match mine (the only option you've altered should be the Deinterlacing), and click on OK.

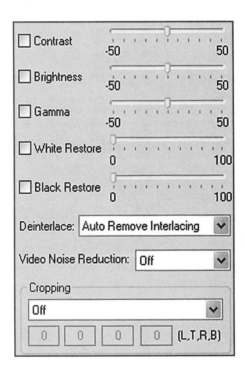

5. We're now ready to export our video as an FLV. Click on the Squeeze It button at the bottom right of the main interface. A Squeezing information window appears (click the Preview On button to see your video hard at work):

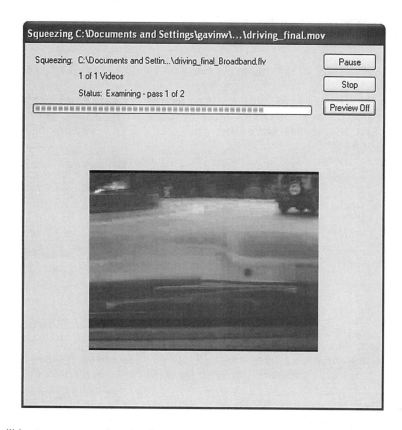

There will be two passes using the Sorenson 2-pass VBR. The first pass will look rather poor, while the second pass will look a lot better, and could take a little longer than the first. Once this has completed, we'll have an FLV video ready for importing into Flash MX. (The FLV format cannot be viewed by itself: it must be viewed inside Flash MX. The FLV format is specifically designed to be called on from Flash as a separate Flash video, or imported into Flash's developing environment.)

One thing to consider at this point is the frame rate, once again. One of the main differences when importing an FLV into Flash is that you will *not* get the choice that we had with Spark earlier to synchronize the FLV with the destination Flash movie's current frame rate. Now that you know this, it may be a good idea to set the frame rate in Flash to match the frame rate of the FLV.

It is true that a *higher* frame rate in Flash, such as 60 fps, will play a 30 fps FLV with no problems, but this isn't necessarily the best way to do things. Either way, if you're looking to lower the frame rate of the video as a way of reducing file size then this must be done in Sorenson Squeeze before you import the video into Flash.

Another important thing to note is that if you decrease the frame rate in Squeeze, the file size may *not* necessarily go down. The reason for this is because Squeeze notices that the frame rate has been reduced and will use the extra data available to improve the image quality. This means that if you want to reduce file size, the most effective way is to reduce the frame rate, the data rate, and the keyframe frequency within Squeeze.

Bringing the FLV into Flash

After this all this discussion, let's conclude our example, and import the FLV file into Flash.

1. Open up the Flash movie you originally imported the video into at the start of this chapter. Open the Library (F11) and double-click on the movie clip's icon to edit it.

2. Select frame 1 and delete the existing video. Remember that this is the original `driver_final.mov`, the QuickTime video file we imported at the start of this chapter.

3. Now it's time to import the FLV file we've just made. Go to File > Insert... and you'll see the FLV file underneath the original source video (notice the immense difference in file size between the source MOV and the compressed FLV):

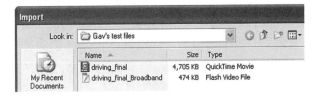

4. Click on `driving_final_Broadband` to import it into Flash.

5. Underneath the timeline, click on Scene 1 to go back into the main timeline. Select frame 1 of the default layer and drag a copy of the movie clip out of the Library and on to the stage.

6. That's it! Go to Control > Test Movie to see your optimized video in all its glory:

7. Save your Flash file and close it

Summary

So there you have it! We have optimized our Flash MX video and it's ready for Internet broadband distribution. We could of course reduce the visual quality and the sound quality and get our video size lower if we wanted to.

There are several things to remember about importing your video into Flash MX. It will probably take multiple sets of trial and error to get your video just as you want it, so be prepared to experiment with lots of different configurations. It's a good idea to keep a log of your findings when exporting video so that you can compare the settings affecting your video size, playback, scalability, and so on.

While doing this, keep in mind where your video will finally be viewed and what kind of hardware and bandwidth the target audience are likely to have. There are usually compromises to make when compressing and importing your video into Flash MX: visual and sound quality versus small, compact, easy to download video files.

What is important is that you make these decisions after having done everything you can to keep file sizes down, and this is what this chapter has covered. Too many people gloss over this kind of detail in their rush to get to the fun bit of using video in Flash and pay the price later when they realise just how big their files are. Now you're ready to go forward to the next chapter, and really have some fun...

Working with Video in Flash

What we'll cover in this chapter:

- *The **streaming** options with Flash Video*
- ***Controlling** video with simple ActionScript*
- ***Masking** video*

The two chapters we've just read have covered the work that we needed to do before we start using the video in Flash. In this chapter, we'll go a step further and see how we can manage and work with video content in Flash. In other words, this is where you'll start to get the payback for the hard work that you've put in over the past two chapters.

We'll start by looking at some ways to ensure that your movie is delivered efficiently, before taking a look at the control Flash has over video clip timelines. With the help of a few simple buttons and a teeny bit of ActionScript, we'll use this knowledge to create some video effects.

Streaming Flash video

Streaming in Flash is a little different from traditional server-based streaming. Streaming servers carefully hand out packets of information when needed by the player. If it's done well, the user will have a little wait for buffering to start, and then a seamless playback of the entire video afterwards. Streaming servers are intelligent enough to calculate the user's bandwidth and serve up different sized content where necessary.

There are ways to do this in Flash, but it's not as easy – streaming video in Flash works on a similar principle to real streaming, but there is no intelligence behind it. Flash simply loads in whatever it can in sequence, and plays back whatever it has loaded. This can often result in jerky playback, where playing pauses, because Flash is waiting for more content to be loaded in. Before we go on to see how to avoid this, let's see the significance of the jerky playback problem first.

Non-buffered streaming

Streaming video in Flash is done on the `_root` (main) timeline. To allow any form of streaming, you must place your video directly on the main timeline. This means that the video cannot be placed within a movie clip.

In this example we'll use 56k as our streaming target.

1. Locate a short video (mine is six seconds long) and make a note of its frame rate. If you want to use the same file as we have for this exercise, download `streaming.fla` from the friends of ED web site.

2. Open a new Flash movie, and change the frame rate to that of your intended import video.

3. Select File > Import to Library and locate the video.

4. On the dialog that appears, select Embed video in Macromedia Flash document.

5. Use import settings depending on the amount of movement and detail in your movie. I've used the settings pictured for the following reasons:

   - Quality: there is not too much intense detail.

   - Keyframe interval: there is a moderate amount of movement.

   - Scale: the original was physically too big for a 56k modem.

- Frame ratio: I can afford to lose a frame every now and again.

- Import audio: there was no audio on my clip.

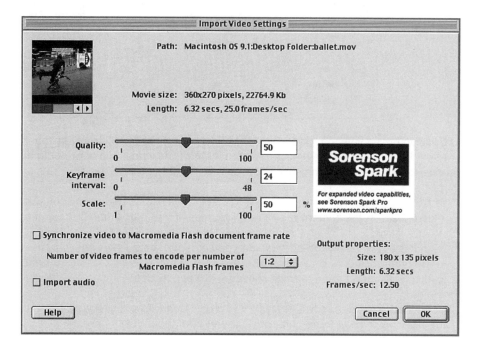

My final imported movie came out as 85kb from a 22.2Mb uncompressed DV-PAL QuickTime movie. This is mainly due to losing 1 frame in 2, compression, and smaller physical scaling.

If you're using a different clip, try to aim for a similar file size of around 100 KB. Don't import any audio with the clip – we're not going to use audio here, as it can be damaging in terms of file size. There's also a jarring 'popping' effect when jumping between different parts of an audio track occurs. We'll be looking at audio in Chapters 6 and 7, so keep reading if you want to find out more about it.

Remember that you can re-import a clip or view its properties by double-clicking on it in the Library:

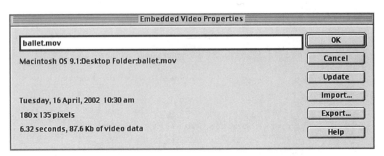

6. Once you have your clip at a reasonable size, drag a copy of it from the Library onto the stage. Allow Flash to extend the timeline to the length of the video, and you should have a video on the stage, and a pretty long timeline.

7. Test the movie using Control > Test Movie (or CTRL+ENTER). The video should now run seamlessly – Flash loads in the content pretty quickly, unless it's told to simulate streaming.

8. Flash has a few bandwidth presets and you can also create new settings from scratch. Still in test movie mode, select 56k(4.7 KB/s) from the Debug menu. We'll use this to simulate a 56k modem loading your movie at an average speed (4.7KB per second).

9. Now select View > Bandwidth Profiler. This will open up a city skyline-like window that displays the size of individual frames and other useful info about your movie:

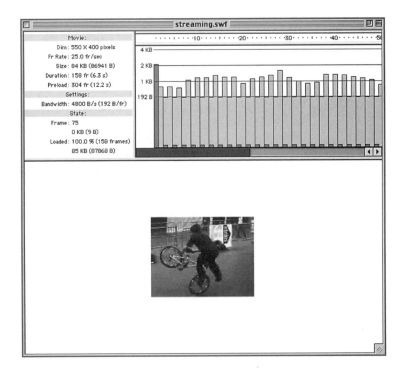

Before we look at the bandwidth profiler in detail, let's do what we set out to do, and stream our content.

10. Select View > Show Streaming. This simulates a 56k modem loading your Flash movie. As soon as you do this, you should notice a green bar growing in the frame graph:

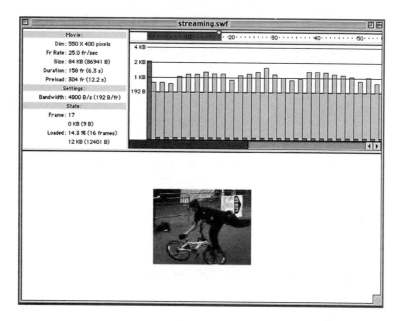

This green bar shows the content that has already been loaded. The tiny little arrow above the frames is the playhead.

If you watch the movie playing, you will notice that it has become jerky and choppy. Content is being played as it would be loaded, and Flash is running out of things to play and is stopping. This results in a stop-start-stop-start movie, not what we want at all!

Save your movie as it is and call it `streaming.fla`. We are about to improve the playback and loading by buffering some content first.

The bandwidth profiler

It might look like gibberish, but the bandwidth profiler is incredibly useful for helping us to manage our playback and loading efficiently.

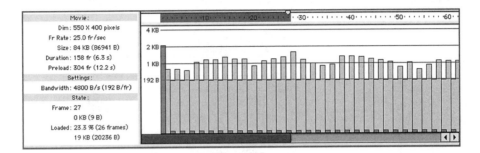

So what exactly is the graph on the right hand side showing us? Well, it breaks down our full file size into individual frames, allowing us to see where the bulk of our movie is. In my example, the movie is quite evenly distributed – with a frame average of less than 1 KB.

The graph bars on the right hand side of the bandwidth profiler are quite telling about my movie. If you remember when I imported my movie, I changed the frame ratio to 1:2. This means that Flash places one new frame, and a duplicate frame following it to fill in the gaps. The peaks and troughs here reflect this and also introduce us to the dreaded red line (in our screenshot, it's alongside the 192 B text).

If a bar is above the red line it means that there is content to be loaded. If the bar is below or shorter than the red line, it means that there is nothing to be loaded for that frame. With my 1:2 ratio of frames, the first frame needs to be loaded and then the following frame does not require any extra load – the content for it has already been loaded.

If loading just over 1 KB every other frame seems quite low, remember that my movie is running at 25fps. A quick bit of maths suggests that we need to load around 12.5 KB every second to load 1 KB every other frame. If you float this against the 4.7 KB per second that 56k modems might give us, it suggests that our modem will not be able to keep up, resulting in our best friends Mr Stop, Mr Start, and Mr Choppy.

This is where buffering comes in and the Preload figure on the left hand side is useful. This takes our frame rate and file size into account and provides us with a suggested number of frames (and time) required to preload and buffer the content, so that the movie can begin playing and the rest of the content can be loaded in comfortably in the background. This is not always totally accurate, but it is a good starting point.

Make a note of this number of frames, and we'll proceed.

Buffering and streaming

What we're going to do here is demonstrate how simple it is in Flash MX to smoothly stream video.

1. Open the streaming.fla movie from the previous exercise if it isn't already open. If you didn't get a preload figure from the bandwidth profiler, go get one now.

2. Insert a new layer and call it 'buffer'. Name the original layer 'vid'.

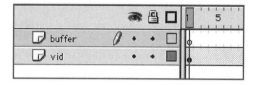

The first thing to do is to move the video content on in the timeline so that it is on the preload frame (as signified in the bandwidth profiler).

3. Double-click on the video in the timeline, so that it is selected. Now drag the video up to the preload frame (mine is frame 304) and release it there.

    This will make our movie start later than before, allowing the Flash Player a little while to load in the rest of the content.

4. On frame 1 of the buffer layer, use the Text tool to place some basic text signifying the preload/buffering, such as that pictured:

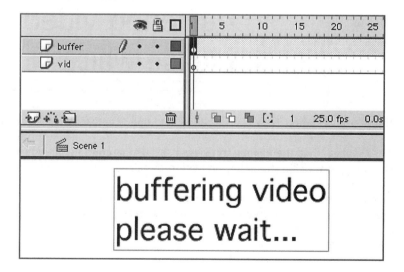

> *When it comes to using video in Flash on the web, it is best to keep the user busy while your movie is buffering. You can do this with some simple animation (nothing so complicated that it too will require a preloader – a preloader for your preloader!), some text for them to read, or some toys to occupy them if you're familiar with ActionScript.*

Now, if you scroll the length of the timeline (or test the movie) you'll notice that the preload text has flowed a little too far and the buffer layer timeline is as long as the whole movie. We need to trim this so that it will disappear when our movie starts playing.

5. Locate the start of the movie in the timeline (as before, mine's at frame 304). On the buffer layer, select the frame before the start of the movie and insert a blank keyframe using Insert > Blank Keyframe or F7. Now, if you run the playhead along this area you'll see that there's a neat crossover.

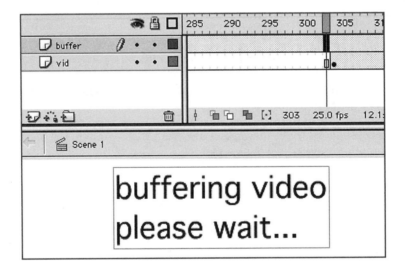

6. Test the movie with Control > Test Movie and open the bandwidth profiler if it isn't already open.

7. You'll notice that the default preview has all our content already loaded – switch on Show Streaming to watch a streaming simulation by selecting View > Show Streaming.

Now keep your eye on the growing *green* bar towards the end of the timeline. If our preloading is precise, as soon as the green bar has finished growing and reached the end of the timeline, the playhead should follow very, very, closely afterwards. If the playhead hits the end a lot later, then we are buffering too much content. If the playhead catches up with the green bar and we get choppy video, then we are buffering too little.

The preload figure given in the Bandwidth Profiler is sometimes a little random and doesn't give us the kind of figure that we need. The best thing to do is to examine the bandwidth profiler during a streaming simulation, and to try and calculate the extra time that it needs to run. Say it needs an extra second of buffering, then add a second's worth of frames, and shift the video along.

This means that we only need keep the user waiting as long as they need to, and no longer. Remember that the example that we have used here is optimized for 56k modem users, and that is likely to be too much buffering for users with faster connections. To counteract this, you could make a number of different SWFs for different users, reducing or increasing the quality, size, and buffering for different bandwidths.

Now for something completely different – a little bit of video management and some neat timeline tricks.

Self-contained videos

In our previous exercise, we had our video placed on the main timeline. As we saw, this is great for streaming content, but like any content not placed within a movie clip, if we want to use it more than once then this will inflate our file size.

To get around this, we need to convert our video into a movie clip. Easy... but there is one thing - doing this removes the potential for streaming the video. Movie clips in Flash must be fully loaded before they can begin playing anything, although you can be strategic about your movie clip loading order. Movie clips are loaded into Flash in the same order they appear in the main timeline (for example a movie clip on frame 1 will load fully before starting to load a movie clip on frame 2).

If the loss of streaming fills you with gloom, just sit back and think about the use of video within the context of your project. There are times when the focus is more on the video than anything else, and in these cases you should probably stream your video and leave it on the main timeline. At other times, the video will be manipulated slightly for a certain effect and will need to become a movie clip (more on effects in Chapter 5).

For now, let's take a look at how our video can become self-contained and multi-purpose.

The video is on the wall

We're going to create an effect similar to those video walls you see in shopping malls or at exhibitions.

1. Open the `halfpipe.fla` file from the download files. The file contains an embedded video file in the Library and nothing else. We've shown you all about importing files in the past couple of chapters, so if you want to use your own video, go ahead and import one into the Library of a fresh Flash movie.

Let's take a quick look at what we're going to make – a number of the same video clips displaying different frames of the clip at the same time:

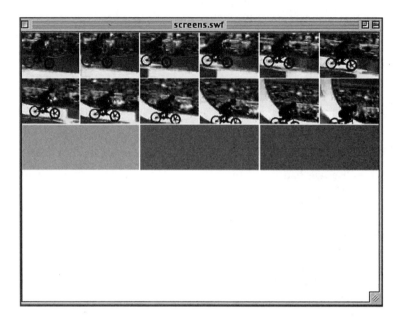

2.   The first thing we need to do is to convert our video clip into a movie clip. Create a new movie clip with Insert > New Symbol. Call it 'halfpipe video':

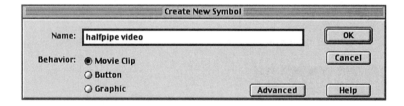

3.   You will then be ushered into symbol editing mode. Drag a copy of halfpipe.mov from the Library and into the movie clip. In the dialog box that appears, click OK.

4. Center the video on stage with the Align panel (CTRL+K to open). Make sure that the Align panel is set to align to stage, as pictured.

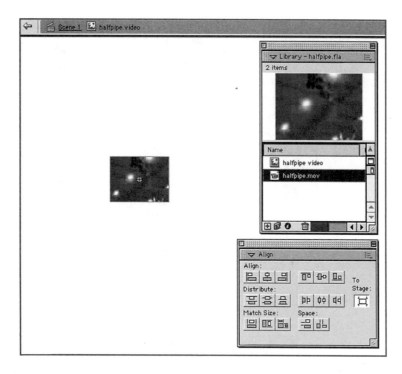

5. Return to the main timeline by clicking on the Scene 1 button below the timeline. This is where we will add our simple magic.

6. Add eleven (yes eleven!) new layers on the main timeline, giving you twelve layers in all. Each of these layers will introduce the video at a different frame to create a staggered effect. Twelve copies of the video will sit quite snugly at the top of our Flash movie's stage.

7. Now, insert a keyframe at frame 2 of Layer 2, frame 3 of Layer 3 and so on all the way up to frame 12 of Layer 12. These frames will create a tight, staggered effect, with only one frame in between each clip:

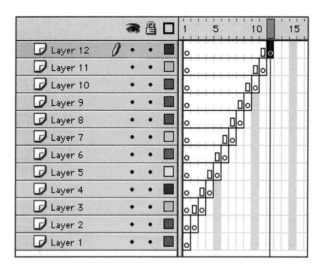

8. Drag a copy of the halfpipe video movie clip onto frame 1 of Layer 1. Position it at the top left of the stage:

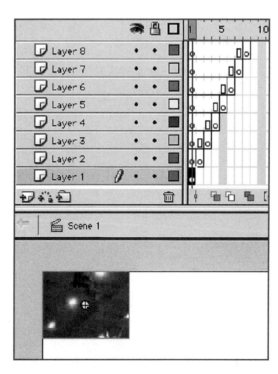

9. Drag a copy of the halfpipe video movie clip onto frame 2 of layer 2 and position it next to the previous one. Don't worry too much at the moment about getting it perfect. Repeat this with every layer until you have six in the first row like this:

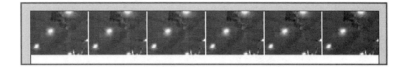

10. Now, let's line them up correctly – evenly spaced, flush to the top of the stage. Select all the movie clips and tidy them up with the Space evenly horizontally and Align top edge options in the Align panel. Make sure the Align tool is set to align To Stage before setting them. Your movie clips should now be tidy and correctly lined up on the stage.

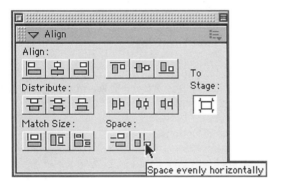   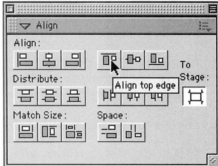

11. Now onto the last six layers. On frames 7-12 of the same layers, drag movie clips onto the stage and line them up in a row, directly below the top row:

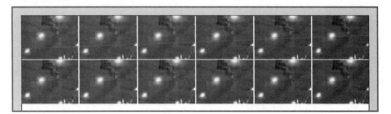

12. Select all of the second row movie clips, and align them horizontally with the Space evenly horizontally option in the Align panel. With all the movie clips still selected, enter '68.5' in the Y value of the Property inspector to place the movie clips directly below the top row in a neat line:

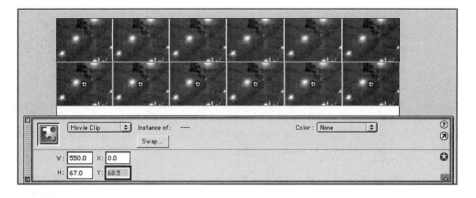

13. Extend the timelines of all twelve video clip layers to frame 60.

14. Now, no need to wait any longer go ahead and test the movie with Control > Test Movie. You'll probably notice that it does not loop like it should, and restarts itself. We need to stop the movie on the last frame so that all the movie clips keep looping.

15. Create a new layer above all the others and name it 'actions'.

16. On frame 20 of the actions layer, insert a new keyframe. We could place one anywhere after or on frame 12, but let's create a little distance and keep our timeline a little less cluttered. Select the new keyframe and open up the Actions window with Window > Actions:

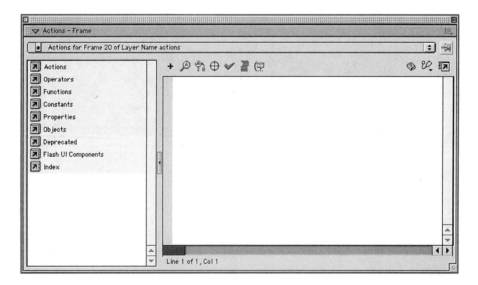

17. In the script pane, enter:

```
stop();
```

18. Now test the movie again. Things should run a lot smoother, with the effect looping until infinity.

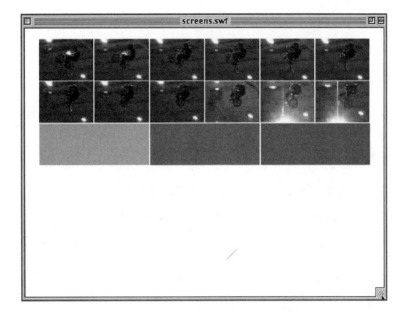

I've added a simple graphic underneath the video instances in my version, as you can see in the screenshots (or in the final file – halfpipe_final.fla), but you can fill the bottom half of your stage with whatever you want.

19. Save the movie. We just might have some use for it in the next chapter... hey - no peeking!

This effect could make a web page really come alive. The whole effect is only 86k because the same movie clip is used over and over again, and movie clips only need to be loaded in once.

Now onto a little bit of timeline manipulation with just a little bit of ActionScript.

Manipulating video timelines

If the idea of a video going forwards at normal speed is a little dull, then you might learn something here. Because video movie clips can be treated in a similar way to normal Flash movie clips, we can play with their timelines with a little scripting. For example, we can tell them to go to a particular frame, back up a frame, or go forward five frames.

We're going to make a video controller to allow us to do a number of things to our video clip:

- Play / Pause

- Fast Forward / Rewind

- Frame Forward / Back

- Go to a random frame

This will create an application similar to the QuickTime Player, the Windows Media Player, or a VCR:

The pause button

Let's start with the pause button

1. Open the `controller.fla` file from the code download for this chapter. As with the last exercise, the file consists of just a video clip and nothing else.

The video clip is big, and hasn't been compressed much. If we were using this for a non-broadband web site, then we'd compress it some more, but we need to be able to see what's happening in our video to check if our controls are working here.

2. Create a new movie clip called 'vcr' with Insert > New Symbol. In the vcr timeline, drag in a copy of cross_ramps.mov. When prompted with the extend timeline dialog click Yes.

3. Center the video in the movie clip with the Align tool. Insert a new layer, and on the new layer insert a keyframe parallel to the last frame on the video layer (this should be frame 117).

4. Click on this new keyframe and open the Actions panel (Window > Actions). Enter the following stop action:

```
stop();
```

5. That's the video movie clip complete, so return to the main timeline, and drag a copy of the vcr movie clip from the Library. Center it on stage, and give it an instance name of 'vid' in the Property inspector:

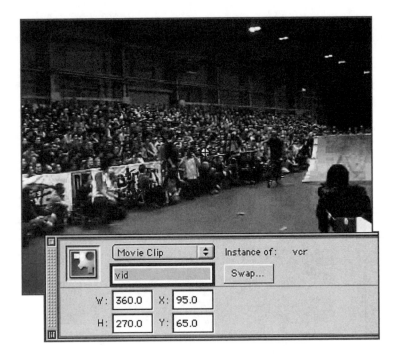

> *An instance name is a unique identifier for a movie clip or object in Flash. Giving a movie clip a unique name allows us to reference it with ActionScript in a little while.*

6. Our video is now ready to be manipulated by some yet-to-be-created buttons. Rename the original layer 'video' and create a new layer called 'buttons'.

7. On the buttons layer, draw a small red square with a black outline (using the Rectangle tool) below our video on the stage. This will be a pause button, the beginning of our button empire.

8. Select the square and its outline and convert it into a graphic symbol (F8) called 'button'.

9. We can use this symbol for all of our buttons. Let's create the pause button first. Select Insert > New Symbol. Make it a Button symbol with the name 'pause button'.

10. Within the pause button timeline, drag in a copy of the button graphic symbol and center it:

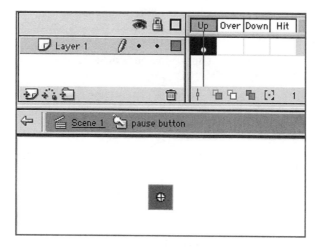

Don't worry too much about the other button states right now. If you want to customize this you can always return here later.

11. Insert a new layer called 'detail' on the button timeline. On this, draw the universal pause sign:

12. Return to the main timeline. You should now have the following:

13. We need to apply a little ActionScript to the button. Select the pause button and open the Actions panel. Enter the following ActionScript:

```
on (release) {
     _root.vid.stop ();
}
```

This script is saying "when this button is clicked on and released...make the video on the main timeline stop". _root refers to the main timeline and vid is the instance name that we gave the video earlier.

14. Now test the movie. When you do this, the video will start to play. When you click and release the pause button, it will stop playing. Unfortunately, at the moment that is the only function. A bit limited, so let's do something about that....

The play button

The next thing we need is a play button.

1. Right-click (CTRL-click on Mac) on the pause button in the Library, and select Duplicate from the context-menu:

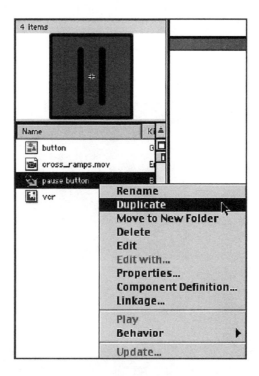

2. In the dialog that appears, enter 'play button' as the name and click OK. Double-click on the newly created play button in the Library to edit it.

3. On the detail layer, delete the current pause symbol and replace it with a play sign:

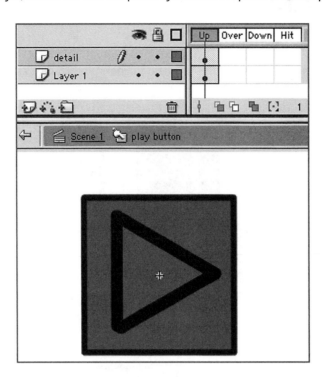

4. Return to the main timeline, and drag a copy of the play button from the Library. Place it immediately to the left of the pause button:

5. Select the play button and open the Actions panel. Insert the following code:

```
on (release) {
    _root.vid.play ();
}
```

This resembles the code for the pause button with only one minor alteration. The stop has been replaced by a play. Pretty obvious huh?

6. Test the movie and try both buttons in sequence. So far so good.

Now we need to add the remaining buttons – frame forward, frame back, fast forward, fast rewind, and random.

7. Go ahead and create these buttons in the same way as you created the play button:

- Duplicate the pause button.

- Give it a relevant name.

- Double-click on the new button to edit it.

- Change the look of the button on the detail layer.

- Drag a copy of the button onto the main stage on the buttons layer.

My buttons look like this:

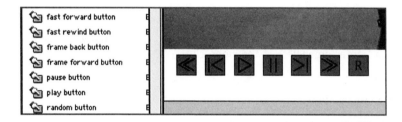

Once you've done them, we need to add a little more script to make them work. Let's start with the frame forward and back buttons.

9. Select the frame forward button on the main stage and open the Actions panel. Enter the following code:

```
on (release) {
     _root.vid.nextFrame();
}
```

As with the previous chunks of code that we've seen, this follows the same pattern but uses a different method to manipulate vid. The nextFrame method is self-explanatory – it tells our video (vid) to go to the next frame in the sequence. So each time this button is clicked on, the video will advance one frame forward.

10. Select the frame back button and type the following into the Actions panel:

```
on (release) {
     _root.vid.prevFrame();
}
```

Again, this code is familiar – with exception to the `prevFrame` method, which is Flash shorthand for "previous frame". This predictably sends the sequence to the frame previous to the current one.

11.   Now we have our frame back and frame forward buttons. Easy, eh? Test the movie and have a go. Remember that only four of the buttons work at the moment.

12.   The last button is the random button, which illustrates the ability to jump to any frame in the video clip. Select the random button on the stage and type the following into the Actions window:

```
on (release) {
      _root.vid.gotoAndStop (Math.round (Math.random ()*116));
}
```

Okay, this looks a little more complicated but it is only because of the horrible number of brackets. This code is simply saying: "When the user clicks the mouse, send the video playhead to a randomly determined frame between 1 and 116."

116 is not a magic number, it just happens to be the number of frames in the video that I'm using! `Math.round` is used to return a rounded number from the result of taking a value between 0 and 1 and multiplying it by 116.

13.   Go ahead and test the movie. Click on the random button, and you'll be magically transported to a random frame somewhere in the video clip.

Now, onto the last two buttons – fast forward and fast rewind.

Fast forward and fast rewind

If you have a cheap or old VCR you'll be aware of sore finger syndrome, brought on by long bouts of having to hold down the fast forward button to find the start of last week's Quincy.

It might seem trivial, but deciding on how something functions is pretty essential when building any kind of application. I've decided to go with the sore finger method – requiring the user to hold down the mouse button to fast forward or rewind – because the clip is so short, and a click-on/click-off option would just mean that the whole clip zooms past before the user gets a chance to stop it.

1.   Select the fast forward button and open its Actions. Enter the following script:

```
on (press) {
      _root.ffwd = true;
}
on (release) {
      _root.ffwd = false;
}
```

This code is split into two mouse button actions: `press` and `release`. The `press` action changes the `ffwd` flag to true – operating the fast forwarding, and the `release` action (when the user releases the mouse button) switches it off. Where is the flag being checked? It will be on the video movie clip.

2. Select the video and add the following actions to it:

```
onClipEvent (enterFrame) {
    if (_root.ffwd == true) {
        frame = this._currentframe +5;
        this.gotoAndStop (frame);
    }
}
```

This time we are attaching code directly to a movie clip. If you find this difficult to comprehend, don't panic. We'll go through it in steps (and you are forgiven if you still don't get it). The code is basically doing this:

■ Do this every frame of the flash movie

■ Check if the flag is true and if it is:

■ Store the sum of the current video frame position + 5

■ Send the video playhead to the frame number stored above

If the flag is not true, the actions in the curly brackets following the `if` command are ignored. `frame` above is a variable – a container for holding information to be used later by the Flash movie. As you might have gathered, my fast forward is a little faster than usual, with a 5 frame increase each time.

3. Test the movie. You should now be able to speed through the video when you hold down the mouse button. When you release the button, it should stop. If you'd like to reduce the speed of the fast forward, simply reduce the 5 in the last section of code.

4. Let's hook up the rewind button in similar fashion. Select the fast rewind button and enter the following code:

```
on (press) {
    _root.frwd = true;
}
on (release) {
    _root.frwd = false;
}
```

As you can see these are the same actions, using a different flag name.

5. Select the video movie clip on the stage and add the following code before the last curly bracket:

```
if (_root.frwd == true) {
            frame = this._currentframe -5;
            this.gotoAndStop (frame);
}
```

This makes the code for the video movie clip look like this in all:

```
onClipEvent (enterFrame) {
    if (_root.ffwd == true) {
            frame = this._currentframe +5;
            this.gotoAndStop (frame);
    }
    if (_root.frwd == true) {
            frame = this._currentframe -5;
            this.gotoAndStop (frame);
    }
}
```

Every frame, this checks both flags to see if they are true and if the user is pressing either of them. Of course, it is impossible to press both at once, but both conditions need to be checked all the same.

6. Before closing the Actions panel, add the following before all of the previous code:

```
onClipEvent (load) {
    this.stop();
}
```

This stops the movie clip from playing when the movie clip is loaded into Flash. So when the Flash movie begins, the vid will be paused on frame 1 and the user can take full control from there.

7. Now test the movie. As you can see, the fast forward button works nicely, but there is a slight problem with the fast rewind button. It's not as speedy as the forward button but it *is* working. Flash appears to buffer video ahead in the Flash Player memory, so it has no problem going forwards but dislikes going back.

That's our video controller finished, all that remains is for a little customization. My final BMX controller `controller_final.fla` looks like this:

In this exercise we have learnt some valuable things about video timelines, and how they can be manipulated in Flash. As you can see, it only involves a little ActionScript, and nothing too heavy (and you should be able to reuse the code we've used in this exercise).

The main point to remember when you come to try this is that you need to give your video movie clip an instance name in the Property inspector, and you need to reference it in its movie location (I used `_root` – the main timeline all the way through mine).

Controlling multiple video clips

We can control the placement of video movie clips, and use some basic buttons to control navigation. This means that we can add an interface to access our video clips in the guise of a television set (for those of you viewing in black and white, the TV in the screenshot is orange and yellow). We'll sort out the video clips first, before adding the buttons to control them, and finally adding some sound.

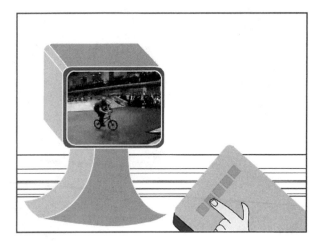

I want my Flash TV

The main timeline for our TV will consist of six frames – one for each of the five clips, and one for the fuzz in between channel changes. The buttons will navigate between them and also shut off the sound of the previous clip – each 'channel' has a separate imported soundtrack that fits with the pace of the clips.

1. Open `tv_clips.fla` from the download files for this chapter. This FLA contains the imported clips and sounds that we will use for this exercise. Again, feel free to use your own files if you'd prefer – we've shown you how to import video files, and Chapters 6 and 7 will cover sound in more depth.

2. The first thing to do is to place the video clips within movie clips. Use Insert > New Symbol to create a new movie clip called '1_ballet'.

3. Within the timeline of 1_ballet, drag a copy of ballet.mov from the Library and drop it onto the stage (BMX fans will point out here that this move is called Flatlands, and not ballet - apologies!).

4. In the dialog that appears, click Yes to extend the frames, and center the video on the stage.

5. Create a movie clip for each of the remaining clips (including TVfuzz.mov), remembering to extend the frames for each clip. Give them the names that you can see in the screenshot:

6. Once you have done that, create a new folder in the Library called 'video movie clips' and drop all the movie clips into it so that our Library doesn't get too messy.

7. Return to the main timeline, and rename the existing layer 'videos'. Insert blank keyframes up to frame 6 with F7:

8. Drag a copy of the TV fuzz movie clip onto the stage in frame 1 of the videos layer. Resize the movie to 180 x 135 pixels using the Property inspector, and center the movie clip on the stage.

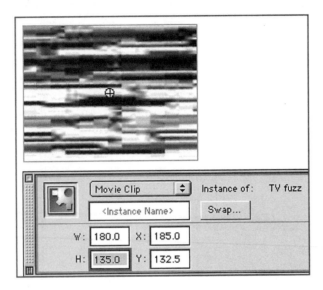

The fuzz clip is now the same size as the other imported clips. The clip is meant to be distorted, so we can scale it as much as we like – distortion can only enhance the effect.

9. Let's draw a TV to add a little realism to our movie. Create a new layer called 'TV' and move it below the videos layer.

10. Lock the videos layer, and use the TV fuzz movie clip as a guide to draw a TV set on the TV layer. If you want a simple TV with curved corners, try the Round Rectangle Radius option of the Rectangle tool. Otherwise, be creative and create your ideal TV, or import a bitmap picture of a real TV.

11. When you are done with your drawing, select the television set and convert it into a graphic symbol called 'television set':

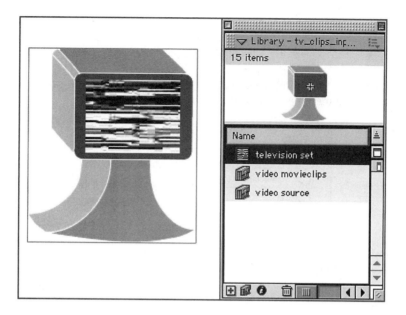

12. Lock the TV layer and unlock the videos layer. Drag the 1_ballet movie clip onto frame 2 of the videos layer and center it.

13. Drag the remaining video movie clips individually onto frames 3-6 in sequence, ending with 5_wallride on frame 6. Center them all to stage.

Now we need to do a few essential things for our movie. Firstly, we need to set up some frame labels for our buttons to access.

14. Create a new layer called 'frame labels'. Place it above the other two layers. As we did before, insert keyframes on every frame of the frame labels layer up to frame 6:

15. Select frame 1 and give it a label name of 'fuzz' in the Property inspector. This will be used when we need to send the playhead back to the fuzz after a clip has played.

16. Select frame 2 and label it 1. As you might notice, this ties in with number prefix given to each movie clip name. Label frames 3-6 with the numbers 2-5 (think of the frame number and -1!). You should now have many red flags on the main timeline. Hey – it's the 4th of July! Err.... Not quite. Just a load of frame labels, sorry.

These labels will be referenced by the channel buttons, which we'll create in a little while. Before we do that, we'll stop the frames in the timeline.

17. Create a new layer called 'actions'. Drag it above all the other layers, and as before, insert keyframes up to and including frame 6 of the layer. It's pretty common to have the actions layer as the uppermost layer as it makes Flash movies easier to decipher.

18. Select frame 1 of the actions layer and insert a stop action. Do the same for all the other frames on the layer, and the timeline should look like this:

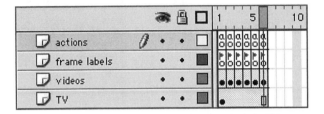

If you test the movie now, you should get a whole lotta fuzz and not much else. The timeline is halted at frame 1 and the fuzz movie clip just loops over and over:

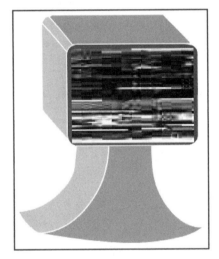

Control buttons

How do you stop all that fuzz and get something more interesting? Time for those buttons...

1. Create a new button symbol called 'change button'.

2. In the buttons timeline, draw a small square on the center of the stage.

3. Return to the main timeline, create a new layer called 'buttons', and move it so that it's the bottom layer. Drag 5 copies of change button onto the buttons layer:

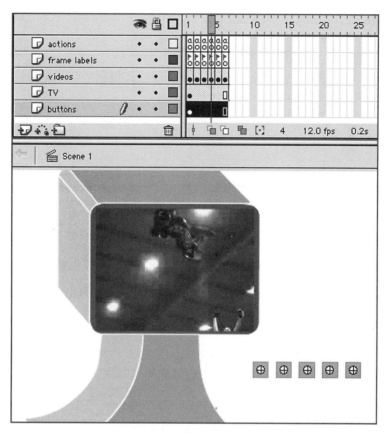

4. Each button has to be programmed to turn to a different channel, so select the first button on the left and open the Actions panel. Enter the following code on the button:

```
on (release) {
    gotoAndPlay ("1");
}
```

This code tells Flash to send the main timeline playhead to the frame labelled '1' (actually frame 2).

> *We could use a frame number instead of a label, but labels sometimes make tasks easier in the long run (for example if you continually shifted your content around on the timeline you would also need to update the destination frame number). We could also use _root.gotoAndPlay ("1"); but because the buttons are on the _root (main timeline), any references we make go straight to it anyhow.*

5. Select the second button and enter the following code in the Actions panel. As with the last button, this sends the playhead to a labelled frame:

```
on (release) {
    gotoAndPlay ("2");
}
```

6. Repeat the steps with all the buttons, incrementing the destination frame label each time, meaning that the last button should have this code:

```
on (release) {
    gotoAndPlay ("5");
}
```

7. Once you've done this, test the movie, and you should now be able to click on the buttons and change the channel. Aren't remote controls great?

    The one major issue is that we only get to see the fuzz once at the start, and the clips are looping because we never told them to do anything. Each video clip now requires a little bit of ActionScript to send the playhead back to the fuzz when they have finished playing.

8. Double-click on 1_ballet in the Library to edit it. Create a new layer and call it 'actions'.

9. Locate the last frame of the video clip and insert a keyframe on the parallel frame on the actions layer:

10. Open the Actions window and insert the following ActionScript:

```
_root.gotoAndStop ("fuzz");
```

This simply tells Flash to go to the fuzz label (frame 1) on the main timeline, when this clip has finished playing.

11. Repeat steps 8-10 for all the video movie clips. Remember to place the keyframe on the same frame as the last video frame.

12. Test the movie – the clips will play, and be sent back to the fuzz after they have finished. Not exactly how television works, but welcome relief from inane adverts.

Adding sound

Our home entertainment system is almost finished. All that needs adding is the sound elements and a little masking to give the television curved corners.

1. On the main timeline, insert a new layer called 'sounds'. Place it just above the videos layer. As with all the other layers, insert keyframes up to frame 6:

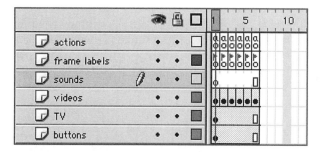

You'll be happy to know that I have saved you a bit of time when it comes to the length of the sound clips. I trimmed them (originally in MP3 format) a little in QuickTime Pro and exported them as uncompressed AIFF files (the Mac equivalent of PC WAVs) for import into Flash.

2. Select frame 1 of the sounds layer and access the sound drop-down in the Property inspector:

3. From the drop-down select `fuzz.aiff`. In the options that appear, set the amount of loops to '9999':

> *The maximum number of loops in Flash is 9999, so lets hope that users don't stare at the fuzz long enough to hear our loop ending!*

4. On frame 2 of the layer, select `train_exc.aiff` from the sound drop-down. Leave the loop to the standard 0 as it will only play once (the sound is roughly the same length as the video clip).

5. Set the other sounds as follows:

    ● Frame 3 : `intro2.mp3`

    ● Frame 4 : `show_yr_colors_nozzle.aif`

    ● Frame 5 : `nozzle_exc.aiff`

    ● Frame 6 : `shootingstar_exc.aif`

6. Once this is done, test the movie. If you try clicking a number of buttons in quick sequence, you'll be greeted by a wall of noise. If you can distinguish it through that racket, you might notice that the fuzz noise is playing throughout.

7. Luckily, one tiny bit of ActionScript can remedy this. Select the left-most button and open up the Actions window. Add this line of code after the first one:

```
stopAllSounds ();
```

All the code for the button now looks like this:

```
on (release) {
    stopAllSounds ();
    gotoAndPlay ("1");
}
```

This magic bit of ActionScript might sound drastic, but because we only want one sound playing at any time, it clears the airwaves before they are filled by another sound.

8. If we want to avoid something that sounds like Musique Concrete, we need to add the code to each button in the same place.

9. Test the movie, and you should have a pretty seamless transition between the sounds. The only noticeable problem area is that the sound of a clip sometimes continues to play for a split second over the fuzz.

10. To remove this, add a `stopAllSounds();` command just before the code at the end of each video movie clip (where we put the `_root.gotoAndPlay ("fuzz");`).

Masking

The last thing I promised to do was to mask the video, and give it curved corners. This involves a fairly standard use of Flash that you'll have seen a thousand times elsewhere. The beauty of the way MX handles video is that it works almost seamlessly with the rest of Flash.

1. Insert a new layer called 'mask'. Place it just above the videos layer. We're going to draw a rectangle with curved corners, to fit our television.

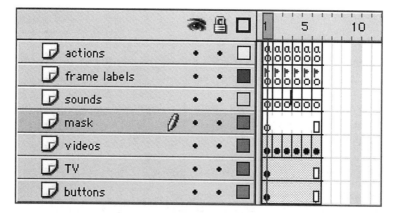

2. To make our job a lot easier, we need to check if Snap to Objects is on. Select the View menu and switch it on if it is currently off.

3. Select the Rectangle tool and choose a disgusting green fill and outline. The idea is to use a color that you'd never normally use so that it stands out during authoring. The rectangle will be turned into a mask where the color will become the transparent 'window' that the user will see, so the user will never get to see our misguided color selection.

4. In the rectangle tool options, select the Round Rectangle Radius option and set it to the same setting you used when you drew the television – 10 in my case – to give our mask soft corners.

5. On frame 1 of the mask layer, line up your cursor to the top left corner of the fuzz movie clip.

6. Now click, and start dragging a shape to cover the fuzz. You will notice that as you start doing this, the shape snaps to the top corner.

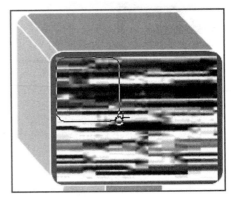

7. Drag down to the bottom right corner and release the mouse button. You should now have a garish green rectangle with curved corners covering the TV screen.

8. Double-click on the paper icon next to the Mask symbol name to bring up the Layer Properties, and select mask from the type list in the window. Click OK, and this will change the icon next to the layer name to a square with an oval in it (pictured).

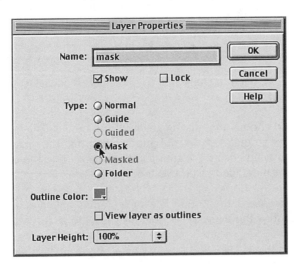

9. Click and drag the videos layer up to below the 'm' of the mask layer:

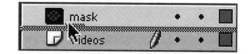

10. Release the mouse – the videos layer icon should changed, and the layer name will be indented. This means that it's now masked by the mask layer. Test the movie and you'll see that our television has a more realistic shape.

That's our TV set done! Go ahead and customize it with your own clips, sounds, and some better graphics. I've added a remote control to mine, and a hand to change the channels. I also added a small border to the video clips to give them a little bit of definition. Here's my super-kitsch attempt, available as tv_final.fla from the download section:

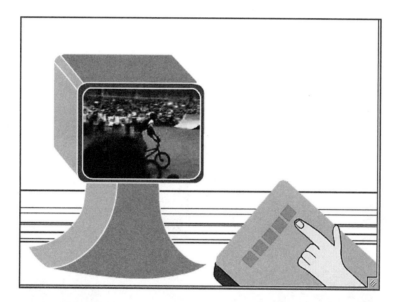

What this exercise shows you is that you can let the user arrange the order of your clips, and not limit them to a linear experience. Normal video on the web simply doesn't allow you to do this, and this is where Flash interactivity comes in.

Summary

In this chapter, we've seen some of the possibilities available to us when we use video in Flash. Thinking of Flash videos as having frame-based timelines can help us to understand them in a Flash-centric way, opening up a number of possibilities for moving content around that the other video players just can't touch.

We've also seen how Flash allows us to easily build graphics and content around video assets, suggesting that building full web sites in Flash with embedded video is easily achieved. Say bye-bye to those pop-ups and external applications and hello to full web site solutions in Flash.

If some of the script in this chapter has scared you a little, don't worry – in the next chapter, we'll be looking at the effects we can create without any scripting.

Adding Effects to Flash Video

What we'll cover in this chapter:

- *Different ways of **masking** video content.*

- *Manipulating a movie clip's **properties**, such as **rotation**, **alpha**, and **tint**, to add creative effects to video content.*

- *Using these properties to enhance the clarity of a video.*

As well as serving up straight video content, Flash gives us the opportunity to use its drawing tools to customize our video. Properties such as color, size, rotation, contrast, brightness, and so on can all be manipulated when a video is embedded in a movie clip. In this chapter, we'll take a look at the available properties (without any ActionScripting) to see how they can be used to create some cool effects, and how they can help to integrate your video content within your overall web site design.

Before we examine these properties, we'll take a brief look at some simple masking techniques, showing how masking your video content can be used creatively to great effect.

Creative masking

In Macromedia Flash MX, video no longer needs to be displayed separately in its common rectangular form. It can sit within an interface, snuggled up to the surrounding web site assets. There are two ways you can achieve successful integration with the other web site elements: clever **layering** and **masking**.

Before we look at some examples, there are some important considerations to take into account when you use either of these techniques: don't cover up too much of your video! This might sound bizarre, after all this is why we use masking, but there is simply no point in covering up large amounts of video that could be trimmed out before importing into Flash – this just adds to the file size for no reason.

> *It is important to point out here that using masks (especially animated masks) in Flash uses a considerable amount of processor power, a resource that you won't want to lose when displaying video. The best thing to do is to test the mask effect on a number of machines and see if there is any considerable lag.*

For instance, imagine using layering to fake a widescreen video. If you're anything like me, then you'll (subconsciously) love those ubiquitous black bars. If we import the following clip into Flash:

...and then fake the widescreen effect by adding two black rectangles, placed on a layer that sits above the video layer in the timeline:

...we'll pay a penalty (in terms of file size *and* by placing unnecessary demands on the user's processing power) for the areas of video covered by the black bars. If you wanted to recreate this effect, the best solution would be to trim the video to the desired size in a video editing application before importing it into Flash (the masking option in QuickTime Pro does a nice quick job). Another option would be to export the movie in widescreen ratio (16:9). Then, you can do some faking in Flash, with the simple black rectangles.

Let's move on and look at using masks creatively with video. All of the source FLAs for the following examples are available at the code downloads section for this chapter at www.friendsofed.com.

Masking with text

Using text as a mask is a quick way to spruce up that boring logo, but it needs to be used sensibly. The amount of physical space that text takes up on the screen is minimal, so if you do use a mask of text over your video, it's quite possible that you'll waste a great deal of the masked video information. This information will still be in the file but the user will not be able to view it, so you'll pay for it with the file size. To justify using this technique, you need to find a good balance and let enough of the video display through the mask to justify the masking text.

Let's look at an example (if you want to look at this effect in detail, the source file is called masking_with_text.fla).

It is quite well balanced, with much of the video on display, allowing enough detail of the video to show through the text:

The mask is made up of a central rectangle, and above and below this, I've used text that has been broken apart into a primitive graphic:

As you can see, it's not difficult to make, but the effect looks pretty good and pulls together both the video and the logo. What is best about this is that the video element really makes the page come alive – a static JPG image just wouldn't achieve the same desired effect on a web site dealing with this kind of subject matter.

Texture

When creating your masks, there are no definitive rules to follow. My advice is to choose the Brush tool, scribble for a while on the stage, and then test the movie. Some of the results you get from just a little improvisation are pretty inspiring and can often lead you to unexpected places.

The following mask example (`masking_texture.fla`) was created simply by drawing a single line, converting it into a graphic symbol, and then duplicating it to cover the whole video clip:

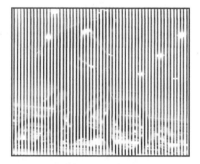

It's worth noting here that you can't make masks using strokes in Flash (such as lines created by the Pencil and Line tools, and any stroke outlines from rectangles or circles). You can get round this by converting your strokes into fills using Modify > Shape > Convert Lines to Fills. If you want to make a mask from freeform lines then you can either follow the step above, or you can draw freehand with the Brush tool (because this tool draws fills not strokes).

This is how the example mask looks on the stage in Flash:

I've extended the previous example by adding a motion tweened mask in `masking_texture_tween.fla`. The mask begins off-stage at the top and then tweens vertically down over the video all the way down until it moves below the stage.

In this example there is obviously the problem that we discussed earlier in the chapter: it is not file size effective. Little of the video is shown at any time, and even though it's a nice effect, it doesn't make for valuable content. Some important questions arising from this are:

- What are you using the video for?

- Is the video one of the focuses of the web site or are you using it for creative effect?

- How does the video add to the user experience?

This next textured mask effect (`masking_texture_edges.fla`) reminds me a little of the texture at the edge of an untrimmed photograph from the darkroom. Besides taking away the dreaded perfect edges, it also gives the clip a little raggedness – which is perfectly suited to my BMX footage:

This mask could be animated – we could add a number of different frames containing various scribbles – to work with the footage and add more motion and character to it. The obvious difference between this example and the last is that this (subtly) enhances the presentation of the video; it does not conceal it nor drown it with overuse of the effect.

The mask was made by drawing a rectangle to cover the whole video clip, and then simply using the Eraser tool to roughly rub out sections of the rectangle:

Multiple masks

If you have the patience to combine multiple masks and video movie clips you can produce endless variations. The truth is that these may be of less immediate use than any of the previous examples we've seen so far, but they're still worth exploring.

This first one (`multiple_mask_skew.fla`) uses two movie clips containing the same video, which are then skewed. Two masks are added to create a shape resembling an open book:

This one requires a little more headwork than the previous examples, but it's relatively quick and easy to build. Both video movie clips were firstly centered, and then skewed to 30 and -30 degrees respectively. The masks were formed using rectangles that were halved and then skewed. Here are the two movie clips and their respective masks:

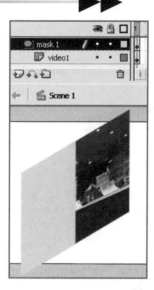

Remember: to check how the mask effect will look before publishing or testing your movie, simply lock the mask and masked layers.

If you are interested in creating some mask effects of your own and need some inspiration, take a look at Lifaros' work with masks at www.friendsofed.com/fmc/lifaros.

Now that we've taken a quick look at masking effects, let's move on to the movie clip symbol properties that we can use to manipulate video in Flash.

Movie clip properties

They might sound a bit dull, but altering movie clips' properties allows you to manipulate your video in a number of cool ways. Properties give you more control over integrating your video in your web site, or just give you a chance to go wild and experiment.

Right now we're going to look at each property individually and do an ultra-quick exercise for each one. You may well recognize a number of these properties as we go along, but as we are leaning towards video, you'll probably learn something new.

If you want follow our examples exactly, we're going to use `properties_base.fla` as the starting point for all of the following exercises, and you can get it from the code downloads section for this chapter at www.friendsofed.com.

None of the properties we're going to look at here will involve scripting (we'll ease off after the last chapter), but if you are interested in using more advanced ActionScript to control video and movie clips, this is covered in depth in Chapter 11.

Let's kick off with the physical properties first (this first one is particularly apt for BMXing).

Spinning around

Everyone has watched TV upside down at one time or another. Fortunately, the novelty soon wears off when the veins at the side of your head start throbbing! If you feel at all nostalgic for viewing video upside down, you'll be pleased to know that you can do it in Flash (and save yourself a headache in the process).

1. Import a video file into Flash or open `properties_base.fla` from the download for this chapter.

2. Create a new movie clip symbol called 'video' and drag a copy of your embedded video file out of the Library onto its timeline. Give the movie clip a central registration point and center the video clip at (0,0).

3. Return to the main timeline and drag out four copies of your movie clip onto the stage. Align them together like so:

We're going to rotate two of these movie clips by 180 degrees to make a weird visual effect.

4. Select the top left movie clip and open the Transform panel (Window > Transform). In the Rotate section of the Transform panel, enter '180' and press ENTER.

5. Repeat this step for the bottom right movie clip, again rotating it by 180 degrees.

6. Test your movie and sit back. Even though you're only watching two angles of rotation, because of the way that the movies are composed and are asymmetrical, it feels like more.

Besides entering numeric values to rotate the movie clips, you can also rotate clips manually using the Free Transform tool or by right-clicking on the movie clip and choosing Rotate and Skew from the context menu. Both options allow you to manually rotate an object – holding down the SHIFT key while doing this constrains the rotation to 45 degree increments.

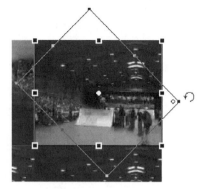

As a quick example of how rotating video can help integrate the video content snugly into a web site, here's a quick interface I came up with using a couple of videos rotated at 30 and -150 degree angles (see rotation2.fla).

Skewing

As with rotation, skewing might only be useful in a small number of situations. One of these could be if you're designing a gallery interface where the videos are hanging on a gallery wall in the movie. You'd need to skew the video to give a false impression of perspective. It can do pretty some pretty wacky distortions and is worth playing around with to see what you can squeeze out of it.

Cubic

Here's a screenshot from the world famous (ahem) web site BMX Cube (it's `cubic.fla` in the download files):

As you can see, the sides of the cube are skewed videos. Let's look at how to make this.

1. Open up `properties_base.fla` from the download example or import one of your own video clips into a new movie.

2. As always, create a new movie clip and drag a copy of the embedded video from the Library into it. Agree to the frame extension dialog and center the video at (0,0) in the movie clip.

3. On the main timeline, drag two copies of the video movie clip onto the stage. To allow more space for the BMX Biogs on the top of the cube, scale both move clips' width up to 130% using the Transform panel (you'll need to uncheck the Constrain box).

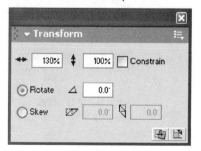

4.   Select the left movie clip and, using the Transform panel, set its vertical skew to 45 degrees. You will need to check the Skew radio button first.

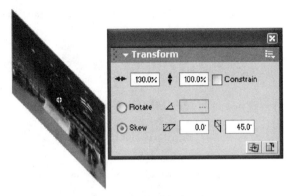

5.   Select the right movie clip and set its vertical skew to -45 degrees. You should now have two skewed movie clips:

6.   Use the Align panel to align the movie clips along their bottom edge. Then position them so that their vertical edges are touching. When moving one movie clip across to the other hold down the SHIFT key to constrain the clip to the horizontal, so that they stay aligned correctly. When they're almost touching, zoom in close, and use the arrow keys on your keyboard to move them pixel by pixel.

7.   When you have them both lined up next to each other and touching, select both clips and group them using Modify > Group.

8.   Center the grouped movie clips horizontally on the stage using the Align panel. Now we've finished the sides of our cube, we need to draw in the lid.

9.   Create a new layer called cube and select the Rectangle tool. Choose an appropriate color in keeping with your video clips and set the stroke width to 2 in the Property inspector.

10. Draw a rectangle above the grouped clips. Don't worry about the size and location on the stage for now.

11. Select the rectangle on the stage and click on the Free Transform tool. Holding down the SHIFT key, rotate the rectangle by 45 degrees:

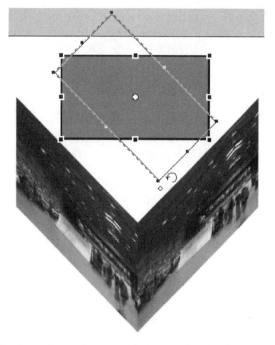

12. With the rectangle still selected use the arrow keys to align it along the top edges of the video clips. Finally, use the Free Transform tool to resize the rectangle into a perfect square that sits on top of the clips, forming the cube shape:

All that remains for you to do is to add some text elements if you want to, and test your movie.

You could replace the current lid with another video movie clip (rotated and scaled) – I tried this, but decided to stick with my colored cube... you can sometimes have too much of a good thing!

Flipping

When you are grappling with an image that doesn't quite fit into a certain composition, simply flipping it horizontally can often help (even though you might look back at it and be aware of the discrepancies). The same idea applies to video – if it doesn't seem to fit, consider flipping it. In most cases you can get away with it, unless of course the video has any obvious distinguishing marks or flaws that makes it unsuitable for mirroring.

On the flipside

1. Open `properties_base.fla` or import one of your own video clips into a fresh movie. As in the previous exercises, create a new movie clip and drag a copy of your video from the Library into it.

2. On the main timeline, drag four copies of the video movie clip onto the stage. Arrange the movie clips into a tight rectangle, closed up around the center point with no gaps visible between them:

3. Select the appropriate movie clips and use Modify > Transform > Flip Horizontal or Flip Vertical to flip each clip as shown here:

    no flips   Flip Horizontal

    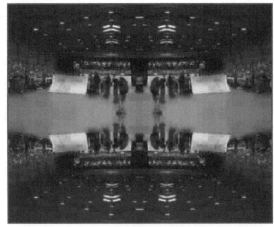

    Flip Vertical   Flip Vertical and Horizontal

4. Once you've done this, test the movie and travel back in time to the apogee of video mixing effects, circa 1972.

Combining rotation with flips can often get you some pretty cool results.

Brightness

If you're working with dark or dull footage, you might welcome the ability to brighten them up in Flash. The Brightness option also allows you to lighten or darken video, as you want. It's set to zero by default, and can be increased or decreased by values up to 100.

You can change the Brightness property of a movie clip or symbol by selecting the symbol on the stage, and choosing Brightness from the Color drop-down menu in the Property inspector:

Tint

If you thought any of the previous properties were cool, then prepare to be blown away by the Tint option. Even though the name suggests a minor degree of coloring, the results you can get from using it are pretty intense. If you work hard enough with this property, you could build that flashing disco floor that you've always dreamt of.

The Tint property is made up of two inputs: color (RGB sliders) and alpha. Here is full red with an alpha value of 36%:

Once you've chosen a color, the alpha setting is used to increase or decrease the overall intensity of the color. For example, a tint alpha of 100% would drown out a symbol with sheer color.

Besides opening up a new world in experimenting with video, the Tint option can also subtly enhance colors in your videos. For example, if your video has a lot of red but lacks yellow you can lift the yellow; or if your video has a lot of blue but you want even more of it then crank up the blue tones. This process in Flash achieves a similar effect as using filters during film shoots, in order to enhance certain tones of the video.

It's murder on the dance floor

Let's try this out in an exercise.

1. Open `properties_base.fla`, or start a fresh movie and import a video clip of your own. Create a new movie clip and drag the video from the Library into it.

2. Return to the main timeline and drop six copies of your movie clip onto the stage. Arrange them in a basic 3x2 grid format:

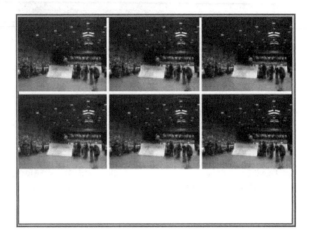

3. Select the top left movie clip and choose Tint from the Color drop-down in the Property inspector.

    Rather than be too fussy with our color choice here, we're going to work with rainbow colors: red, orange, yellow, green, blue and violet (admittedly, we've left indigo from the list!)

4. Choose red from the color selector and give it a tint alpha of 40%.

5. Select the remaining movie clips and set their tint to orange, yellow, green, blue, and violet, working in a clockwise direction from the top center clip. Give each one a tint alpha of 40%.

    When you are doing this, select a tone of color that lifts the video clip, rather than dulling it. Remember that we're representing the rainbow here and he likes to make people happy.

6. Once you've done this, they should already look quite inviting. Save your movie as `tint1.fla` and then test the movie. You'll see that the tint alpha value we gave them is just enough – although the tint colors take over, they still preserve some of the original color. If you feel this is too much (or it might even be too little) go ahead and play with the tint alpha value.

If you take the tint alpha value much higher, you'll veer into The Smiths album cover territory (*The Queen is Dead* is a good example), but this might be the effect you are looking for.

Okay, this isn't the disco floor that I suggested earlier, but imagine that you're with Lionel Richie circa 1986 getting down on the ceiling and looking down at the dance floor. Or you could apply some skewing to make a good old isometric dance floor. Darn it! Pixel Boy has escaped and is strutting his stuff at the video disco (take a look `tint2.fla` included in the download files):

Alpha

The Alpha property is one of the most commonly used properties for all sorts of effects in Flash, ranging from simple tweening to ActionScript-driven animation. The simple reason for this is that it allows you to make an object appear out of nowhere, fading in from nothing into your web site or movie. In truth, the scaling-and-fading-in-text trick is a little overused, but we can apply this old trick to video and give it a new lease of life.

> *As with masking, the alpha effect is also very processor-intensive so you need to think carefully about how you go about using it in your movies.*

Fade in fade out

Right now, we're going to use the Alpha property to create a cross dissolve transition in Flash. We'll create a sequence of two different video clips and then manipulate the alpha properties of each clip to create a dissolve between them. (If you want to compare your file with ours as you go along then you can refer to `fade_in_fade_out.fla` in the download files.)

1. Open `alpha_base.fla` from the download files for this chapter or locate two of your own video clips and import them into a new Flash movie.

2. Create a new movie clip called 'clip1'. Drag a copy of one of the videos into clip1. When you're greeted with the extend frames dialog, make a note of the length of the clip and click OK. Center the video in your movie clip.

3. Insert a new layer called 'actions' on the movie clip's timeline. Locate the end of the video clip and insert a keyframe (F6) above it in the actions layer. Add a stop action to this last frame (in our example this is frame 206):

4. Double-click on the clip1 name in the Library and add the number of frames (the length of this video) to its name:

5. Repeat the previous three steps for the other video clip in Library, placing it in a new movie clip called 'clip2' initially, adding a stop action to the last frame of its timeline, and renaming the clip.

    You should now have two movie clips in the Library, with each name suffixed with the number of frames in the clip:

6. Go back into the main timeline and insert two new layers. From the top down rename the layers 'actions', 'clip2', and 'clip1':

7. Now we need to line up our clips on the stage. Drag a copy of the clip2 movie clip onto the clip2 layer, and drag a copy of clip1 onto the clip1 layer. Align both clips to the center of the stage.

8. We have to increase the frame length in the main timeline to equal the actual frame length of the movie clips. So, if you're using our source file, on the clip1 layer we should have 206 frames and 89 frames on the clip2 layer. If you are using your own video clips then these values will be different.

9. Insert a keyframe (F6) in the last frame of both layers. These keyframes will be used as tween points.

Because my clip2 is much shorter than the other clip (89 frames compared to 206 frames), I've decided to put it first in the sequence. We'll let the shortest movie clip run from the start, so we need to move the other clip further along in the timeline.

Because of the length of my clips (and a little experimentation), I've decided to use a 30 frame crossover, which equates to just over a second at 25fps.

10. Select the clip you want to place second in the sequence (clip1 in my file), and drag it along the timeline so that it begins 30 frames before the other clip ends (at frame 59 in my file).

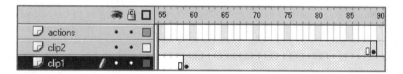

Now we need to create the fade in and fade out. Let's start with the fade out.

11. Insert a keyframe (F6) at frame 59 of the clip2 layer (or the layer containing the first clip in your sequence).

12. In the same layer, select the keyframe at frame 89, and then select the movie clip on the stage. Go into the Property inspector and choose Alpha from the Color drop-down menu. Set the alpha to 0%.

13. Select any frame between the two keyframes and use the Property inspector to add a motion tween. Your timeline should now look like the one pictured:

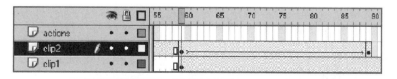

If you now scrub the playhead over the frames containing the tween, you'll see the first clip fade out revealing the clip in the layer below.

14. To get a perfectly smooth cross dissolve, we need to fade in clip1. Hide and lock the clip2 layer to prevent us accidentally working with it. Insert a keyframe at frame 89 of the clip1 layer (or at the frame corresponding to the end of the other clip's fade out tween).

15. Select the video at keyframe 59 of the clip1 layer and set its alpha to 0%. Now select any frame between 59 and 88 and insert a motion tween. Our clip1 will now fade in between frames 59 and 89:

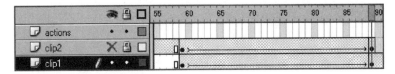

16. That's the visual elements of the movie finished. The last thing to do is to halt the movie at the last frame to round off the sequence. Add a keyframe to the actions layer at the last frame of the sequence (frame 264 of the source file). Add a stop action to this frame.

17. Now test the movie to see the neat cross dissolve transition take effect.

And that's it on the Alpha property. Even though the alpha fade effect is used so frequently, the simple reason for this is because it is quick to create and produces good results. You don't always have to combine it with a tween as we've just done here; you can also use it create subtlety (as a faded video background) or for overlaying different video objects.

Advanced Effect

The final option in the Color drop-down menu we'll look at is the Advanced Effect options. This is basically a combination of the Tint and Alpha options, presented in a separate dialog box allowing us to accurately enter these values.

Besides the obvious tinting and wild coloring, the Advanced Effect option can also help you to subtly enhance your image or video. In the following exercise, we'll go through a number of options to explore the creative possibilities available to us using the Advanced Effects settings.

Sharpening a video

1. Open the properties_base.fla. As normal, place the video in a movie clip, extend the frames and center it at (0,0).

On the main timeline, add a new layer called 'control'. Rename the existing layer 'test'.

2. Drag out two copies of the video movie clip from the Library and place one copy on each layer. Position the clip on the control layer to the right of center stage, and place the clip on the test layer to the left of center stage. The video on the right will act as a control clip to compare the effect against, and the one on the left will have the effect applied to it.

Lock the control layer so we don't accidentally change any of the content on it.

The first thing we are going to do is sharpen up the video clip slightly, adding a little brightness and changing the contrast.

3. Select the left clip and choose Advanced from the Color drop-down menu in the Property inspector. Click on the Settings button and make the changes shown in the screenshot to the settings in the Advanced Effect dialog:

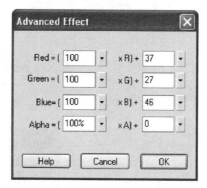

4. Click on OK to apply the settings. Save your movie as `advanced_sharpen.fla` and then go ahead and test it. You should see that the test video is lifted and altogether much improved and clearer than the control clip:

The only negative point about this particular clip is that the test clip does appear to show more effects of the compression because it is brighter, so it's worth bearing this in mind when applying this technique to your own video.

Close down the test movie, and leave the main movie open for the next quick exercise.

Color inversion

Because the colors in the Advanced Effect window can also be have a negative value, it allows us to suck the specific color completely out of the graphic (down to 0%) and then begin to invert the color when we set it below zero.

1. With the movie open from the last exercise, save it as `advanced_color_inversion1.fla`.

2. Back in the main timeline, select the test clip and apply the following settings in the Advanced Effect dialog:

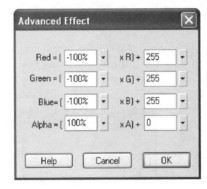

3. Test the movie and you'll see that black has now become white, and vice versa:

This feels like an aged analog effect, usually seen in a low budget movie's dream or madness sequence. This effect can be useful in quick bursts to signal some kind of tension or approaching moment.

We'll try out one more quick effect before we finish. This last effect strips out all of the colors in the video except for black and red.

4. Close down your test movie; go back into the main timeline, and save the movie as `advanced_color_inversion2.fla`. Select the test clip and make the following adjustments to the Advanced Effect settings:

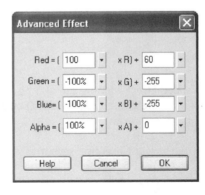

5. Test the movie and you'll see that the clip has a red and black monotone look. This is because we've stripped out all the green and blue again. If you reverse the –255 value of the green, you'll see that the green replaces the black and looks a bit like a tie-died T-shirt – not pleasant! It does show that the Advanced Effects dialog is a powerful beast and it's probably best to keep experimenting with these settings to see what you can come up with.

You can of course tween with the Advanced Effects settings, as with any of the other movie clip properties. You could fade your clip to black (turn everything down except the alpha) or create a transition between reality and a psychedelic dream sequence.

Summary

Even though we've looked at manipulating these properties in a fun way, they can be very beneficial in making your video sit neatly within a web site interface. The Advanced option for example, can be used to tint a video so that it matches a company's brand color or the background color of the interface. The rotation property can be used to orientate the video so that it fits in with angular graphics and unconventional interfaces.

The main benefit of manipulating your content within Flash is that you can quickly test the effect (no rendering is required) and you don't have the expense of having to buy an editing application (such as Adobe's After Effects). Controlling your content in Flash, for instance coloring your videos, also means that you save on having to import a number of different video clips specifically for the job.

So far, we've spent a fair amount of time dealing with the visual side of using video in Flash. It's time to move on and take a look at the equally important topic of sound…

Sound

What we'll cover in this chapter:

- *Using **wave editor** applications to manipulate sound outside of Flash.*

- ***Importing** sound files into Flash.*

- *The different ways sound can be incorporated into your Flash movies.*

- *Setting sound **properties** from within the Flash interface.*

So far, we haven't given any attention at all to using sound with your videos because we've focused on illustrating how video works, without getting bogged down in any sound issues. In the following two chapters, we'll look at how Macromedia Flash MX works with sound files and how it can be combined with video files in your presentations.

In this chapter we'll address many of these sound issues, and look at when it's best to leave sound attached to video files, or if it's better to import sound files separately.

As you've learnt in the book so far, the quality of the original *source* video file before we bring it into Flash is of crucial importance when it comes to maximizing the quality of our presentations. This same concept is equally important when it comes to working with sound.

We'll begin by looking at how to prepare your sound files for importing into Flash using external **wave editing** software.

Wave editors

Wave editors deal specifically with sampled audio, allowing you to cut and paste sound (at the most basic level) and apply all sorts of filters and effects to it. Wave editors might help you when you need to trim one of your sounds, amplify them, or need to clean them of any rogue audio.

We're going to look at two wave editor programs separately: Sonic Foundry's **Sound Forge 5.0** for Windows, and for Mac users we'll be using **Sound Studio 2.0** by Felt Tip Software. This section won't be a comprehensive guide, as they are both complete applications in themselves, intense enough to warrant a book each! We'll concentrate on the basic skills you need to get sound files ready for Flash.

For the following exercise, there is a lengthy download time for PC users (23.1 MB for the trial version of Sound Forge 5) and a much smaller download for Mac users (1.2 MB for Sound Studio 2). If you're already confident using wave editors, after using free shareware or software bundled with your machine for example, then you may want to save time and move on in the chapter to the section headed 'Sound in Flash'. If you do want to investigate these applications then read on!

If you are interested, the sound file we'll be using for this exercise is a recording of the good old Mac voice from the Speech control panel:

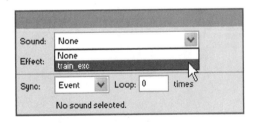
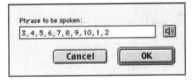

The voice was recorded using Snapz Pro (by Ambrosia Software) set to MOV capture with Record Mac Audio on. It was saved at CD Quality (44kHz).

First though, some basic notes on cleaning.

Sound cleaning

Both of the programs we're about to use have numerous tools to clean up digital sound, but they aren't magic! If you record an interview with someone standing in the middle of a highway, it's unlikely you'll be able to do much to save those precious words – even digitally. Unfortunately, there is no Photoshop for sound, but waveform applications go a long way to eradicating those curious pops and buzzes. Here are some of the common tools that'll help your sound on its way:

- **Normalization** is used to boost the overall output level of an audio file. It works by scanning the whole audio section to determine the highest level of output, and then boosts the level of the entire file to a user-defined figure. You should usually apply normalization to all your recorded sound files.

- **Equalization (EQ)** is used to boost certain sound frequencies within an audio file. The user controls the EQ manually, reducing or boosting individual frequencies of their choice. You'd do this if you wanted to make audio sound less bass-heavy (reduce the lower frequencies) or if a file was too tinny. The EQ can also be used creatively to single out and reduce dull sounds that appear during recording in certain environments.

- **Compression** is used to lower the volume of individual sounds that extend above a defined level, so that the overall volume output is smooth rather than fluctuating wildly up and down. A potential use for this is if you're recording speech using a static microphone, and the person speaking moves closer or further away from the microphone (or whispers, or even coughs). Compressing the higher volumes to bring them down to the same level as the rest of the speech will give you a constant volume throughout.

Okay, now on to using the sound application Sound Forge 5 for Windows. If you're using a Mac, feel free to skip on a few pages to the next section headed 'Sound Studio 2 for Macintosh'.

Sound Forge for Windows

Sonic Foundry's Sound Forge is the perhaps the most popular wave editing application for Windows. It is a hugely comprehensive application with all sorts of bells and whistles for the audiophile. There is also a cut-down Studio version for $60. Don't panic though – you can pick up a save disabled trial version from www.soundforge.com/download to use in this exercise to see if it agrees with you!

Also, we'll be using the source file counting.mp3 which is in the downloads section at www.friendsofed.com.

Working at the forge

1. Open up your version of Sound Forge and choose File > Open. Select the `counting.mp3` source file.

   You should now see the following:

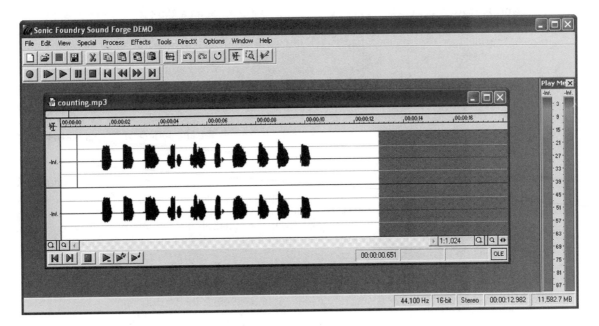

The two layers represent the two (left and right) audio channels, and the dark shapes are waveforms: visual representations of the sound. Each clump represents one spoken number, with nicely defined gaps in between each to make them visually clear.

2. Press the Play Normal button, located at the bottom left of the active window. Your file will play once and then stop:

While listening to this you may have noticed that the counting is a little screwy, starting at 3 through 10 and ending on 2! The numbers have just been deliberately muddled so we can practice rearranging the sound into the right order. So, the first thing to do is shift the numbers 1 and 2 to the start of the file to make the numbers run in sequence.

3. Click just to the left of the second-to-last waveform and drag your mouse across to highlight the last two distinguishable numbers (the last two waveforms), including a little free space after the last number:

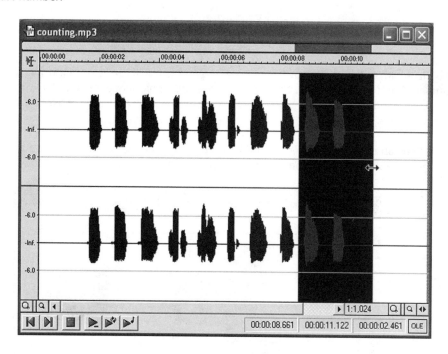

4. Now cut these numbers out using Edit > Cut. They should disappear from the timeline and will be stored on the clipboard (as with normal text or images).

5. Place the timeline cursor before the first number in the list and paste the sound back in with Edit > Paste.

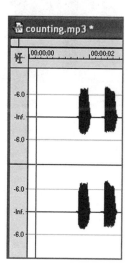

6.   Okay, now press the Go to Start button to rewind the sequence and then play it again:

This time our numbers play in the correct sequence, but there is an annoying pause between numbers 2 and 3. Let's remove the gap and make the whole sequence sound a little more regular. Firstly, we need to measure a typical gap, to see how long we need to make the space between numbers 2 and 3.

7.   Select the gap between numbers 3 and 4 (you may find it easier to do this if you zoom in a little) and take a look at the selection information boxes in the bottom right of the active window:

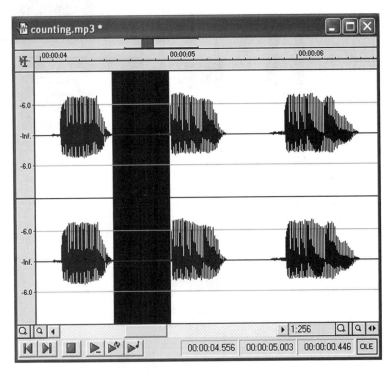

The first two boxes display the start and end points of our selection, while the third box shows us the total length of the selection – perfect!

As you can see, most of the sounds have approximately 0.4 seconds between them, so we'll use this as a rough figure. Before we use it though, we need to trim the current gap between numbers 2 and 3.

8. Select the silence (the empty space) between numbers 2 and 3:

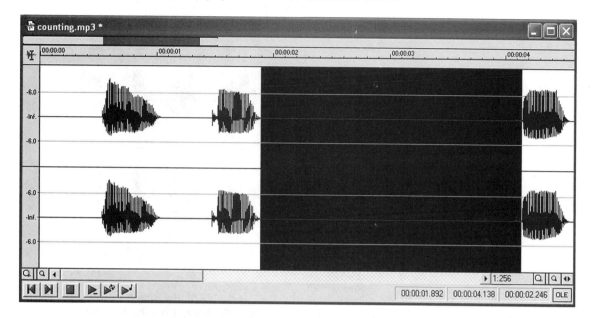

If this were a real project, you'd be *very* choosy about making this selection and zoom in much closer to make it as accurate as possible, but a rough selection will do for now.

9. When you're happy with the selection, cut out the silence with Edit > Cut.

Now our numbers 2 and 3 are getting pretty close to each other. Too close! So, we'll insert the average length of silence that we measured before. Luckily, the cursor is already placed at the exact point where we have just made the cut, so we can go ahead and insert the silence here.

10. Go to Process > Insert Silence..., and in the window that appears, set the silence length to '0.4' seconds in the Insert field:

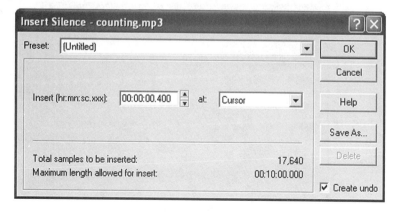

11. Now click OK. When we return to the main window, we see that the sequence now looks ordered – cool! Play the file again to check how it sounds.

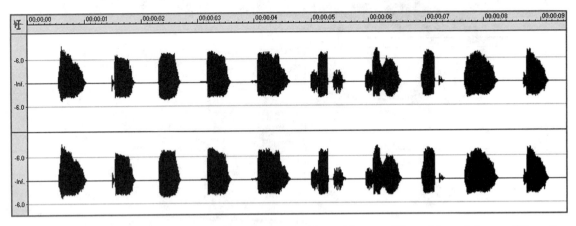

OK, that's our sound done! Now let's have a bit of fun with one of Sound Forge's insane filters, the **Time Stretch**. You might have heard this used before in *every* electronica song. Ever.

12. Firstly, trim off the excess silence from the start and end of the sequence by highlighting the silence and then using Edit > Delete (Clear), leaving a clean cut. Now the fun part...

13. Select all of the sound (Edit > Select All) and use the Process > Time Stretch... menu option. You'll see another gray dull window, but you don't know the magic that this window can do!

14. Choose AO9. Speech 3 (fast) from the Mode drop-down menu (this is just a list of presets to play with) and crank the Final Time slider all the way to the top. Overkill! Your settings should now look like this:

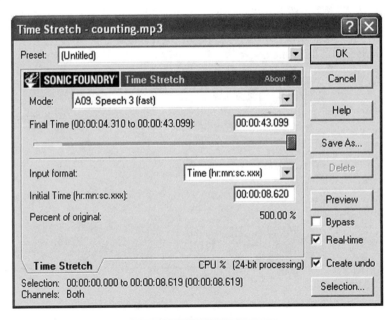

15. Click on Preview to have a quick listen to the effect. If you like it, click OK, otherwise feel free to experiment with this and the other filters and effects.

Sound Forge has some really neat effects to work with, and also a number of clichés just waiting to happen. However, it all depends on how you work with them.

I'd strongly suggest that you keep playing around and see what you can come up with. Some of you may unlock hidden musical talents, while others may have a chuckle at the backwards effect at least!

Besides being a haven for sound effects, one neat thing that Sound Forge does is that it enables you to open an AVI file and then edit your sound to it visually. You might find this really useful when it comes to orchestrating your video files as traditional video editing applications just don't give you the same flexibility with sound.

Now we're done with this mega-brief introduction to wave editing using Sound Forge. You can skip the Mac application if you wish and go straight to the following section headed 'Sound in Flash'.

Sound Studio 2 for Macintosh

Sound Studio is a shareware wave editing application made by Felt Tip Software for the Mac. Version 2 was built specifically for Mac OS X, but will run on any Mac OS from 8.1 onwards. You can download a 14 day fully working trial version from www.felttip.com/ss for this exercise (a 1.2 MB download).

Until using Sound Studio, I had always remained loyal to Macromedia's SoundEdit for manipulating sound. Unfortunately, SoundEdit is no longer supported and is unlikely to see any updates. If you are new to sound editing on the Mac, I'd suggest starting with something like Sound Studio.

Work in the studio

1. Open Sound Studio and choose File >Import with QuickTime. We're going to use `counting.mp3`, available in the downloads section at www.friendsofed.com.

At the prompt, stick with these suggested settings:

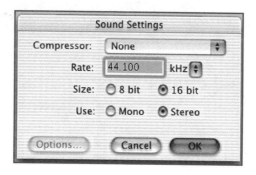

2. Click OK. You'll be greeted with the main interface:

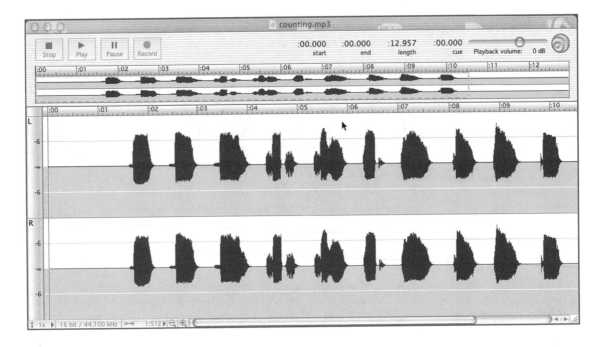

The two layers here represent the two (left and right) audio channels. The dark shapes are waveforms – visual representations of sound. Each dark clump represents one of the spoken numbers, with gaps of silence in between each number to make them clear.

3. Press the Play button to listen to the imported file.

Yep, you got that right – either Fred has lost his marbles or he just can't count! The insane number sequence runs from 3 through 10, and then 1 and 2. This was done simply to give us something to practice on, so that we can edit the sound back into the correct sequence.

4. Select the last two waveforms in the sequence by clicking your mouse between the channels and then dragging it across. Cut the sounds with APPLE+X (or Edit > Cut).

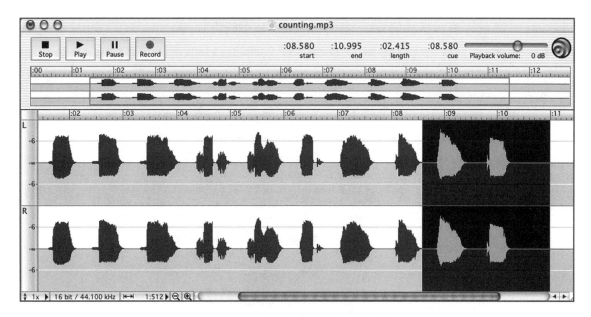

We're going to put 1 and 2 in their rightful place, at the beginning of all the other numbers. Don't be afraid at this point to cut a little too much silence along with the sounds, as we'll trim more thoroughly in a moment.

5. Click to the left of all the other numbers, so that you see the flashing cursor appear in the timeline:

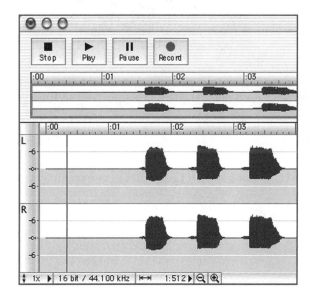

This is where we'll paste our numbers 1 and 2.

6. Press APPLE+V (or Edit > Paste) to paste the numbers back in. This will place them before all the other numbers – the right place for them (or at least the way I was taught to count!)

7. Press Play to listen to the numbers in the correct sequence.

8. However, there's a lengthy pause in between 2 and 3, so let's try and edit this gap to make the whole sequence run much smoother.

9. Select the gap between numbers 3 and 4 and take a look at the selection information at the top of the window (you may need to zoom in at this point to get a better view):

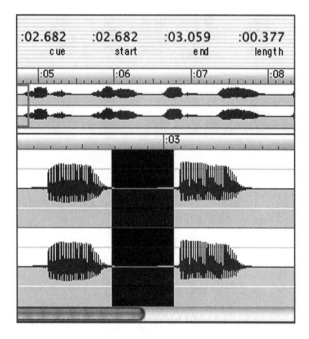

The fourth information field, length, tells us how long (in seconds) our selection is – the amount of time in between each number utterance. The average for all the gaps in the sequence is just under 0.4 seconds, so we'll go with this figure for editing the gap between 2 and 3. Firstly, though, we need to reduce the current gap.

10. Select all of the silence between numbers 2 and 3 and delete it with the BACKSPACE key:

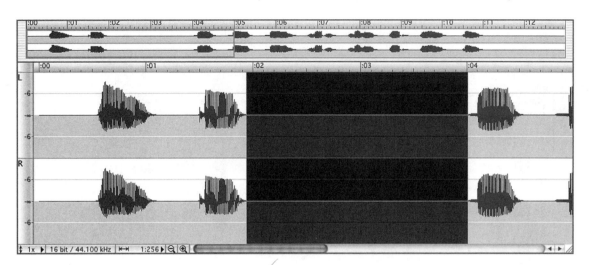

Okay, now numbers 2 and 3 are very close friends! Sadly, we have to break up their little party before it's even begun. You might notice here that the flashing cursor is positioned exactly where we just deleted the silence, so this the perfect position for inserting the new, correct, amount of silence:

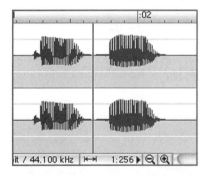

11. Select Insert > Silence and type '0.4' seconds (the figure we worked out roughly earlier on) in the Duration field of the following window:

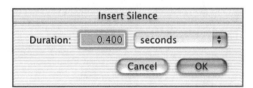

12. Now, if you click OK, zoom out fully, and look at all of the sequence, you'll see that the waveforms are evenly spaced out:

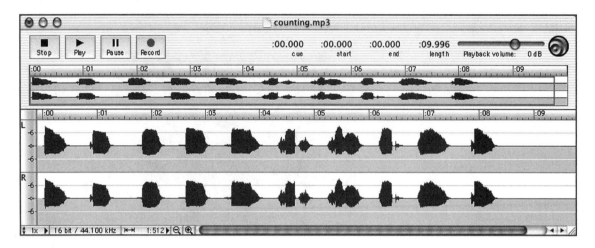

13. Press the Play button to have a listen to the reorganized file, and you'll hear that Fred can count again.

As a concluding flourish, let's make him sound like a Dalek using the Flange effect.

14. Trim off the excess silence from the start and the end of the clip.

15. Now select the whole sequence using Edit > Select All and choose Filter > Flanger.... In the window that appears, select Fast Flanger from the Preset drop-down menu and click OK:

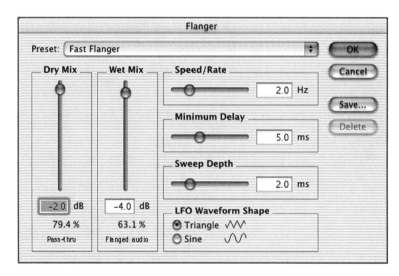

After the small rendering time has finished, press Play to listen to the effect. Fred is doing his famous Dalek impression!

And that's it for our quick introduction to Sound Studio. As you can see the application has a lot more to it than what we've covered here, but this is just a nice way to show you the environment and some of its capabilities. You can stick with this and play with some of the sound effects for a while, or you can whiz onto the next section where we'll start working with our sounds in Flash.

Sound in Flash

There are a number of ways to work with sound in Flash, and in reality sound is far more flexible to work with than video. This flexibility becomes clearer when you use ActionScript to control the sounds (in a similar fashion to how we controlled video in Chapter 4). We'll look at manipulating sound with ActionScript in depth in the next chapter.

Before looking at sound in conjunction with video, let's take a quick look at the different situations when you would want to use sound.

Music

Music is often used in Flash web sites to enhance the overall experience. However, if it doesn't have a particular focus, background music can quickly become annoying and repetitive – especially when small sections of music are looped over and over. It's in cases like these where the user will either the leave the web site or turn down the volume.

Besides simply providing an extra dimension to your web site, the style of music also says a lot about it and the expected viewing audience. I'll leave this choice up to you, as it's pretty obvious what works where and it's a matter of individual taste. Just imagine you're dressed in your best New Romantic velvet suit and makeup, and accidentally walk into a specialist hardcore punk record store, 3-chord riffs are blasting out – you're bound to feel a little out of place and run back out the door.

Before using background music on your web site, you need to be clear about why you are using it. Ask yourself a couple of questions during the planning stage:

- What does the music add to the experience and how does it fit in with the site's content?

- Is it worth the extra download time?

- Is the chosen music likely to segregate your audience? Is this what you want to do?

If you intend for the music to accompany your video, then it already has a focus. As proven in cinema, if music is used correctly, it significantly adds emphasis and emotion to video content. If you strip a movie of its sound, it quickly exposes all of its flaws (as I found out when my university lecturers made us watch famous Hitchcock scenes without sound!). Although there is no narrative structure to my BMX project, without the appropriate music the videos are incomplete and lack the live energy of the event.

When it comes to using music in Flash there are two different ways of bringing in the music: either importing a separate sound file (such as an MP3, WAV, or AIFF) or using the sound already attached to a video clip. So, which is best?

Well, if your music is synchronized or features vocals, it's best to import the music with your video clip. This way you wouldn't have to then try and sync the video and audio together in Flash – a mammoth task!

If your music is supplemental to your video and doesn't need to be strictly synchronized (as is the case with my BMX video), then think about using a separately imported soundtrack. This will allow you to control the sound as a separate asset, potentially giving the user the ability to change the volume, mute it, or skip a track.

If the idea of using two separate files sounds like a hassle, there is another major benefit of using this method: performance. When sound is synced to a video clip, the visual elements always try to keep up with the audio. On slower machines this means that the video will skip frames in order to stay synchronized with the sound. When your sound and video files are separate, the video will run much smoother because it isn't tied to anything.

Thinking about the use of music in cinema again, slashing all of the music from a film will leave you with the dialog, incidental sound effects, and atmosphere. A great deal of work goes on in the cutting room to make sure that these sound elements go in *exactly* the right place. If we have similar needs in Flash, syncing the audio and video is very important. This is an occasion where importing sound with video is better than a separate sound file, despite the performance issue mentioned previously.

There are other situations where your sound and video sync will be thrown out, most notably when using ActionScript to manipulate the video timeline. Let's consider an example: imagine you are creating an interactive video where the user must choose where to go next in the video. There is one video clip featuring all of the possible destinations, and ActionScript is being used to send the video timeline to the correct places when prompted by the user. In this scenario, when you send the video timeline to a particular frame, the sound will often trail behind and you will lose your careful syncing. An obvious way around this, of course, is to use many video clips embedded in their own individual movie clips, with each video representing a different destination. This might mean a larger file size, but you'll be able to keep your carefully crafted sync.

Working without a script

Besides the scripting options available, there are also some manual ways to work with sound in Flash. One of the benefits is that it will allow you to have streaming audio. Let's take a look at the sound options available in Flash in a quick exercise.

1. Open a new Flash movie and rename the default layer 'audio'.

2. Go to File > Import and locate a reasonably long sound file on your machine, or use `train_exc.mp3` included in the download files for this chapter at www.friendsofed.com.

3. Click on Open to import the sound file into Flash.

    Remember that you can import a number of sound formats into Flash, including the standard MP3, WAV, and AIFF.

4. Select frame 1 of the timeline, and the Sound options will appear in the Property inspector. Click on the Sound drop-down menu and choose your sound file:

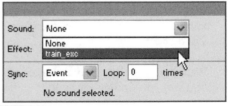

5. This menu displays all of the sound files in the Library. Leave all of the other settings as they are, but make sure that Sync is set to Event. We'll see why in a moment.

6. Deselect frame 1, and you'll now see a blue squiggle in it – this is our sound file. Extend the timeline with F5 so that you can see all of the waveform:

7. Trim off the excess blank frames from the end of the waveform, so that the frames only extend to the end of the audio track.

8. Test the movie (CTRL+ENTER).

    The eagle-eared amongst you might notice that the sound is a little different to the original source. This is because Flash applies a standard amount of compression to each sound unless we tell it any different. These general settings are located at the bottom of the Flash tab of the Publish Settings menu (File > Publish Settings):

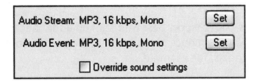

    If you're unhappy with the amount of compression that Flash has forced on your beautiful music, then you can individually set the compression type and amount for each sound file. Let's take a look...

9. Open up the Library (F11) and double-click on your sound file's icon. This will bring up its Sound Properties window:

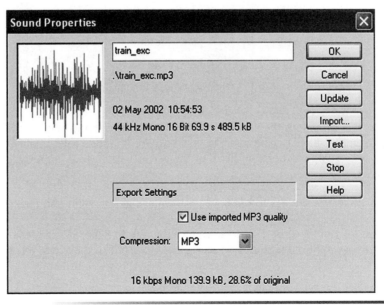

At the top of the window is the file's original information, export info at the bottom, and a whole load of buttons on the right. At the moment though, there isn't much to write home about in the export department – this is because it is usually the default quality as defined in the Publish Settings window.

10. Click on the Compression drop-down and you'll see a number of compression codecs listed:

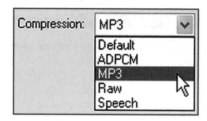

Let's take a brief look at two of the most significant codecs on the list:

- **MP3**: The codec that has taken the Internet by storm because it produces such small file sizes. This is best used for music.

- **Speech**: This codec works best with spoken audio because they both have a low frequency. This allows you to reduce the maximum frequency down to 5kHz. This codec is useful for narrated tutorials, for example.

11. Select the most appropriate codec for your audio file. I'm using music in this example, so I've chosen MP3:

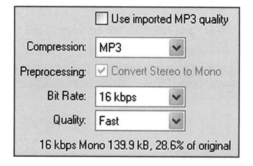

A number of options then appear showing the export settings, along with useful information about the exported file size (you need to uncheck Use imported MP3 quality to see these). As you can see, this example exports at 28.6% of the original size, which is pretty good, but it is still 139 KB overall.

Let's tweak the settings to see how small we can get it ... and also hear the difference!

12. Select the Bit Rate drop-down and reduce the rate to 8kbps. Already the export information shows a decrease in file size, but it's obviously best to listen to the file at this setting.

13. Click on the Test button to preview the file with the new settings. You'll see a progress bar that might take a little while to complete, as Flash is encoding the file into MP3 format with the settings that we gave it.

   Once the encoding is finished, have a listen. Be incredibly picky at this point and listen out for any digital gargling and kerfluffing (highly technical definitions).

   To get down to this low file size, Flash has converted the original stereo file to mono, as well as reducing the quality of the sound. As you can hear, this setting has made our music sound quite poor. As a general guide, don't go below a 20kbps bit rate when compressing music in order to keep a reasonable level of quality (although rates below this are fine for effects such as button clicks).

14. If the quality is acceptable, click Update and OK. If it's not in fine fashion for your ears, increase the Bit Rate, and then click Update and OK.

15. Save the movie as `audio_import.fla` for use later on in the chapter.

Okay, now that we've taken a little look at compression, it's time to look at the different ways to use sound in Flash MX.

Streaming and events

Like video, there are several methods of implementing sound in a Flash movie, and they're are called **Sync** types. These types are Event, Start, Stop, and Stream. These options are located on the Sync drop-down menu of the Sound options in the Property inspector:

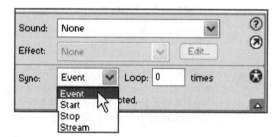

Stream

Streaming sound is treated in the same way as streamed Flash video and is buffered before playing. However, unlike video, it has built-in buffering, so you don't have to fill up your timeline with frames to buy it time to load – streamed sounds are synchronized to the timeline.

Buffering in Flash is set as standard to 5 seconds, but it can be changed with a tiny bit of ActionScript using the **_soundbuftime** property. As with video, sound can only be streamed on the main timeline. If you wanted to lower the buffer you would type something like this on frame 1 of your movie:

```
_soundbuftime = 3;
```

This would give you a 3 second buffer, meaning that Flash will pause 3 seconds before starting to play your sound. Also remember that _soundbuftime is a global property so there is no need for the traditional _root prefix.

One good thing about the Stream setting is that the movie will only load in the required amount of the sound file. So, if your timeline stops short before the end of the audio file, this excess is ignored saving you some valuable file size.

To test your streaming, use CTRL+ENTER to test your movie and then choose the View > Show Streaming menu option.

Event

Just as the name suggests, an Event sound is played at a significant point when an event occurs. This makes event sounds suitable for button press sounds, game death, intro music, or any other sound that is required on demand.

Event sounds though cannot be streamed in; like a movie clip, they need to be fully loaded into the movie before they can be played back.

Also, Event sounds can be set to loop a certain number of times in the Sound options area of the Property inspector:

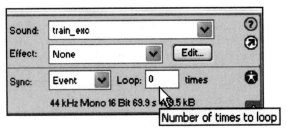

One thing that is important to know about Event sounds is that they will keep on playing until they reach the end of the sound. Trimming frames from the timeline or issuing stop commands have no effect on halting playback. Here's a timeline where the sound frames have been trimmed down from the full 840 frames, and a stop action has been inserted at frame 15 where we want the sound to stop playing:

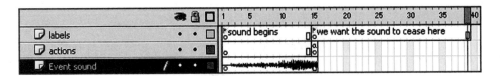

Believe it or not, but the sound clip will still play to its full conclusion, despite all our resistance! It can however be stopped with a blank keyframe (placed on the sound layer in the last frame) or by using the **Stop** sound type...

Start and stop

These options simply extend on the Event type, allowing you control over where your sound starts (this is the equivalent of Event) and also when it should end. If we added a new layer called 'Stop sound' and a keyframe at frame 15, using the previous example, we can halt the sound with the Stop event:

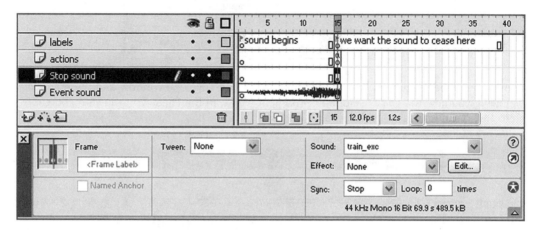

To be honest, although this method will save you a frame on your movie, it is far easier to halt sounds with a blank keyframe in the same layer as the Event sound.

Of all these Sync types, the Stream and Event options are definitely the most useful for different purposes. If a sound is frequently used in a movie – such as a game start jingle – then stick with the Event type at all times.

If you have a long audio file and want to broadcast the complete file in one go, your audience will benefit if the sound file is streamed – they don't have to wait for the whole file to load. Before you come to test your buffering, keep your audience's bandwidth in mind and set Show Streaming to the lowest required download speed when testing your movie in Flash.

The MP3 format though is likely to make sound streaming much easier and users should not have to wait too long before the music starts to play back smoothly.

Now that we've seen some of the basic timeline sound options, it's time to see what effects we can add to our audio files within Flash.

Flash sound effects

Let's get this straight right away: when we say 'effects' we don't mean the kind of effects seen in waveform editing applications like those covered earlier in the chapter (that sure would be something!). Flash has control over volume and panning, allowing you to control these properties in the Edit Envelope environment.

You access the Edit Envelope window by first selecting your sound in the Property inspector and then clicking on the Edit... button:

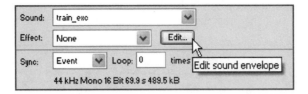

Flash has a number of presets that are available in the Edit Envelope window and these are very useful in showing you how the Edit Envelope environment works. In the Effect drop-down menu choose Fade Left to Right, and let's take a closer look:

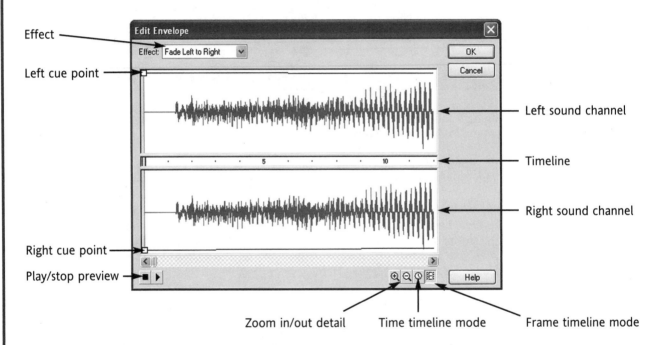

Effect

Left cue point

Left sound channel

Timeline

Right sound channel

Right cue point

Play/stop preview

Zoom in/out detail   Time timeline mode   Frame timeline mode

If you look at the left sound channel, you can see that the left cue point is right at the top of the window, meaning that it is at full volume, whereas the right channel volume is set to zero. This preset makes the sound shift across from one channel to the other over the whole length of the sound (you need to zoom out as far as possible to see the whole effect):

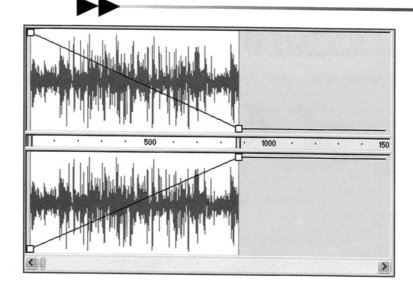

The cue points can be dragged around as much as possible, and new cue points can be added by clicking on the line. By doing this you could, for example, make the crossover point occur in the latter stages of the movie instead of starting the effect right at the beginning of the movie (also notice that the Effect drop-down has now changed to Custom):

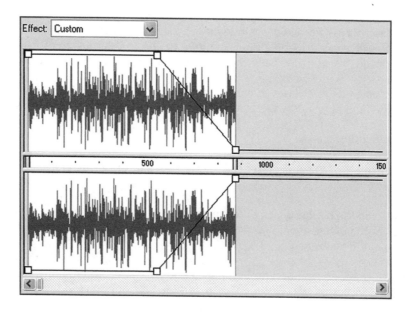

You can add up to 8 cue points for any separate instance of the sound on the stage. You might find that the presets are perfectly adequate for your needs, but you can go ahead and edit these to suit your own movie. For example, a quicker fade out might be necessary if your accompanying video action cuts out suddenly.

Now let's use all that we've learnt and apply it to our own sound file.

Getting the sound right

1. Open up the `audio_import.fla` you were working on earlier in the chapter.

2. Insert a new layer called 'actions' and insert a keyframe (F6) on the very last frame of this layer (frame 840 in our example). Place a stop action in this frame.

   At the moment, my sound cuts off suddenly at the end, so I want to soften the ending with a little fade out.

3. Select frame one of the audio layer, and choose Fade Out from the Effect drop-down menu in the Property inspector:

4. Use CTRL+ENTER to test your movie.

   The fade out for my audio is a little bit too long and needs to be shorter. To shorten it, I need to decide where to start fading from, so I have to find this starting point. There are a couple of ways you can do this: using the Bandwidth Profiler and keeping an eye on the playhead, or we can cheat.

   The simple way to cheat is to change the Sync type to Stream. Flash will then give you a preview of the sound as you drag the playhead along the timeline (also known as scrubbing).

   Let's do just that.

5. With frame 1 of the audio layer still selected, go into the Property inspector and change the Sync type to Stream.

6. Now scrub the playhead along the timeline and locate the point at which you want to start fading. After a little examination, I opted for frame 775 to start the fade out, but feel free to choose your own point if you want.

7. Change the Sync type back to Event and click the Edit... button in the Sound options area of the Property inspector. We're now going to edit the fade out point in the Edit Envelope window.

8. Click on the Frame timeline mode button so that we can view the sound in relation to the Flash movie frames:

9. Drag the cue point from its current position to approximately frame 775. It doesn't matter which of the channel points you drag, as Flash will always keep them parallel with each other (don't worry if you accidentally add more cue points, as you can remove them simply by dragging them out of the channel window):

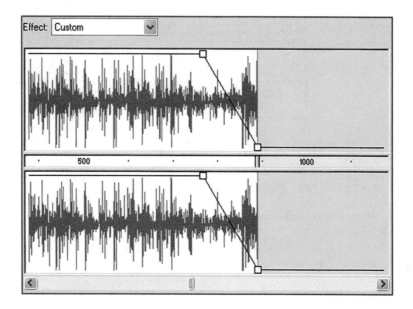

10. Now zoom in so that you can accurately position the cue point at exactly frame 775. Click OK when you are done to confirm these changes.

11. Test the movie to see if this sounds better.

Now that we've done a little sound editing, let's see how streaming and buffering works...

12. Close down the test movie, and back in the main movie change the Sync type to Stream (again!).

As we mentioned earlier, the standard buffer set by Flash is 5 seconds. Let's see how our music streams with this amount of buffering.

13. Test the movie and select 56K from the Debug menu. Now select View > Show Streaming. The green bar should whiz up the timeline and, after 5 seconds, the audio will start to play.

14. Scroll along the timeline while the sound is playing and you'll see that all of the sound has finished loading by frame 374.

The result is a very smooth play-through with no stops and starts:

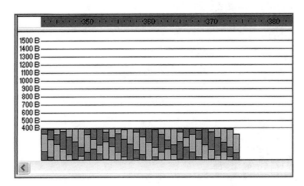

So what does this all mean? Well, we can afford to use a lower buffer time than 5 seconds! Normally 5 seconds isn't too long to ask the viewer to wait, but let's be bold and give them even less! Let's try the magic number – 3.

15. Close the test movie window to return to the main timeline.

16. Select frame 1 of the actions layer and open up the Actions panel (F9). With Expert Mode selected (CTRL+SHIFT+E) type in the following code:

```
_soundbuftime = 3;
```

17. Easy. Test the movie and select View > Show Streaming again.

If you watch the green bar again, you'll notice that the sound finishes loading way before the playhead even gets close to it, resulting in smooth playback again. We could push our luck here but perhaps it is best to quit while we're ahead!

18. Save your movie and close it.

Summary

Like all other media within Flash MX, there are ways to make sure that we create the right balance between quality and file size - and what you do to the sounds before and during the import is of great, well, import.

There is a certain amount of control available purely from the Flash MX interface and the Property inspector - but not probably as much as you'd like, so in the next chapter we're going to move on to some more advanced sound manipulation, looking at the Sound object and using ActionScript to control our sounds.

The Sound Object

7

What we'll cover in this chapter:

- *The **properties** and **methods** of the Sound object.*

- *How to use ActionScript to control the Sound object.*

- *Using ActionScript to create a **dynamic MP3 player**.*

In the last chapter, we looked at how sound can be placed on the timeline, streamed, and manipulated a little using the Edit Envelope window. All of this can be done with the **Sound object**, but with the advantage of allowing us to control its properties on the fly using ActionScript.

ActionScript is now a fully object-oriented programming (**OOP**) language, enabling it to both work with and dynamically create various objects. Basic objects in Flash include movie clips, text fields, components, and obviously sound. In the previous chapter, the sound was left in its rawest form (a bit like a broken-apart circle on the stage) and subsequently could not be controlled by any ActionScript. In order to control the sound with ActionScript, the sound needs to be made into an object.

Introducing the Sound object

In the following script example a new Sound object is declared, filled with a sound file called 'rockSong' from the Library, then called and played:

```
mySound = new Sound ();
mySound.attachSound ("rockSong");
mySound.start ();
```

If this looks confusing, try not to worry – we'll be using this script frequently, so you'll become familiar with it.

The Sound object has a number of useful built-in methods including:

start

This makes the Sound object begin to play at a specified point. For example:

```
mySound.start (5);
```

will start the mySound object playing at the 5-second mark. If the seconds parameter is not set, then mySound will begin to play immediately from the beginning by default. This method also allows you to specify an optional loop value after the starting position parameter. For example:

```
mySound.start (5, 2);
```

will loop the sound twice from the 5-second mark starting position. The sound is set to loop once by default.

stop

This halts playback of the sound. If you don't specify in your ActionScript which sound you want to stop, then Flash will stop *all* currently playing sounds.

setPan

This method is used to set the left and right balance of the Sound object. It accepts values from -100 (panned fully to the left) through to 100 (panned fully to the right). By default setPan is set to 0, so sounds will be panned centrally unless you alter this.

setVolume

This allows you to set the volume of the Sound object anywhere between 0 (silent) through to 100 (full volume). The default setting for this is 100.

loadSound

Flash MX now allows you to import an MP3 file with this new method... and it gets better! Not only can Flash import MP3 files, but it can also stream them. The following example shows how you would specify an MP3 file to stream in your movie:

```
mySound.loadSound ("http://www.yourhomepage.com/discopop.mp3", true);
```

With the `isStreaming` parameter set to `true`, the sound will stream in. If it is set to `false`, Flash will import an MP3 as an event sound that has to be fully loaded before it can be played.

This means that building a dynamic MP3 player is now possible with Flash MX.

Additional methods

The Sound object also has a number of methods to extract some values from itself, including getPan and getVolume. But more importantly, Flash is able to retrieve a couple of key properties from instances of the object, namely:

- **duration**: the length of the sound file.

- **position**: the location of the playhead in the currently playing clip.

If all this technical detail has passed you by, fear not – we'll be using a number of these methods in our next exercise so you can see them in action. Once we're done, you'll feel like old friends!

Dynamic sound

In this exercise, we'll start building a mini sound application to show off some of the functionality available when using the Sound object partnered with object-orientated ActionScript. We'll start off with the two most basic sound elements, volume and pan (balance).

1. Open a new Flash movie and import a reasonably long sound file (CTRL+R). In this example we're going to use the same `train_exc.mp3` that we used in the previous chapter (located in the code downloads section of www.friendsofed.com), but you can use any of your own sounds if you prefer.

2. In order to control our MP3 with ActionScript we need to give it a Linkage name. Open the Library (F11) and right-click (Control-click on the Mac) on the sound file name. Select Linkage... from the menu.

3. You'll see the Linkage Properties window. Check the Export for ActionScript box and two things will happen: the Export in First Frame box will also become checked, and the file name will appear in the previously grayed-out Identifier field:

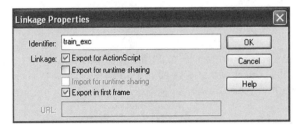

4. Change the Identifier to 'music' and click OK.

5. Next, let's get our sound hooked up. Rename the default layer in the timeline 'actions' and, with frame 1 selected, open the Actions panel (F9). Type in the following code:

```
mySound = new Sound ();
mySound.attachSound ("music");
mySound.start ();
```

This code is very similar to the script we saw at the start of the chapter. The only difference is that I am calling a different Linkage name in the second line of code. Let's look at this code line by line. We're telling Flash to:

- Create a new Sound object called mySound.

- Get the audio file with the Linkage name of music from the Library, and place it in mySound.

- Start playing mySound from the beginning, and do not loop it.

> Even though I've used mySound several times in this chapter, you can call your Sound object almost anything. However, you should try and avoid using variable names, ActionScript commands, or other Flash-reserved words, as this may cause problems in your script.

6. Now, test the movie and you'll hear your sound. Just remember that we've done all this simply using a bit of ActionScript and our newly created Sound object, and without creating any long timelines.

Let's not get too complacent – after all, it's only playing the sound. Instead, let's begin our dynamic sound manipulation. We're going to create simple input fields where the user can enter values to control the pan and volume values of the currently playing sound.

7. Close down your test SWF. Back on the timeline, create a new layer called 'text'. In frame 1, use the Text tool to draw two static text fields, and type 'VOLUME:' and 'PANNING:' in them:

8. Alongside each of these, draw an input text field roughly the same size:

9. Select the input text field next to the VOLUME text. Click on the Show Border Around Text button in the Property inspector and type 'volumeChange' in the Var (variable) field:

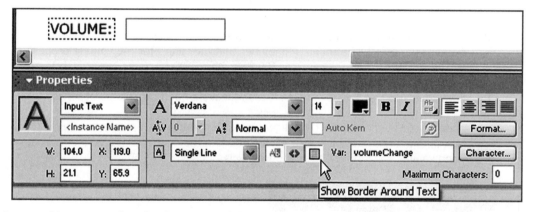

10. Repeat this process for the input text field next to the PANNING text, this time entering 'panChange' in the Var field.

11. Okay, now that we've made our input fields we need a button that, when pressed, will tell Flash to change the sound properties accordingly. Insert a new layer called 'updateButton'.

12. Select frame 1 of the updateButton layer. To save us some time, open up the Components panel (CTRL+F7) and drag out a copy of the PushButton component on to the stage, placing it alongside your input fields:

13. Select the PushButton on the stage, go into the Property inspector, and give it an instance name of 'update_mc'. Then click in the Label field and enter 'UPDATE':

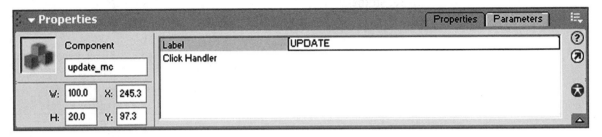

14. Now we'll add some more ActionScript to make this button control the Sound object. Select frame 1 of the actions layer, open the Actions panel, and enter the following code beneath the previous three lines:

```
this.update_mc.onRelease = function() {
    mySound.setPan(panChange);
    mySound.setVolume(volumeChange);
};
```

This code uses the setPan and setVolume methods that we've already looked at in this chapter to update the volume and pan properties of the mySound object (our sound file) when the instance of the PushButton component is pressed.

15. Test the movie, try entering some values in the input fields, and then click the update button to see how this affects the sound. Remember that the values for the volume property are 0 through to 100, and the values for pan are -100 through to 100 (extreme left to right).

16. Save your movie as sound_app_1.fla and leave it open for the next exercise.

At the moment our application isn't intelligent enough to know the limits of volume and pan, as it allows us to crank up the levels into the realms of distortion. In the next exercise, we'll insert constraints so that the pan and volume can't exceed their proper levels.

Adding a graphic interface

We can improve this little application with some plus and minus buttons, in order to make it feel more like a GUI and allow the user to return to the comfort of their mouse when changing the levels.

1. With sound_app_1.fla still open from the last exercise, save it as sound_app_2.fla before we go on and build our interface.

2. Insert a new layer called 'small buttons'. In frame 1, draw a small square and convert it to a graphic symbol (F8) called 'small square'. This will form the graphic base for our four buttons.

3. Now select the square graphic symbol and convert it into a button symbol called 'plus volume button'. In the plus volume button timeline, add a new layer and draw a plus sign in its Up state:

4. Create three other buttons by duplicating the 'plus volume button' and changing the plus symbol to a minus symbol, an 'L', and an 'R'. Call them 'minus volume button', 'left button', and 'right button' respectively.

5. You can also add some pan value signifiers to give the user a hint on values to enter. Here's the full interface positioned correctly on the stage:

VOLUME:

– +

UPDATE

PANNING:

L R
-100 100

Now each button has to be given an instruction. I've decided to make all the buttons increase or decrease their associated value in increments of 5, so that the user doesn't have to make too many mouse clicks.

6. Select the minus volume button and attach the following code to it:

```
on (release) {
    volumeChange -= 5;
}
```

This subtracts 5 from the volumeChange variable (the equivalent of volumeChange = volumeChange - 5).

7. Add the following code to the plus volume button:

```
on (release) {
    volumeChange += 5;
}
```

8. Select left button and add this ActionScript to it:

```
on (release) {
    panChange -= 5;
}
```

9. And finally, add the following code to the right button:

```
on (release) {
    panChange += 5;
}
```

Okay, that's the small buttons finished. Remember those limits I mentioned? If you're click happy like me and try testing your movie now, then you'll have sent the volume way past 100. There are two sets of two constraints that we need to set:

- Volume cannot exceed 100 nor go below 0.

- Pan cannot exceed 100 nor go below −100.

10. Select frame 1 of the actions layer and add the code in bold, so that your ActionScript for frame 1 looks like this:

```
mySound = new Sound();
mySound.attachSound("music");
mySound.start();
this.update_mc.onRelease = function() {
    if (volumeChange>100) {
        volumeChange = 100;
    }
    if (volumeChange<0) {
        volumeChange = 0;
    }
    if (panChange>100) {
        panChange = 100;
    }
    if (panChange<-100) {
        panChange = -100;
    }
    mySound.setPan(panChange);
    mySound.setVolume(volumeChange);
};
```

This new code is simply saying 'if the user enters values that are above or below any of the specified limits, then set the pan or volume variable back to the limit'.

11. Test the movie and use the buttons to change the Sound object's properties.

> You'll probably find yourself using the buttons exclusively from now on – there's nothing wrong with this, and it's a lot easier on the digits. Ideally, this application would have slider bars for pan and volume, but I'll leave these for you to integrate into your application.

12. Save your movie and close it.

Okay, that's the panning and volume controls done. As you can see, even at this basic level, ActionScript has already opened up a number of possibilities for controlling sound in your movies.

Sound and video in flux

The last exercise showed some of the possibilities for manipulating sound using ActionScript. Even though we described our little application as dynamic, it was also *undynamic* in one respect – the application was reliant on the user's input. This next exercise will show you how to build something a little less reliant on the user.

Using setVolume

We're going to control the setVolume method to create sound that fluxes in and out of audible range as it plays.

1. Open a new Flash movie and import a reasonably long sound file. We're still using `train_exc.mp3` from the downloads section, but you can use any sound or music you like.

2. Right-click (control-click on the Mac) on the sound in the Library and choose Linkage... to open the Linkage Properties window.

3. Check Export for ActionScript and change the linkage name to 'fluxer' in the Identifier field.

4. All we need to do is add some ActionScript to control this sound. Change the name of the default layer in the timeline to 'actions' and add the following code to frame1:

```
speed = 1;
volumeChange = 100;
volumeAdd = speed;
mySound = new Sound ();
mySound.attachSound ("fluxer");
mySound.start ();
```

The first three lines initialize a number of variables for the movie:

- speed – the amount by which volume will increment/decrement in one step.

- volumeChange – this sets the volume to 100 at the start of the movie. During the movie, this variable is used to store the volume level.

- volumeAdd – this stores the actual amount added or subtracted to the volume in each step.

The second chunk of code should be familiar by now. This creates the Sound object, pulls in the sound file with a Linkage name of fluxer and begins to play it.

5. Now add the following line:

```
createEmptyMovieClip ("mc", 1);
```

This creates an empty movie clip on the stage and gives it the instance name (identifier) of mc. This is ActionScript's way of making a normal movie clip, just as you would in Flash.

6. Carry on and add this code:

```
mc.onEnterFrame = function () {
    if (volumeChange >= 100) {
        volumeAdd = -speed;
    }
    if (volumeChange <= 0) {
        volumeAdd = speed;
    }
    volumeChange += volumeAdd;
    mySound.setVolume (volumeChange);
};
```

The first line uses the empty movie clip called mc to set up an event that occurs in every frame of the movie. The code that is processed every frame follows inside the curly brackets.

The if statement is similar to the code we used in the last exercise; it checks to see if the volume has reached the maximum or minimum volume allowed. If either limit is reached, then the volumeAdd variable is inverted, making the volume continuously climb (or flux) up and down.

The last section, after the if statement, does two things: it updates the volumeChange variable, and then uses this new value to change the volume of the sound accordingly.

7. Okay, if you did or didn't quite get all of that, test the movie. If you didn't quite get all of the code, maybe it'll make more sense as you listen to it. The volume continuously changes between the maximum minimum level and back again:

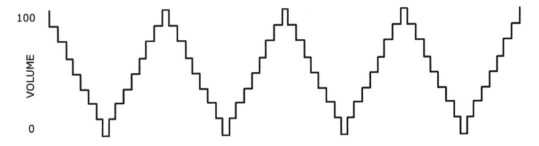

If you feel the flux is too slow, try increasing the speed variable and you'll see the result straight away. From here you could easily manipulate the effect so that you can flux the pan, directing the sound from extreme left to extreme right and back again. All you need to do is change the checking parameters in the if statement to work with values of -100 and 100, and change the last line of code to mySound.setPan (volumeChange);.

You could also give the variables more accurate names such as panChange and panAdd, but I'll leave this up to you. If you do try this pan flux effect, remember to place your speakers apart to get the full effect.

We'll now move on and spice up this flux movie with a visual element, a video!

Video and sound in flux

In a similar style to the previous sound exercise, we're going to make our video's alpha value flux between 0% and 100%. Luckily, we can use the same variables to control both the sound and the video.

1. Still working in the same movie, create a new movie clip (CTRL+F8) called 'video'.

2. Import a video file into the video movie clip. I've used `halfpipe.mov` from the code download for this chapter.

3. Go back into the main timeline and insert a new layer called 'video'.

4. With frame 1 of this layer selected, drag a copy of the video movie clip onto the main stage and give it an instance name of 'myVid':

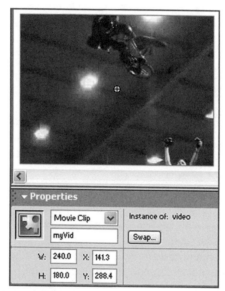

5. Now, open up the Actions panel for frame 1 again. Insert the following script after the last line of existing code, but just inside the very last curly bracket:

```
myVid._alpha = volumeChange;
```

Your final code should look like this:

```
speed = 1;
volumeChange = 100;
volumeAdd = speed;
mySound = new Sound();
mySound.attachSound("fluxer");
mySound.start();
createEmptyMovieClip("mc", 1);
mc.onEnterFrame = function() {
    if (volumeChange>=100) {
        volumeAdd = -speed;
    }
    if (volumeChange<=0) {
        volumeAdd = speed;
    }
    volumeChange += volumeAdd;
    mySound.setVolume(volumeChange);
    myVid._alpha = volumeChange;
};
```

6. It's finished! Go ahead and test the movie. Now our ActionScript is controlling both objects at the same time: the video movie clip and the Sound object.

7. Save your movie and close it.

We can already see some of the benefits of using the Sound object over traditional timeline based sound, but we won't ignore timeline based sound completely. Let's see how to sync sound to some video.

The position property

If you ever need to sync video with sound, then it's usually best to bring in the video's accompanying soundtrack when you import the video into Flash. If there are instances where you do need some loose syncing, and want to optimize and treat the sound differently, there is a way to do this using the **position** property of the Sound object.

The position property constantly updates while the Sound object is playing, and can be retrieved like this:

```
whereItsAt = mySound.position;
```

The variable whereItsAt asks the mySound object where its playhead currently is. The result is returned in milliseconds (yuck!) so if, for example, the playhead were at the 6 second position, then it would return a value of 6000.

In this next exercise, we are going to use this in conjunction with the **start** method of the Sound object, and send the parameter to it. Awkwardly, the start method accepts parameters in seconds, so if we sent it a value of 6000 (1 hour and 40 minutes) it would probably be looking for the latter bars of a movie soundtrack. To get around this and make position return a value in seconds, we just need to divide the figure produced by position by 1000:

```
whereItsAtInSeconds =  mySound.position / 1000;
```

Problem solved. On to the exercise...

Me and my sync

In this exercise, we'll be using separate video and sound files, and stopping and starting them simultaneously to show ActionScript's syncing capabilities.

1.   Open a new Flash movie and import a longish video clip (I'm using halfpipe.mov, the same video from the last exercise). As usual, import the video into its own movie clip, and give the movie clip a suitable name.

2.   Drag a copy of the movie clip onto the stage and give it the instance name 'myVid'.

3.   Import a long sound file (I've used train_exc.mp3 again here) and give it a Linkage name of 'music'.

4.   Insert a new layer called 'buttons' and create three simple buttons on the stage for Play, Pause, and Stop. You can draw the buttons yourself or, to save time, use Flash's built-in buttons located in the Playback **folder** at Window > Common Libraries > Buttons.

I've dragged out instances of gel Stop, gel Right, and gel Pause:

Let's consider the buttons' functionality. In this exercise, we're going to use a variable to check if the video and sound are playing. This variable will be used by the play and pause buttons, so that only one of them will be functional at any time – having a video simultaneously playing and pausing is a bit difficult.

5. Create a new layer called 'actions' and open the Actions panel for frame 1. Enter the following code:

```
playing = true;
mySound = new Sound ();
mySound.attachSound ("music");
mySound.start ();
myVid.play ();
```

We've seen most of this before so I won't go over it again. The only new addition to the standard Sound object initialization is the first line of code: this is the variable that we just talked about. The last line of code tells the instance of the video movie clip to start playing at the same time as the sound.

6. Select the pause button and give it an instance name of 'pause_mc'. Select frame 1 of the actions layer and enter the following code beneath all of the previous lines:

```
pause_mc.onPress = function () {
    if (playing==true) {
        pausePos = (mySound.position)/1000;
        mySound.stop();
        myVid.stop();
        playing = false;
    }
};
```

Let's run through this ActionScript in plain English:

When I, the pause button, am clicked {
   if (the video and sound are playing (this is the variable check)) go and do this {
      set a variable called pausePos to hold the current position of the sound divided by 1000
      stop playing the sound
      stop the video
      Change the variable called playing to say that the video is not playing
   }
};

Calling this a pause button is essentially trickery. It is actually stopping and resetting the sound timeline, while also pausing the video timeline (with the stop command!). Before it resets the sound timeline, it stores its current playhead position, dividing it by 1000 so it can say where it is in seconds.

7. If you're wondering why we bother to do this, you're about to see. Select the play button and give it an instance name of 'play_mc'. Enter the following code beneath the previous lines (in frame 1 of the actions layer):

```
play_mc.onPress = function () {
    if (playing==false) {
        mySound.start (pausePos);
        myVid.play ();
        playing=true;
    }
};
```

This translates as:

When I am clicked {
   If (the video is not playing) do this {
     Start the sound at the stored position
     Restart the video
     Change the playing variable to say that the video is currently playing.
   }
}

We stored the point at which we stopped the music in the pausePos variable in the last step. Now, when the user starts things up again, the sound can start off in exactly the same place that it was stopped.

8. Select the stop button, and give it an instance name of 'stop_mc'. Add the following actions underneath the previous code:

```
stop_mc.onPress = function () {
     mySound.stop();
     myVid.gotoAndStop (1);
     pausePos = 0;
     playing = false;
};
```

This code stops the sound file dead but this time does *not* store the playhead's position. Then, it sends the video timeline back to frame 1 and makes it stop there. The next thing it does is to set pausePos to 0. We've done this because the play button always tells the sound to play from the stored position. Finally, it changes the playing variable to false. If the user presses play now, both sound and video will run from the beginning.

9. Test the movie. One thing to notice is that if your video file is longer than your sound file then the sound file will loop. If you want to fix this to keep your sync, simply add these two lines to the last frame of your video movie clip:

```
_root.mySound.stop();
gotoAndStop(1);
```

This will halt both the video and the sound when the end of the video clip is reached. But what if the end of the sound file is reached first? Onto the next trick...

It's not over 'til the onSoundComplete

The onSoundComplete event is another great piece of ActionScript that you can use to help you keep your sound and video synced up. This event is new to Flash MX. As its name suggests, this event occurs when a sound playing within the Sound object comes to an end. The code is a little more complex than some we've seen:

```
mySound.onSoundComplete = function () {
     }
```

This checks to see if mySound has finished playing and, if this is true, tells Flash to do whatever we put in the curly brackets. This event could come in useful when your sound is driving your video or if you need some intro music before displaying the video file.

In this exercise, we're going to make a streaming MP3 player that displays a different video to accompany each audio track. For this, we'll use the onSoundComplete event to trigger the change in video. For this video, we'll use a couple of BMX video files and leave them to loop.

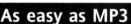

As easy as MP3

In the following exercise, we're going to dynamically call two MP3 music files into our Flash movie. If you want to follow our example exactly, there are two tracks available in the code downloads section for this chapter at www.friendsofed.com. They're called `recordsback.mp3` and `nowewon.mp3`. They're 2MB and 2.5MB respectively, so those of you on slow connections might want to use your own MP3 files.

There's quite a lot of ActionScript to get through here, but stick with it – we'll go through it in separate blocks.

1. Open a new movie and import two video clips, and don't import the sound with them. I've used `cross_ramps.mov` and `halfpipe.mov` from the source download for this chapter. As usual, remember to place these videos inside their own movie clip.

2. On the main timeline insert two new layers called 'video1' and 'video2', and drag each of your movie clips on to its own layer.

3. Select frame 1 of the video1 layer and drag it to frame 2, then select frame 1 of the video2 layer and drag it to frame 3. Your timeline should now look like this:

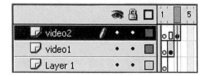

   We're now going to add ActionScript to our movie to dynamically call in the MP3 files to accompany our video. We'll also make each video clip loop until the end of the first audio track and then, when the next MP3 track starts, we'll play the second video.

4. Rename Layer 1 as 'actions', select frame 1, and open the Actions panel. Enter the following code carefully:

```
i=1;
songArray = new Array ();
songArray [0] = "recordsback.mp3";
songArray [1] = "nowewon.mp3";
songCount = songArray.length;
```

   First, we initialize the `i` variable. This is used to store the current song that is playing.

   Next, we create an array of song file names. The second line of script creates the new array, and the next two lines inhabit cells of the array with song file names. If you're wondering why our playlist appears to start with 0 rather than 1 as you might expect, this is simply because arrays always begin counting at 0.

   Arrays are a little like variables because they store information, but they can also store more than one piece of information. If you imagine that an array is like a paper grocery list, then you might ask your partner when you're shopping in a store 'what's first on the list?' or 'what's next on the list?'

As variables can only store one piece of information, you'd have to store one shopping item on each tiny bit of paper and it's therefore much harder to find what you are looking for: 'what's on the pink post-it note – no, not that one, the other pink note!'

Looking back at the array in our script above, you can easily add extra MP3 files by just extending the list. If you wanted a third track you would simply insert the line:

```
songArray [2] = "myThirdTrack.mp3";
```

... and so on. The last line of code in this section stores the number of cells inhabited in the array. In its current state, the variable songCount has a value of 2.

> *You can see in the code above that we've entered the file names for our example MP3s. If you're using your own files then replace the existing files with your own file names inside the quotation marks.*

5. Underneath the previous lines, type in these two lines of code:

```
mySound = new Sound ();
mySound.loadSound (songArray [i-1], true);
```

Okay, the first line is familiar: we're setting up the Sound object. The second line uses the loadSound method to pull in an MP3 sound file. We've previously only used attachSound to pull in files, but as mentioned earlier, you can dynamically call in external MP3 files for use in Flash MX. The loadSound method accepts the following parameters:

```
mySound.loadSound (<URL/Filename> , <Streaming Flag>);
```

If the Streaming Flag is set to true, the MP3 file will stream in to the movie, and if set to false then the MP3 will be imported as an event sound. For this exercise, we're going to use streaming, so we've set it to true in our code.

6. Onto the section of code. Type in the following:

```
mySound.onSoundComplete = function () {
    i++;
    if (i>songCount) {
        i=1;
    }
}
```

As we've seen previously, this first line checks to see if the sound has finished playing using the onSoundComplete event. If the sound has finished, Flash will go and on and follow the instructions inside the curly brackets... which is next.

When a song has finished, we need to increment our count variable, `i`. This second line of code is the shorthand equivalent of saying `i = i +1`.

The third line checks to see if the count variable `i` is higher than the actual amount of songs (stored in `songCount`). If `i` is higher, then the count variable is reset to 1, meaning that our MP3 playlist will be looped back to the first song when it reaches the end of the list.

7. Now type in the last chunk of code:

```
mySound.loadSound (songArray [i-1], true);
gotoAndPlay (i+1);
};
```

The first line here should be familiar as it loads in an MP3 file, using information from the `songArray` list. If you're wondering why this is set to `[i-1]`, it's because computers start counting from 0 - remember?

The second line sends the main timeline to another frame so that it displays a different video. We've used `i+1` here because our video clips are sitting on frames 2 and 3.

8. The last thing to do in Flash is to insert a stop action in both frames 2 and 3 of the actions layer:

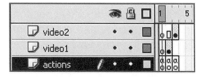

9. There's something you need to do before you can test the movie. Locate the MP3 files you are using for this exercise on your hard drive, and place them in the same folder as this FLA. Now save this Flash movie as `mp3_player.fla` in the same folder as your MP3s. This is important - if they're not in the same folder, then Flash will not be able to locate them when you test your movie.

> *It's always best to avoid using odd characters in your file names (such as spaces or slashes). Stick to underscores and hyphens if you must use them, as this will make it much easier to avoid errors in your ActionScript when naming files.*

10. Now go ahead and test your movie.

The first video will continue to loop while the first track plays, and then, when the first audio track ends, Flash will go and play the next video and audio track simultaneously. The changeover isn't the smoothest thing in the world, but this is down to the MP3 files being loaded in. If you want to sync sound and video in your movie (i.e. you're not just making an MP3 player), then it is usually best to import the sound file into the Library and use the attachSound method, as this minimizes the pause during the changeover.

This may not be the most sophisticated MP3 application, but it's relatively quick to build and very easy to maintain: you don't have to do too much work to add more tracks or videos to it, and this application will happily keep playing through a whole folder of MP3 files. If you want to expand on the video elements, consider building separate Flash movies for each video clip and using ActionScript to load in these external SWFs into the main movie.

To take this further you could use some creative ActionScript to color or distort the video timeline. You could also introduce some skip track buttons so that the user doesn't have to wait for each track to finish before they can listen to a new one, or see a different video. I'll leave this up to you to go ahead and experiment.

Summary

In this chapter, we've looked at some different uses of sound in Flash, as well as how external sound files can be used creatively with video using ActionScript. We've looked at the advantages of dynamically calling in MP3 files and when it is better to import the soundtrack at the same time as your video. We've also looked at how importing sound separately into Flash can give you more control over it as a separate entity, and helps you to keep things in sync when skipping through your video timeline with ActionScript.

All of this proves the creative diversity and possibilities available through controlling the Sound object with ActionScript, whether the object is used alongside video, animation, or simply on its own.

This chapter rounds off the first, and most important section of this book. If you've read this far, you've now got the skills that you need to go away and create some blinding Flash presentations. Don't leave, though, because the next section is all about how to use these skills together and create a real on- and offline project...

section 2
Case Study

8

The case study: planning, production, and post production

It's time to really get your hands dirty. Enough talk – let's make a Flash presentation which can be delivered as a microsite on the web, and as a CD-Rom. Over the next three chapters we'll plan, build and export a Flash MX promo for Livingston Skatepark in sunny Scotland.

The first thing I do is plan out some rough sketches of what the promo might look like. I'm not looking to make any final decisions on layout, but I want to work out a production strategy of what content the promo should contain, what interactivity there will be, and a rough plan of how it will be built.

These bullet points and the rough sketch on the next page are my production strategy:

- Design will be minimal, with video taking the lead visual role.

- It must contain video of skating at Livingston.

- The message is very simple, and simple bold typography will back this up.

- Livi is a concrete skatepark that has a bit of a reputation for hurting people. This roughness should come through but not be dominant.

- There is a busy local scene, giving it a lot of personality – this should come through. This is NOT California.

- Sound is very important, but this is a low budget (well, no budget actually!) number, so publicly available and homemade sound will feature heavily.

- Even though it uses video, I want the promo to work well with low bandwidths. Maybe the user should be offered a choice of connection speed at the start?

- Video is traditionally a linear content element. Its addition to Flash opens up new possibilities with regards to interactivity. This could be explored.

- It should be viewable in a browser on a screen set to 1024x768 without scrolling. It will be an advantage if the CD-Rom version could be viewed on an 800x600 screen.

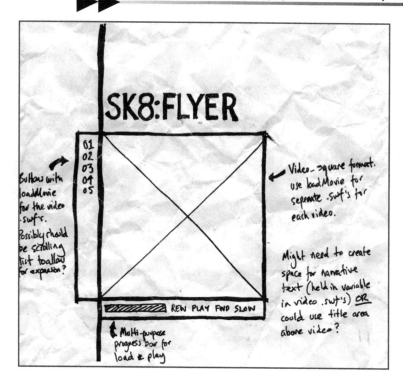

Some of these are very rough concepts, but they gave me a base to work on.

After this, I waited for a nice sunny afternoon and headed down to Livingston, tooled up with my digital video camera and tripod. The most obvious reason for taking the tripod was to get very steady footage, which is a good thing - if your source footage is steady, then you'll end up with higher quality video at smaller file sizes. Also, if there was any aggro - someone wanting to 'borrow' the digital video camera, for example - it would make for a pretty good weapon.

Failing to plan is planning to fail

Normally, before going out to shoot video, I'd recommend writing down a list of planned shots that you can tick off as you film them. It's a pain having to go back at a later date to shoot more footage just because you missed one critical camera angle. This said, however, all I can plan for is the type of shots I *want* – I'll just have to wait and see whether what I want is on offer.

Stylistically, I decided not to go with the traditional skate footage format, where the camera dives about a lot with very fast pans and cuts. It's not that I'm against this – far from it – but it will make it too difficult for me to create a modem-friendly version of the footage. Remember – the more static the footage, the higher the quality, and the lower the file sizes.

I shot about an hour's tape, which sounds like a lot, but in reality will only contain about five minutes worth of really good footage. Additionally, I chatted with a couple of groups of locals about the skatepark and some of the spills they had witnessed. For various reasons nobody was prepared to allow me to film them chatting – only skating, so my plan to background video interviews had to be binned, although I got a lot of good stories.

Herein lies a golden rule of filming: not all your plans will work out. Stuff will happen, equipment will break, and people will get shy. The flipside of this is that mad and unplanned stuff will happen that you couldn't expect, but if you can get it on camera then you'll have extra valuable content. (Ever tried to video an interview between two people in a public park when a dog runs up and knocks over one of the subjects? Priceless stuff. You could do a lot more with it than just hope for fifty bucks from one of those 'home video bloopers' shows.)

I had a problem, though – sixty minutes of footage from which I want about 10 to 15 clips. In an ideal world they would all be one after another... but this is not an ideal world and they are littered throughout many minutes of dull footage.

Reviewing the footage

It is very, very, very tempting to dive in and start capturing and cutting the video footage when I'm just back from Livi and I've another couple of hours before going to meet some friends - just long enough to start capturing the footage. This would be a bad idea. Video files are really big and cumbersome.

Or, at least they are if you keep them relatively uncompressed, which is something we want to do when capturing the footage. We'll be compressing the clips as we import them into Flash, so we want to keep our source files of as high a quality as we can manage. Ten minutes of digital video captured at full resolution with DV compression (almost no compression) will take up about 1.6 Gigabytes of hard drive space. Even if you have a huge hard drive, files of this size are unwieldy and slow down applications on all but the fastest computers.

So what do I do instead of jumping in and capturing the footage? I plan. Forget the computer for a second. Get a comfy seat on the couch, with a nice cup of something, paper, pen, and a digital video camera. What I'm going to do is review the hour long masterpiece and take a note of the start and end times of the best bits (I don't have to be too accurate at this stage). This will force me to watch the footage several times and I will start to become more familiar with what I've got to work with. My advice is to watch it until most of it really bores you and you know it off by heart.

After doing this, I've decided on nine clips, which show a good mixture of what the skatepark has to offer. This has given me an idea for the interactive element of the video. I like the idea of being able play part of the footage in slow motion, perhaps by clicking a button. And maybe it would add to the suspense to have the sound go quiet during slow-mo and return to full volume when normal speed is resumed? I'll come back to these ideas later.

Capturing the video

After that, I needed to get the footage onto my computer. There are loads of different ways of doing this, depending on what software you've got and whether you're using a Mac or a PC. I normally use Moto DV to capture from the digital video camera and then process the footage in Cleaner 5. That software isn't cheap though, so here I'm going to use Windows Movie Maker, the software that comes as standard with Windows XP.

The best way by far to capture video from a digital video camera is using FireWire. It gives the highest quality and is fairly cheap to install if it didn't come as standard on your computer.

Fortunately for me, my soundcard has a FireWire port on it, so I use it to connect the digital video camera to my PC, and then turn the camera onto Playback mode. After a few seconds, a dialogue box appears offering me the option to 'Record Video using Windows Movie Maker'. Clicking OK opens the record screen with several options. I want to capture the highest quality footage we can, so I used the Setting drop down to select Other... which makes another drop down appear, from which I selected DV-AVI (25Mbps).

This setting will capture the video with only very slight compression using the DV codec - fully uncompressed video at this size would produce files four times bigger. Assuming you're using a home computer without fancy video hardware, then this would create files way too big to handle.

At the bottom of the Movie Maker window there are some blue buttons that control the playback of the camera, allowing me to get the tape to the start of each section that I chose during my couch session earlier. Now is when I can really benefit from having the timings written down – I can go straight to the required footage. I'm not worried about being too accurate, as it's actually worth capturing a little too much before the start, and a little too much after the end. Pressing the Record button starts the capture and hitting stop brings up a save dialog box, allowing me to tell the program where to store the captured footage.

After a bit of processing, I'm faced with a basic timeline editor. I have now completed the capture, but I want to do some tidying up of the video, like trimming the start and end to remove unwanted footage.

By default, Windows Movie Maker splits the video into 'Clips,' which are its attempt at guessing different camera cuts. Don't let this confuse you though; I am still working off just the one file. I click on each clip and then play it in the preview window. I tend to find that the first and last couple of clips are not required, so I click on the first clip that starts my chosen section and then Shift-Click on the clip that ends my section. Now I can drag all the selected clips to the timeline at the bottom of the screen.

The following steps are all I need to do to save out my file ready for Flash import.

1. Choose File > Save Movie...

2. Set Playback Quality to Other... > 'DV-AVI PAL (25Mbps)' (or the NTSC alternative if that's your country's TV standard).

3. Click OK.

4. Give the new video clip a file name and hit Save.

I followed this process for all nine of my selected video clips, and then congratulated myself with a hot beverage. Don't be worried if the video seems very jumpy when played back on your computer in its current form. It isn't compressed for playback yet, and most computers struggle to play full resolution DV codec video at the correct frame rate. All will be fine once we get it into Flash.

As you saw in my sketch of the interface earlier in the chapter, I decided to go for a square video format. The actual size is dictated by a combination of file size expectations, processor performance and the available screen area. Because the video is the main focus of the project, I opted for a quite big 360 x 360 pixels video area.

I used Adobe After Effects to resize and crop down my video files to this size from the captured originals of 720 x 576 (PAL) – I used After Effects because I own it, and it's easy, but there's a whole bunch of other software you can use to do this, some of which are a lot cheaper.

> *Generally speaking, it's a good idea to make your video dimensions a multiple of 4 because the Sorenson Spark codec compresses the video in 4 x 4 segments. This means that, if your video is 157 x 157 pixels, it will add an extra 3 pixels to the width and height to allow the compression to work properly. The extra size isn't visible in Flash, but it does add slightly to the file size.*

Tune!

I need to hold back a bit longer before starting Flash. I needed to get some sounds together first, so I made a list of my sound requirements as follows:

-   Intro loop – quiet, background, heavy bass.

-   Scratchy, bleepy spot FX for text animations.

- Fat, lazy beat loop for main part of site.

- Scratchy 'ting' spot fx for buttons.

- Fat, loud, hyped beat loop for video sections.

- Quiet version of above loop for video slo-mo.

There may be some additional spot effects required, but this list gave me a great place to start. Starting sound creation/gathering without clear goals can be an extremely time consuming job. You'll have noted that my English isn't very good in the above list, but it's more important to get down some key words – even if they are made up phonetic words – so that you know what you are looking for. This is especially important if you are building a project as part of a team and someone else is getting the sounds together for you.

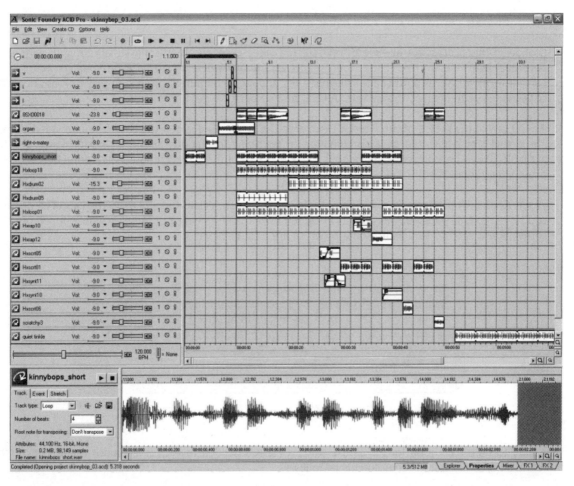

I've built up a fairly large collection of spot effects over the years from a combination of purchased CD collections, and freeware files downloaded from the web. There are loads of sites on the web with spot effects and music for you to download for free, but be careful - just because a site allows you to download a music clip for free, it doesn't mean that they necessarily obtained copyright permission to put it there. If you're caught using it on your site, you could be held responsible, so better safe than sorry.

Better still; why not invest in a decent microphone and some sound software? This will allow you to create many of the sounds that you'll require. I use Sonic Foundry's Sound Forge for recording and tweaking my spot effects, and Acid Pro for creating music loops. Demos of both are available from their site at www.sonicfoundry.com/downloads, and more details on sound editing are available in chapters 6 and 7.

As usual, my sound creation doesn't go exactly to plan and my files don't all sound exactly like they were intended to, but happy accidents are inevitable, and that's all part of the creative process.

Summary

You should have found this chapter a bit frustrating. You want to get your teeth into the project, dive into Flash right from the start, and skip all this planning.

Don't. You'll save so much time and effort by going through the above steps first. If you don't, you may still end up with a great project, but the chances of you being on time and within budget are slim.

Plan what your project is about and what you want it to achieve. Then determine what content will be required. Is video really relevant and not just a tacked on extra? Make lists of the content required, including text, video, still images, music, sound effects, and voice overs.

It can seem hard to do this much planning from such an early stage, but the key to success is to not worry about getting it exactly right first time. Just make sure you give yourself something to go on. Now that we've done that, we can move onto the next stage.

Inside Flash

What we'll cover in this chapter:

- *Learning how to organize our Flash movies using **abstraction***

- *Importing our video into Flash*

- *Using ActionScript to create a **dynamic** Flash video player*

Now the moment you've been waiting for – time to open up Flash and start building. Well, sorry to disappoint you, but we're still not ready to open the program. First we need to get pen and paper back out and plan the construction of the project.

There are loads of different and equally valid ways to structure a Flash project, and the decision sometimes comes down to personal preference and your level of knowledge of Flash. For example, I can think of two main ways to approach this project, both of which would give a similar end result. The tricky bit is determining which is best, and nothing is better to help you decide than hindsight.

What am I talking about? If you're fairly new to Flash then you might not see where I'm going with this, so let me explain. The most obvious option for building this project is to have one big Flash file with a bunch of scenes. Being the most obvious, it requires the least amount of planning and therefore is the route that most people go down, but it has its problems. These are hard to realise without hindsight – something you won't have if you are new to Flash – so here, borrow some of mine.

An experienced person is just someone that's made lots of mistakes. This makes me very experienced, and one of the lessons I've learned the hard way is to make all my projects as modular as possible, making them easy to modify and expand. Towards the end of a project, and after completion, you tend to have requests to add new content and modify what's already there. Forward planning will make a big difference to how easy this will be.

Picture this. Six months on from now, Livingston hold a big skate event and supply me with a bunch of new video footage to update the promo. There's very little budget to do this work, so I want to do it as efficiently as possible. I open up the Flash file, which I haven't looked at for six months. It takes a good ten minutes to open and slows my computer down to a snail's pace. That's because the file is huge with all the video in it. Every time I export the file for the web, it takes another ten minutes because it's got to compress all the sound (including the video soundtracks). This is a nightmare that I am not going to wake up from. There must be a better way.

There is. It's centered around a concept I call 'abstraction'.

Abstraction

Legendary jazz bassist Charles Mingus is famous for the wise words, 'Making the simple complicated is commonplace; making the complicated simple, awesomely simple, that's creativity'.

The key to abstraction is simplification. Keep your files simple. This is the single most important concept to get into your head if you want to work efficiently with Flash. The addition of potentially large video files to projects makes abstraction more important than ever, but you'll be glad to know that Flash MX goes a long way to making this possible.

In Flash, being able to put buttons inside movie clips, which in turn are nested inside other movie clips, means that you can quickly end up with a complex hierarchy of timelines with your script and scattered throughout your animations. By abstracting your ActionScript from your animations, and keeping all your ActionScript in one place separate from your graphics, it makes it a simple task to change graphics without messing with the code.

Break everything down to as simple structures as possible. You might be surprised to know that the most highly complex web sites that I've been involved in actually have Flash files with relatively simple file structures – lots of simple items combined together in clever ways.

Please don't panic if you are starting to feel out of your depth, with all this mention of file structures and programming. Abstraction is a simple concept that takes a bit of a mind-shift to grasp, but once you get it, you'll save yourself loads of time and effort in the long term.

Flash structure

It's time to put all this theory into practice in the planning of the Livi skatepark promo. If we don't plan the structure, we will go down the most obvious route that reflects our linear thought process. First we think about what is contained in the promo as shown.

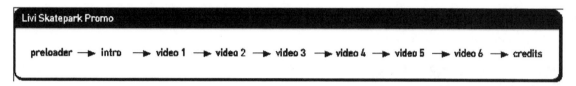

This simple file structure would work fine. Each element of the promo would exist in the one file, perhaps in different scenes. You would have buttons on screen that would allow you to jump to the different videos on the timeline. The problems start to appear when you get a lot of video in, increasing the file size, reducing your efficiency and increasing the complexity of your file.

I'm not going to explain how to build this basic structure here. There are lots of other good Flash books that will explain how to build simple Flash sites like this, those that deal less with byte hungry video – Foundation Flash MX from friends of ED (ISBN: 1903450101) for example. I want you to take a sidestep with me and invest a little more thought into coming up with a solution that will save you a lot of blood, sweat, and tears in the long run. How do you know that your client won't turn round a week before completion and ask to increase the number of videos to 200?

The core elements of the skatepark promo are video clips and an interface that we can use to select and control the video clips. In addition to this, I want an intro animation and a credits section. That's it.

Abstraction is most relevant to elements of a project that are likely to change in any way. The promo is likely to require new video clips added to it in the future, with the total number of clips possibly increasing significantly. We could start out planning for six clips, but this might grow to sixty, so we need to plan for this.

The basic structure we've just looked at has the flaw that, if someone wants to specifically watch video 6, they have to wait for the other five to load first. Because video files can make for some long downloads, this would be a bad thing – although not as bad as having to wait for videos 1 to 59 to load so that you could watch video 60!

Time to touch base

Flash allows us to have a movie that loads other movies into it. This isn't as confusing as it might at first seem. We can have a 'base' file that has the code and the interface buttons to load and control video clips, but it does not actually have any video in it.

Open the file `video_base.fla` (contained in the download files for this chapter) for an example of this technique.

What's the first thing you notice? There's only one scene with one frame on the timeline. This may go against how you may have worked in the past, or how other Flash books have taught you, but with the movement towards object-orientated design and programming in Flash MX (more on this in chapter 11), it'll become more and more relevant. Stay with us and we'll show you the light.

I'm not going all the way with the theory of abstraction in the skatepark promo. For example, I'm keeping my buttons as actual Flash buttons, as opposed to self-hiding movie clips that inherit their abilities from functions written on the root timeline.

Preparing for video

So, what do I have in this file? There are two white boxes, one of which is empty, and the other has a couple of text buttons, titled Video 1 and Video 2. When I publish the file, I create a SWF that is less than 1KB in size. This isn't surprising, bearing in mind how simple the file is. But simple doesn't mean powerless, as we are about to see. We'll step through the creation of the `video_base.fla` file, allowing you to see the concepts and stick to the original as much as you like.

1. Open a new Flash movie, call it `video_base.fla` and save it.

2. Add two new layers, and rename our layers (from the top downwards) video, buttons, and boxes.

    The boxes layer contains our basic outline, or background for the player. The left hand column will contain our video selection buttons. The right, when we play it, will contain the video!

3. Draw your own box, or copy ours. The boxes have a stroke thickness of 10 pixels, meaning that for our proposed 360 x 360 videos, the right hand box needs to be 380 x 380 pixels.

4. On the buttons layer we're going to add two buttons. First, draw whatever you like for the video1 button - you can be as intricate as you like with your design, but ours is simply the words VIDEO 1.

5. Select the text and press F8 to convert it to a symbol. Make it a button and name it 'vid1But'. Make sure it has a hit state that covers the area of the text.

6. Back on the main timeline, select our VIDEO 1 button and in the Actions panel enter the following code:

```
on (release) {
    loadMovie("video1.swf", "video_mc");
}
```

This simple code says that when someone clicks and releases their mouse on this button, Flash should load `video1.swf` in the place of the movie clip called `video_mc` that we'll come to in a moment.

7. Duplicate vid1But in the Library, changing its name to 'vid2But' in the process.

8. Visually alter the button so that it looks like you want it to. Drag an instance of it onto the stage, below our VIDEO 1 button in the first frame.

9. With this instance of vid2But selected, open the Actions panel, and enter this ActionScript:

```
on (release) {
    loadMovie("video2.swf", "video_mc");
}
```

Only the file name of the video's SWF is different to the script on the VIDEO 1 button. Like the last button, the video SWF will replace a movie clip called `video_mc`, so let's create that.

10. Create a new movie clip, call it 'emptyMovieClip', and do nothing within it. That's right, nothing at all.

11. Go back to the main timeline, and drag an instance of emptyMovieClip onto the stage in the video layer. Line it up with the top left corner of the right-hand box. In the Property inspector, give it an instance name of video_mc.

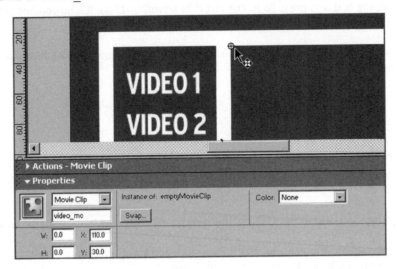

What's the point? The location of the empty movie clip marks the top left point of where our video will be, and this is where our video files will load in. Now we need to create our two video files. I plan for the video to fill the big empty white box in the base movie, so our video needs to be 360 pixels by 360 pixels.

Picture this

We've prepared our video clips and cropped them down to the right size, now let's import them. The file I'm using is way too big to download, so either use your own, or copy it from the Library in my video1.fla.

1. Create a new Flash file and set the size to 360 x 360 and the frame rate to 25 or whatever the frame rate of your clip is.

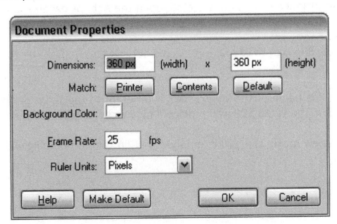

2. Save your file with the file name `video1.fla` and make sure it is in the same location as the `video_base.swf` file.

3. Select frame 1 and choose File > Import.. . Select the video file and choose Embed video in Macromedia Flash document in the pop-up dialog box.

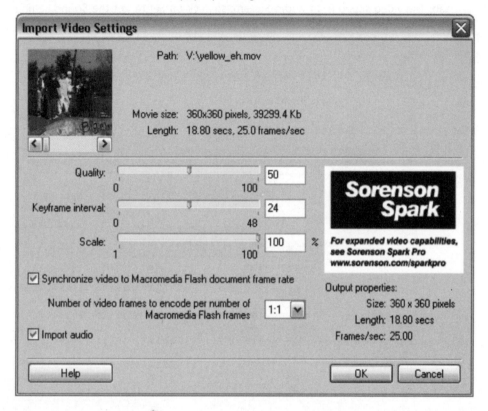

4. For the purpose of this example, I am going to leave the Import Video Settings at their defaults, and click OK.

Remember that Flash now uses the Sorenson Spark codec to compress the source video file into a new video file inside Flash, so this could take a wee while depending on the size of your clip and the speed of your computer. Kick back with a nice cup of tea and read the paper until you see this dialog box:

5. Click Yes and you'll be presented with the first frame of the video on my timeline. Make sure that the video is centered in the movie by adjusting its X and Y coordinates in the Property inspector. If your video is not 360 x 360, you can scale it here too.

6. The only other thing we need to set is the audio quality in File > Publish Settings… on the Flash tab. The video sound is an Audio Stream, so click on Set to get the Sound Settings dialog.

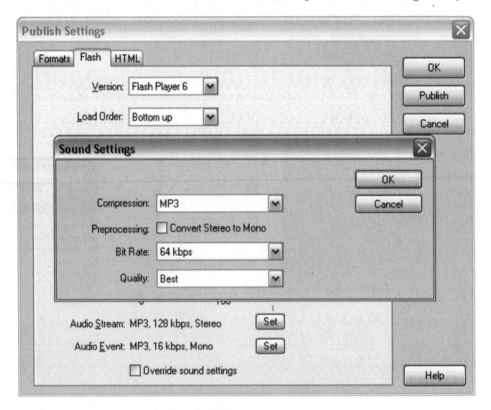

7. Set this to the quality you require, bearing in mind that higher quality means bigger files means longer downloads. I'm going to set the compression to MP3, 64kbps, Stereo. Flash compresses video, but not its soundtrack, when importing video – the soundtrack is compressed when exporting the SWF file.

> *Remember that making your MP3 sound stereo does not double the file size, as the compression only stores the differences between the left and right channels. As video tends to have similar sound on both left and right, this makes for very efficient stereo compression.*

8. While in the Publish Settings, click on the Formats tab and uncheck the HTML option. Because this file is for the base movie's use, we are not going to need to embed it directly into an HTML page – so all we need is the Flash SWF.

9. Now publish your movie.

I've got `video_base.swf` in the same location as the `video1.swf`, which you should just have created. If you double-click `video_base.swf`, then you get the basic interface of two boxes side by side, one with two buttons and the other empty. There is an empty movie clip there as well, but we can't see it because it's empty.

10. Go on then, you know you want to – click the VIDEO 1 button. The video plays perfectly in the base movie. Clicking the button ran the code that told Flash to replace our empty movie clip called video_mc with the other Flash file `video1.swf`.

This technique of loading external files into a base movie is not unique to working with video. It's the most efficient way to build large projects of any kind, as they allow you to break the project into simple objects that can be built in isolation. This has the advantage of allowing several people to work on one project at a time, with each person creating separate modular components that are loaded when required by the base movie.

Clicking on the VIDEO 2 button removes the video because it is trying to load in the file `video2.swf`, which we haven't built yet. This is your next task – to create individual SWF files (and buttons within the main movie) for each video clip that we plan to use.

You should now be starting to see the advantages of abstraction of the project. We could have thousands of videos accessible through a scrolling list, and the user would only have to download the files they wish to view, in the order they want to view them – not the order you placed them in your Flash file.

We have abstracted the 'content' (the video clips) from the 'interface' (the controls) giving us a simple modular structure on which to build. And now we have a basic prototype for the promo.

Take control

The next thing to do is to add some extra functionality. The main thing I am missing is some VCR style controls. I want to allow users the following functionality:

- Fast forward

- Rewind

- Play

- Stop

The obvious way to do this would be to add buttons that directly control the video clips by adding them to each of our video clips. There is nothing wrong with this – it would work fine. But imagine the extra work I'll have on my hands when I need to add another sixty video clips – I'd have to add buttons to each of the sixty clips.

And then the real nightmare would start, because after reviewing the project, I decide that I'm missing another feature: slow motion. That would mean that I would have to sit down and go through all of the video clips adding this functionality, file by file, having to re-export the video file each time.

Fortunately, I'm using an abstracted approach that minimizes the extra effort required to carry out everything I have just described. The video clips are the variable in the promo. It is very likely that more will have to be added, and exporting these clips can be slow due to the processing required by the computer. I therefore only want to export them once, even if I'm going to change the functionality of the promo itself.

So I'm going to keep the video files 'dumb' or 'raw'. This means that I am not going to place any functionality within the video files – all the intelligence will live in the controls in the base movie. This has the advantage that if I need to add or remove functionality, I only have to do it once to one file, which is tiny in size and therefore fast to export.

Starting and stopping

Before we go any further, open `video_base_2.swf` and have a play around with the new VCR style buttons to get a feel for what we're about to create.

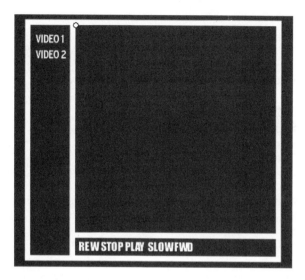

1. Open your `video_base.fla` and alter the boxes layer – you can see how I've altered mine in the screenshot. Just remember that our videos are mostly going to be 360 x 360, so give them enough room to appear.

2. Create five new buttons and place them on the stage in frame 1 of the buttons layer. Again, like the video selection buttons, mine are just text with a rectangle for their hit state.

3. Click on the PLAY button first, and in the Actions panel add this code:

```
on (release) {
    video_mc.play();
}
```

This button is nice and simple. The first line tells Flash that I want something to happen when someone clicks and releases their mouse over this button, and the next line says what I want to happen. Let's break the next line down into its parts.

The first part, `video_mc`, tells Flash that I am referring to the video (remember this is the name I gave to the empty movie clip, which means it is also the name for the video clips that load in its place).

The next part is a full stop which tells Flash that whatever comes next relates directly to `video_mc`. Think of it as a way to link code in this instance, although it's actually a wee bit more complex than this.

The third part is `play()`, which means exactly what it says. In this instance it is saying that I want `video_mc` to play.

So you kind of need to read the line backwards to understand that it means 'play video', which is exactly what I want our button to do. See – it's simple! The key to this code is that we gave the empty movie clip the instance name video_mc and because it has a name we can tell it to do stuff.

4.   The next button to script is the STOP button. It has to have this code attached to it:

```
on (release) {
        video_mc.stop ();
}
```

You can see that it is just like the play button, but instead of telling video_mc to play, it is telling it to stop.

Forwards, backwards, slower

Now that we've got our simple stop and start buttons sorted out, we can move on to the more interesting buttons.

If you take a look at the FWD button in video_base_2.fla, you'll see that there's much more code than the PLAY and STOP buttons, and it looks much more complicated. Don't be put off, it's simpler than it appears.

The main difference is that telling the video to stop and play are events that happen in an instant – one click and you get the result you are looking for. Our forward and rewind buttons are special, in that I need them to carry out a task while I hold our mouse down and stop that function when released. We therefore need two sections of code.

1.   This is the first section – this code starts the task of fast forwarding when the user presses the button. Select the FWD button on your stage and add this to its Actions panel:

```
on (press) {
        video_mc.onEnterFrame = function () {
                video_mc.gotoAndStop (video_mc._currentframe + 5);
        };
}
```

Let's analyze the code. This is what is technically known as a callback function, I'll explain it without getting too techy.

The first line indicates that I want something to happen when someone presses and holds down their mouse button.

The next line says that I want to add a 'function' to the video clip. A function is a bit of code that adds functionality – in this instance, forward-winding the video. I am also indicating that this function should be carried out onEnterFrame, which means that it should happen on every frame of our movie.

The next line is the function itself – it is the actual instruction to be carried by the function. The first bit is video_mc.gotoAndStop, which means I am telling the video clip to go to a specific frame and stop. The second bit is `(video_mc._currentframe + 5)`, which specifies the frame that we want the video to go to. It is actually a simple equation that adds 5 to the current frame of the video. This will have the effect of the video skipping forward 5 frames at a time, as opposed to normal play, which skips forward at 1 frame at a time.

2. After the code you've just added, add this code, which stops the video forward-winding when the button is released:

```
on (release) {
    video_mc.onEnterFrame = null;
    video_mc.play ();
}
```

The code here is much simpler. The first line indicates that we want something to happen when someone releases their mouse button.

The next line removes the forward-wind function I added to the video clip when the user pressed the button.

The last line you will recognise from the PLAY button. It tells the video to start playing again.

3. If that seemed like hard work, you'll love the RWD button. Add this code to it on the stage:

```
on (press) {
    video_mc.onEnterFrame = function () {
        video_mc.gotoAndStop(video_mc._currentframe - 5);
    };
}

on (release) {
    video_mc.onEnterFrame = null;
    video_mc.play ();
}
```

Look familiar? It should do, as it's almost identical to the FWD button. The only difference is the frame that I am telling the video to go to as part of the function. Instead of adding 5 to the current frame of the video, we subtract 5 to make the video go backwards.

4. Last but not least is the SLOW button. It'll keep the video playing, but play it at one-third normal speed whilst the user holds down their left mouse button on it so that they can pick up some new moves from the Livingston crew. Add this code to the Slow button's Actions panel:

```
on (press) {
    video_mc.stop();
    counter = 0;
    video_mc.onEnterFrame = function () {
        counter ++;
        if ((counter % 3) == 0) {
            video_mc.nextFrame();
```

continues overleaf

```
            };
        };
    }

on (release) {
    video_mc.onEnterFrame = null;
    video_mc.play ();
}
```

Some of this you'll recognise from the FWD and REW buttons. It adds a function to the video when the button is pressed and removes it again when it is released. In fact, the release code is identical to that in the FWD and REW buttons.

The press code is a little more complex:

```
on (press) {
```

Indicates that I want something to happen when someone presses and holds down their mouse button.

```
video_mc.stop ();
```

The next line is similar to one from the STOP button. It stops the video.

```
counter = 0;
```

This sets a variable called counter to equal zero. Think of this as an actual counter that has been set to start at zero.

```
video_mc.onEnterFrame = function () {
```

This says that I want to add a function to our video clip. This is the same line of code as used in the FWD and REW buttons.

```
counter ++;
```

This time our function consists of more than one line of code, but they still all run on every frame of the movie. The first line adds one to our counter, meaning it goes up by one on each frame of the movie.

```
if ((counter % 3) == 0) {
    video_mc.nextFrame ();
```

The next lines are a wee bit more complex, but translated into English they say 'tell the video to move on to its next frame, every 3 frames'. This makes the video run at a third of the speed of normal. Obviously, if you changed the 3 to 10, it would move on every 10- frames meaning the video would be playing at a tenth of its normal speed.

You don't need to understand fully how the slow motion function works to use it, but in case you're that way inclined, here's the lowdown. Each frame we increment the counter so that it reads 1, then 2, then 3 and so on. After incrementing the counter, we calculate `counter % 3`.

The old familiar percentage sign, as you will know, actually has a secret double life in the world of ActionScript. Here it is called a **modulus**. What it does is tell you the remainder after dividing the first number by the second. So 5 % 3 is calculated to be what's left over after 5 is divided by 3 – namely 2. The function advances the video to its next frame every time the counter % 3 equals zero. This happens every third increment (i.e. 3,6,9,12, etc). It's a very neat solution to an often encountered problem.

When you're done, export the movie and open the SWF to see it all in action. Our prototype is nearly complete...

Summary

Many of you reading this may be new to programming, and are put off instantly at the thought of it. This chapter has shown you how simple and logical ActionScript can be. There are very many ways to do things in Flash, and no one way is always the best.

If you can get into the habit of planning your projects to keep them as abstracted and simple as possible, you will be able to take on bigger and bigger projects without too much trouble, as you will still only be working with simple building blocks (albeit lots more of them).

This chapter may have been quite technical, but take another look over the final files, and compare them to Flash projects you have produced in the past. What strikes you? Hopefully it's the simplicity and cleanliness of the structure. There almost nothing to what we've done here. That's always the best way.

10

Adding Sound and Distributing the Project

What we'll cover in this chapter:

- Adding **sound** to our video project.

- Creating a **loading indicator** and a **playhead**.

- **Distributing** the finished project via CD and the web.

There are three main parts to this chapter, which cover the final steps needed to finish off the skatepark promo. First, we'll take a look at using sound to complement our video clips, before taking a look at giving the user some feedback about the state of the video, and publishing our files for the web and for CD.

Sound

There are two ways to add sound to the project. The first method is simple, and you may already be familiar with it. It involves specifying that a sound should play on a keyframe on the timeline of the movie. If all you need to do with your sound is start and stop it, then stick to this technique. It's simple and transparent, but does not offer as much control as you may need.

On the other hand, if you want to do anything interactive with the sound then there's another technique, which involves adding the sound using code. This technique is covered in a bit more detail in Chapter 7.

Adding sound

In the last chapter, remember that we put an empty movie clip on the stage and named it video_mc? This allowed us to add buttons that interacted with the video, because if something has an instance name, we can control it. Sound is exactly the same. ActionScript allows the designer to add sound to a movie, giving it a name, so that we can order a pan from speaker to speaker or fade in and out – amongst other things.

1. Open up your version of the case study FLA. If you'd like a sneak preview of what we're going to do here, you can open `video_base_3.fla` from the download files.

2. Let's tidy up our Library. Create a new folder in your Library, call it 'buttons', and drag all of your buttons into it.

3. Import your sound loop with File > Import... I've used the main sound loop that I've created, which is called `skinnybop.mp3`. Of course, you can either use this, or any other sound.

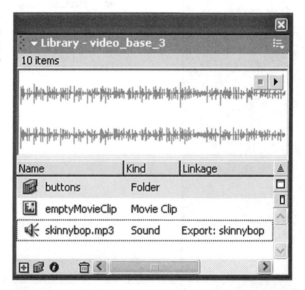

4. Select your file in the Library and choose Linkage... from the drop-down menu at the top right of the Library. The Linkage Properties for `skinnybop.mp3` are shown in the screenshot – I've specified that it be exported for ActionScript and given it the name 'skinnybop':

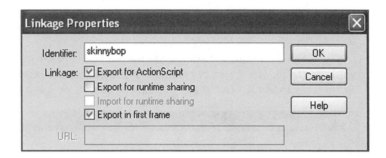

> *Unless you wish to have to remember to alter every occurrence of this name in the ActionScript that follows, use the same name here, even if you're not using the same sound file.*

5. Close this dialog box and look at our MP3's properties by clicking on the small blue circle with the i in it at the bottom of the Library window:

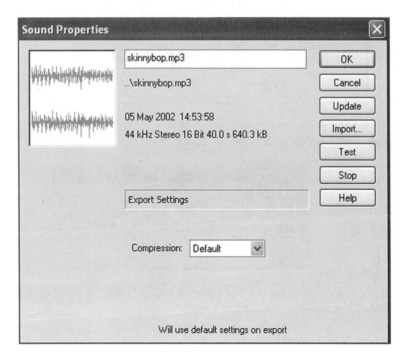

When you import an MP3 into Flash it sets the compression to Use imported MP3 quality. The original MP3 file that I imported was of high quality, and was therefore a bit big to put on the web, and there's every chance that yours will be too.

6. To compress it, make sure that the Compression in the drop-down is set to Default, which means that the sound will be compressed with the settings I specify in the Publish Settings window.

7. Open this window with File > Publish Settings, set the Audio Event MP3 compression to 32 kbps stereo. This will keep the file size down, but maintain a decent sound quality. It doesn't matter what the Audio Stream is set to as I haven't got any streaming sounds or video in my file:

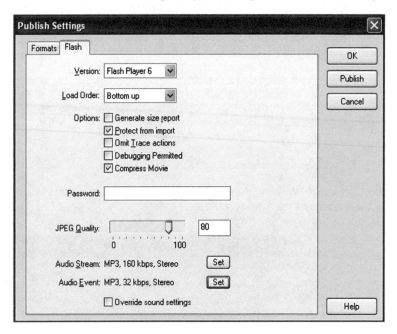

8. Create an empty movie clip called 'emptyMovieClip' at the top left of your movie (see the screenshot). Give it an instance name of 'sound_mc':

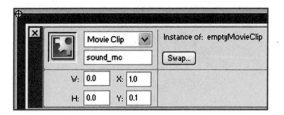

9. Open up the Actions panel for the first frame of the code layer. It could look like a lot in one block, so let's break it down. Add these three lines:

```
tune = new Sound(sound_mc);
tune.attachSound('skinnybop');
tune.start(0, 690);
```

The first line creates an object called 'tune' in the empty movie clip with an instance name of sound_mc, which the second line attaches the sound file to. The third line tells tune to start playing, specifying that it should play the sound repeatedly (in a loop) six hundred and ninety times.

Why 690? No specific reason – any high number would be fine, as long as it makes the sound play for longer than someone is likely to spend looking at the project. In this instance the sound clip is 40 seconds long – meaning that it will take over 7 hours to play 690 times.

> *In this example I have specified a target* (sound_mc) *for the sound object that I create. This isn't strictly speaking necessary as* tune = new Sound(); *would also work fine, but it is good practice to use targets as this allows you to have different volumes for multiple sound objects, and saves potential difficulties when you use* loadMovie *more extensively.*

I have used the name I gave the sound file (skinnybop) to attach it to an object that I have created (tune). The difference between my sound object and the empty movie clip I used earlier is that the sound object exists only in the code – there isn't a physical representation of it in my movie. Because the sound is attached to an object that has a name, we can control it easily with ActionScript. Let's do that now.

Fading the sound

What I want to do is fade the sound down while the user holds the SLOW button down and then play back at full volume when they release the button to watch the video at full speed. All we are going to have to do is add a little extra code to the code we already have on the SLOW button.

1. Select the SLOW button now and look at the Actions panel. Add the **bold** script to the on (press) function:

```
on (press) {
     video_mc.stop();
     counter = 0;
     tuneVol = tune.getVolume();
     video_mc.onEnterFrame = function () {
          counter ++;
          if ((counter % 3) == 0) {
               video_mc.nextFrame();
          }
          if (tuneVol > 0) {
               tuneVol --;
               tune.setVolume(tuneVol);
          }
     };
}
```

Let's look at the press code that activates the fading down of the sound first. The first new line creates a variable called `tuneVol` and stores the current volume of the sound in it. You don't really need to understand how variables work for this, just think of this as Flash taking a note of the current volume of our `tune` sound object. The volume of the sound object is merely a property similar to the alpha of a movie clip that can be tested and set by Flash. This is done when the button is initially pressed.

In the next section of new code, the line `if (tuneVol > 0)` checks to see if the volume that we're setting the sound to in the `tuneVol` variable is above zero, and if it is, then it runs the next two lines.

The next line decreases the variable `tuneVol` by 1, and the line after that sets the volume of the sound object to our new setting stored in this variable. This has the effect of reducing the volume of the sound object `tune` by 1 every frame. The normal volume is 100, so it will take 100 frames to fade the sound out completely.

What I have done here is expand the slow motion video function so that it also fades down the volume of the sound object. Because of this, when the existing release code removes the function from the video clip with the line `video_mc.onEnterFrame = null;` it also removes the sound fading code.

2. All I need to add to the release code is a line to put the volume of `tune` back up to 100, and that's exactly what the line `tune.setVolume(100);` does. This code is within the function that we add to the video clip called `video_mc`, so it therefore runs every frame of the movie until the release code removes it. Add it, and the rest of the **bold** script shown here:

```
on (release) {
      video_mc.onEnterFrame = null;
      video_mc.play();
      tune.setVolume(100);
      if (tuneVol == 0) {
            tune.stop();
            tune.start(0,690);
      }
}
```

The last few new lines are an extra finishing touch. If someone holds down the SLOW button for long enough then the volume of `tune` will reach zero, and there is silence. I have noticed that I tend to do this on sections of video where a skater gets some big air, and I release the button as they hit the ground.

The start of the sound loop is the most powerful/loud, so I decided it would be cool for the sound loop to play from the start if the volume gets to zero during a slow motion scene. That's what this code does – it checks to see if the volume of `tune` is 0 and if it is, it runs the next two lines which stop and start our loop so it plays from the beginning.

As an extra, you could try fading up a second, quieter sound loop as the main one fades down and then stop it when the SLOW button is released and the main loop comes on full volume. This would create a cool cross-fade effect. You'll need to create two sound objects to hold each of the loops (empty movie clips will do), and you'll need to specify named movie clips for each of the sound objects to target in order for them to have independent volumes.

Has it loaded yet?

The promo really is taking shape, but it's easy to forget that not everyone is going to be viewing it from our hard drive. Look back at my original planning and you can see that this has to work as a web site as well as a CD-ROM. I also specified that although it uses video, which traditionally means very big files, I don't want to exclude modem users. This means that we need to do some testing on the web.

We have used the Bandwidth Profiler earlier in the book to check how your movie will load over the Internet by simulating various connection speeds. Although this is a fantastic tool, it is of almost no use to us in this project. That is because it only simulates download speed for the movie you are exporting and not any other loaded movies. Most of our content is in loaded movies so the only way to see how this is going to stream over the web is to actually put it on the web.

As soon as I did this I noticed that something was missing. I don't get any feedback as to how much there is left to load of the current video. Depending on the Internet connection I use, I am able to view some of the video playing quite quickly and then it stops and starts playing to the end. This is because Flash is streaming the video, allowing us to see the bit that has already downloaded while the rest continues to load in the background.

Adding a progress bar

What we need to add is a progress bar to indicate how much of the video has loaded.

1. Open `video_base_4.fla` to see the next version of the prototype. You'll notice a white box at the bottom right of the movie.

    It is simply that – a white box, but it is embedded in a movie clip, which means we can give it an instance name, `vidLoadBar`. You know what an instance name means – we can control it with ActionScript, and change its width in relation to how much of the video has loaded.

2. Open your version of our case study and add another line to the boxes layer as I have, to divide the loading indicator from the buttons.

3. Create a new movie clip, call it 'vidLoadBar' and draw a white strokeless rectangle within it.

4. Add a new layer called loader between the buttons and boxes layers.

5. Drag an instance of vidLoadBar out onto the stage on the loader layer. Using the Property inspector, place it as shown. Give it a size of 139 x 20 pixels, and an instance name of vidLoadBar:

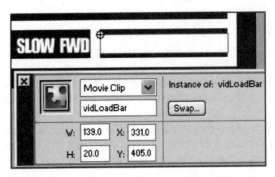

6. Open the Actions panel on the first frame of the layer named code. Add these few lines of script:

```
vidLoadBar.onEnterFrame = function() {
    total   = video_mc._totalframes;
    soFar   = video_mc._framesloaded;
    loaded = soFar / total * 100;
    vidLoadBar._xscale = (loaded);
};
```

The first line is similar to the code I used for the FWD, RWD, and SLOW buttons, in that it is adding a function to an object, which will run the code every frame. In this instance it is vidLoadBar that will receive the function.

The next line finds out the total number of frames in the video that's loading, while the third line finds out how many frames have loaded so far. The fourth line does some simple arithmetic using the info from the previous two lines to calculate the percentage of video that has loaded.

The last line tells the white box progress bar to change its width to the percentage that the previous line calculated. This means that when 100% has loaded the box is at its full width of 100% wide.

7. As a finishing touch I've put the text 'LOADING' underneath the progress bar so that it is only visible when the bar is less than 100% wide. To do this, add a new layer called loading text below the loader layer and add the text in the appropriate place.

If you test this from your hard drive, you're not going to see anything other than a full width progress bar because Flash is loading the video so fast. For the reasons discussed earlier, the Bandwidth Profiler isn't going to be any use to you, so you are going to have to put your SWFs up on a web site – something I'll cover later in this chapter. So that you can see this effect working without having to alter all your files, the video_base_4.fla file is altered to load the video files directly from a URL.

Where are we in the video?

Now we can see the progress of the video loading, but we haven't a clue how far through the video we are when watching the video. Well, *we* have – because by now I'll bet you know the video files that you're working with off by heart – but our eventual audience won't. What we need is a playhead to indicate the video's progress.

Adding the playhead

Open `video_base_5.fla` and have a look at how this will work. If you click on the small playhead image on top of the progress bar, you'll see what is shown in the screenshot below. You guessed it – another movie clip, called playHead.

1. Close the `video_base_5.fla` and open up your version of the FLA.

2. Create a new movie clip called 'playHead', and draw something appropriate to use as a playhead marker.

3. Add a new layer called playhead between the buttons and loader layers. Drag an instance of our playHead movie clip onto it, and give it an instance name of 'playHead'. The correct _y position on the stage is important, but the _x value will be determined by the ActionScript that we add next.

4. The ActionScript for the playhead is again placed on the code layer on the main timeline. Add the following code below the progress bar code:

```
playHead.onEnterFrame = function () {
    fTotal      = video_mc._totalframes;
    fNow    = video_mc._currentframe;
    fPos    = fNow / fTotal * vidLoadBar._width;
    playHead._x = fPos + vidLoadBar._x;
};
```

You can see a lot of similarities between this and the progress bar code. It attaches a function to the movie clip with an instance name of playHead. The second line finds out the total number of frames in the video while the third line finds out the current frame that we are watching.

Line 4 is similar to the progress bar code that calculated the percentage loaded. It divides the current frame by the total frames and multiplies the result by `vidLoadBar._width`, which is the width of the progress bar. This means that when the video is at the start we will get a very small number and when it is on the last frame we'll get 139 (the width of the loading bar in our file).

The last line adds the _x position of the loading bar (its left side) (conveniently, this is where I want my playhead to start its journey) to the position calculated on the previous line. This means that, during the length of the video, the playhead will move from the left side to the right side of the full width progress bar.

Test the movie and watch a video to see the playhead in action.

Can we show it to everyone else yet?

Now that we've got all my videos in place, we're almost done. As I mentioned earlier, the plan is to put the skatepark promo on the web and on CD-ROM. Let's deal with the downloading version first as it's almost ready to go.

Preparing for the web

To get our project suitable for the web, we need to do three things. We need to publish our files, make sure that they load in for the user, and upload them onto our server.

1. First things first, open your FLA (I'm using video_base_5.fla), and select File > Publish Settings...

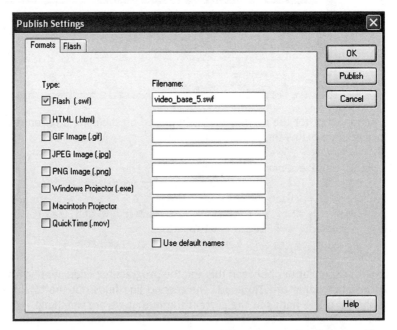

2. Uncheck the Use default names box so that you can change the names of the published files. We've been working with incremental file names as we've added functionality, and this is a good habit to get into as it allows you to go back to older versions if you make a mess of the latest file. The final web site, however, requires a Flash movie called video_base.swf, so change that now.

3. Click on the Publish button to publish the movie.

The observant of you will have noticed that I have missed something out. The `video_base` movie is nearly 150 KB, and we need a preloader. The problem is that almost all of that file size is due to the sound file `skinnybop.mp3`. As you may remember, in its Linkage Properties I specified that it should be exported for ActionScript in the first frame of the movie, meaning that the whole sound file will load before anything else, including the preloader.

The answer is a preloader movie that loads in the `video_base.swf` in the same way that `video_base.swf` loads in its movie SWFs. You can see the finished product in `preloader.fla`.

4. Create a new movie called `preloader.fla`, and give it the same dimensions as `video_base.fla` (500 x 460 pixels).

5. Create a large white box in the middle and convert it into a movie clip. Give it the instance name 'loadBar':

6. Put an instance of the emptyMovieClip at the top left of the stage and give it the instance name 'video_base_mc'.

7. Insert a new layer called 'code', and enter the following code:

```
loadMovie('video_base.swf', video_base_mc);
```

This is very similar to the code on the buttons that load in the video clips. It tells Flash to load our `video_base.swf` movie into the place of the emptyMovieClip called `video_base_mc`.

8. Enter some more code:

```
loadBar.onEnterFrame = function() {
    total  = video_base_mc.getBytesTotal();
    soFar  = video_base_mc.getBytesLoaded();
    percent = soFar / total * 100;
    loadBar._xscale = (percent);
```

Compare this code to the code I used a few pages back for the progress bar for the video clips. It's almost the same, except I'm monitoring how much of the `video_base` movie is loading, and using the movie clip with an instance name of `loadBar` to display the progress by adjusting its width. The other change is that instead of monitoring frames loaded, I'm monitoring file size loaded.

9. The last bit of code is:

```
if (percent == 100 && total >10) {
    loadBar.onEnterFrame = null;
```

continues overleaf

```
                    loadBar._visible = 0;
            };
    };
```

Here, the first line tells Flash to run the following code if the `video_base` movie has completely loaded. The code that follows is simply a little housekeeping. I remove the function that is attached to `loadBar` and then make it invisible.

In the first line, I'm also checking that the total size of the file to be loaded is greater than 10 bytes. The empty movie clip registers as having a total size of 4 bytes, so `total>0` would not be any good.

> *I'm loading the* `video_base.swf` *movie into an empty movie clip, because it's a technique we've already used, and we're keeping things simple. In reality, I would normally load* `video_base.swf` *into a* **level** *rather than a* **target**, *because the loaded movie is of the same size and positioning as the preloader movie. This wouldn't require an empty keyframe, and would simply use the code* `loadMovieNum ('video_base.swf', 69);`. *To further simplify things, I'm using physical instances of empty movie clips from the Library rather than the* `createEmptyMovieClip` *method.*

10. Select File > Publish Settings... and specify a Flash movie of the preloader and an HTML page to hold the movie. Call the HTML file 'index.html':

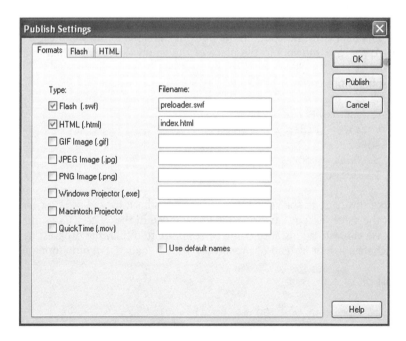

11. The last step is to upload our files to a server. You should have the documents shown in the screenshot: four Flash documents, four Flash movies and one HTML document. We need to leave the FLAs behind, and upload the SWFs and the HTML file.

Name	Size	Type ▲
preloader	22 KB	Flash Document
video1	1,830 KB	Flash Document
video2	4,392 KB	Flash Document
video_base_5	2,187 KB	Flash Document
preloader	1 KB	Flash Movie
video1	322 KB	Flash Movie
video2	1,240 KB	Flash Movie
video_base	155 KB	Flash Movie
index	1 KB	HTML Document

12. Because we've called our HTML file `index.html`, we can simply use the directory we've uploaded stuff to as an address. I copied the files into a new directory called `sk8flyer_tutorial` on my site www.h69.net, so I can use the URL www.h69.net/sk8flyer_tutorial.

> It's important that all files are put in the same directory, otherwise the video won't load. If you do need to have lots of videos it might be neater to have a sub directory called 'video' and put all the video SWFs in there. If you do this, you will have to change the code on the load buttons by adding 'video/' before the file name. For example, `loadMovie("video1.swf", "video_mc");` would have to be changed to `'loadMovie("video/video1.swf", "video_mc");'`.

Theoretically, all we have to do to create the version for CD-ROM is create a standalone projector, which is a simple task that we'll look at in a minute. The idea here is to create a dual format (Mac and PC) CD-ROM, which means that we'll need access to a CD writer with appropriate software.

There's also some nice touches that are definitely worthwhile taking the time to add, and we'll take a quick look at these first.

13. Re-save your FLA as `video_base_cd.fla`, because we're about to make some changes, and look at these Publish Settings (File > Publish Settings…):

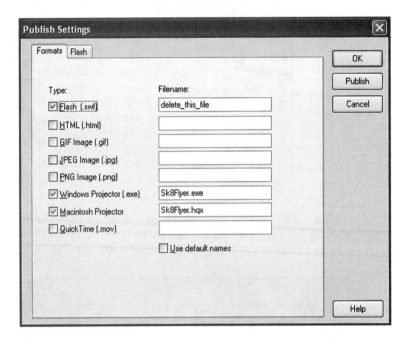

14. I'm doing this on a PC, but on a Mac the process is almost identical. The files that we want are the Windows and Macintosh Projectors. As you'll see from the screenshot, we also want to create a SWF with a name to denote the fact that it's going straight to the bin. Why do this? It's a quirk of Publish Settings that if you do not choose to export a SWF, then the Flash tab is removed, making it impossible to set the sound quality and other settings for the projectors.

15. Click OK, go into the main timeline, and select frame 1 of the code layer. At the top, we need to add two lines of code specifically for the standalone version of the promo. They are:

```
fscommand('fullscreen', 'true');
fscommand('allowscale', 'false');
```

The first line tells the projector to go full screen and fill the screen area with the movie as opposed to it sitting in a window. The next line prevents Flash from scaling the movie up when it goes full screen. Instead, Flash will fill the area around the movie with the movie's background color.

If we allow the movie to scale, and if someone is viewing the presentation on a slower computer with a screen resolution of 1024x768 (or higher) the video will scale up, making the file more processor intensive, which can in turn make the video play choppily. That said, personal preference does come into it as well. Try changing the second line to `fscommand('allowscale', 'true');` to see the scaled up version for yourself.

> *When in full screen mode you can always press the Esc key on your keyboard to switch back to window mode.*

16. One important feature has to be added to the promo that wasn't required in the web version because it wasn't full screen – a quit button. Many people (including myself) often forget to add this. Create a new button (CTRL+F8) called 'quitBut', and draw something appropriate – an 'X' or maybe in keeping which what we've been doing so far, simply the word 'QUIT'.

17. Drag an instance of the button from the Library onto the buttons layer of the stage.

18. Click on the QUIT button and add this code in the ActionScript panel:

```
on (release) {
    fscommand("quit");
}
```

This one's easy to understand. It says that when someone presses and releases their mouse on the QUIT button, the projector should quit.

19. It's time to select File > Publish to create the projectors. As the Mac projector is in a compressed format, I need to take it onto a Mac and expand it.

As long as the video_base.swf and video SWFs that we created earlier are in the same folder as the projector then they'll load without any problems. If you have a bit of time on your hands then you could remake your video SWFs by importing the video at a much higher quality, and exporting with high quality sound. This will produce bigger files, but that shouldn't be an issue with CD-ROM content.

Alternatively, if you'd rather spend more time out partying, you could just use the same video SWFs as you've put on the web. To keep things nice and neat on the CD-ROM, make all the files except the projectors invisible so that the end user just sees one file. The movies will still load when they're invisible.

Summary

Although there's a lot in this chapter, it only really covers the fundamentals. This is no bad thing however, as they are the most important building blocks for your future projects. Pull apart the files and cannibalize them to make your own video promo.

The last three chapters have explained how to build the prototype for the skatepark promo. The final promo has some more tweaks and wee bits of attention to detail, not to mention the intro and interface typography. It could take a full book to explain the final file in detail, but it is available for download with the rest of the files mentioned here, from www.friendsofed.com.

The file is heavily commented and after having worked your way through this book it should be easy for you to understand what's going on. There's nothing complex – it's just lots of simple building blocks added together to create something that is far more than the sum of its parts – something you should always aim for in your own projects.

We've had fun in this case study and have kept it simple, but you can always get deeper and more involved, which we'll do in the next chapter. Good luck!

section 3
Advanced Concepts

Scripting with Video and Sound

What we'll cover in this chapter:

- An introduction to **object-oriented programming** (OOP).

- Building your own reusable **components.**

- Constructing a sound and video player.

If you've got this far in the book, you'll have acquired all of the skills that you need to effectively master the new world of Flash MX video, and you'll have seen how to use those skills in a real project setting. This last section is a step forward into what happens when you take all this knowledge, and really push it to the max.

We're not going to lie to you and tell you that this section isn't difficult. It is. Those of you without any previous ActionScript experience are going to have some seriously sore brains by the end of this section, and even those of you with ActionScripting experience are going to encounter some new concepts.

The point, though, is that a book on Flash MX and video would be incomplete without this – it would be like going on holiday, staying on the beach all day every day, and never exploring the exotic country you've flown to. Even more importantly, if you work through this chapter and follow our instructions, you're going to end up with a fully customizable sound and video player as a Flash component.

What's that mean? That means that you've got a customizable video and sound player that you can drag and drop into any Flash project you create in your future design career, and then easily change to fit in with whatever project the player is needed for. Take a look at the screenshot to see what you're getting.

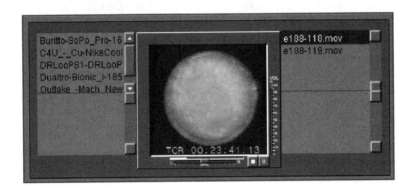

We're going to start this chapter with a brief run through some of the theory behind our building strategy before we start with the practical building of the project.

Objects and object-oriented programming

When most people hear the terms 'objects' or 'object-oriented' they instinctively think 'programming'. This is largely due to the fact that these terms have been inseparable since conception. Object-oriented programming (OOP) started in the early 1960s, when a need developed to organize code in such a way as to make complex programming tasks more easily understandable by humans.

This need has evolved over the years resulting in not only a large number of object-oriented programming languages, but pre-built **drag and drop** objects too. Not only do these new objects make their functionality easily understood, they also eliminate the need to code altogether. One of the biggest proponents of these drag and drop reusable objects is Macromedia Flash. You don't have to tell Flash what a movie clip is, you simply create one, and use it. You might not have known it before, but when you use movie clips, what you're doing is practicing OOP.

The basic premise of an object is that it keeps related data and code in one location. The beauty of an object is that a user doesn't need to know what actually takes place inside of the object; they just need to know what to feed into it and what it should then produce. This concept had been commonly referred to as a **black box,** since you should never need to peek inside, and you don't need to worry about what's inside either – as long as it produces the expected results.

Ultimately, every good object was originally programmed by somebody – so in this chapter we'll not only reuse and configure pre-built objects, but we will program our own reusable object: a sound and video player component.

The simple object

In Flash the most generic object is the object Object. Whenever any new object is created, it ultimately inherits the methods (behavior) and properties (characteristics) of the original object. Essentially, any new object gets the 'genes' of the object from which it is created. For example, meet Fred:

```
fred = new Object();
```

Here, Fred is a new object and he has inherited the genes of the object Object. Fred is now an object, but unfortunately he is still pretty bland. Alternatively, Fred could have become a new movie clip:

```
fred = new MovieClip();
```

Now Fred has some personality! He inherited all of the properties and methods of the MovieClip object – which in turn inherited all the properties and methods of the object Object. So Fred is now that much cooler. Using ActionScript, we can access a variety of built-in methods such as play, stop, and enterFrame, and also multiple properties including _x, _y (which refer to Fred's position on the stage) and _width, and _height.

Before Macromedia Flash MX, the main method used to create a new movie clip was by using the Insert > New Symbol menu option and then adding graphics to the timeline of the new symbol. This new symbol is an *object*, in the sense that its code and variables can be centralized to that timeline, but it is always more 'object-oriented' when you don't need to have a fixed graphic image or piece of code for that object.

Dynamic Fred

In previous versions of Flash you could change the appearance of a movie clip from the Library using the attachMovie method. Now in Flash MX, as well as changing a movie clip's image, you can dynamically create the movie clip as well. So, let's create a dynamic Fred and give him an appearance.

1. Make a new graphic symbol using Insert > New Symbol. Draw any kind of graphic on the stage to represent Fred:

2. Go into the Library and select the graphic you've just created. Choose Linkage… from the Library menu (at the top right-hand edge of the Library panel). Check Export for ActionScript and type 'appearance' in the Identifier field:

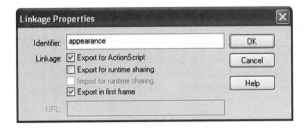

3. Next, type the following code in frame 1 on the main timeline:

```
fred = createEmptyMovieClip("fred", 1);
fred.attachMovie("appearance", "newAppearance", 1);
```

Now Fred is not only an object with the properties and methods of the MovieClip object, but he has gained a visual appearance that hasn't been created using the Create New Symbol dialog box: it's been taken from the graphic symbol.

4. Save your movie as fred1.fla.

Methods and properties

So we've mentioned methods and properties, but what use are they really? A method is essentially a function within an object that performs a specific task for that object. Properties are, well, just that - properties that the object has, like position and dimensions.

The most basic method that Flash users know is play. If any object has been made into a MovieClip object, either through ActionScript or just by using Insert > New Symbol, then it already has play and several other methods pre-built into the object.

We can also create a new method for an instance of an object, for example:

```
fred.rotate = function(n) {
    this._rotation += n;
};
```

So, anytime we make a call to `fred.rotate(number)`, Fred rotates the given number of degrees. The function `rotate(number)` is a *method* of Fred.

Rotating Fred

Let's test out our new method:

1. Open up `fred1.fla` if it isn't still open from the last exercise. Add the following functions to the main timeline, immediately below the previous two lines of ActionScript:

```
this.onEnterFrame = function() {
    fred.rotate(5);
};
fred.rotate = function(n) {
    this._rotation += n;
};
```

2. Save your movie as `fred2.fla`.

3. Now test your movie (CTRL+ENTER), and you should see Fred rotating in a clockwise direction:

If you can't see this, take another look in the Linkage Properties window of your graphic symbol and ensure that Export in first frame is checked.

What actually makes Fred move is setting his `_rotation` property. A property is an aspect or characteristic whose value is specific to an instance of an object. All MovieClip objects have a `_rotation` property, but the value of the property is unique to each instance. So, if `fred._rotation` is equal to 5, that does not mean that `fred2._rotation` must also equal 5.

Classes and inheritance

As mentioned earlier, inheritance simply refers to the 'genes' that are passed from one object to another. These genes are the methods and properties inherited from an Object, or more specifically, from the **class** of an Object. In Fred's case, we could make Fred represent a class from which we could make other instances of Fred.

That's my boy, meet Fred Jr

1. Open a new movie and add the following code to frame 1 of the main timeline:

```
Fred = function () {
    this._x = 100;
};
```

> The names of **classes** generally start with a capital letter, and **instance** names should start with a lower case letter. This helps to keep them separate and organized in our ActionScript.

In this case `Fred` is a very simplistic class, but if we make a `new Fred()`, we can then see how the properties of `Fred` are inherited by a 'fredJr'.

2. Add the following code directly beneath:

```
fredJr = new Fred();
trace("fredJr._x = " + fredJr._x);
```

3. Now test your movie and look in the Output window:

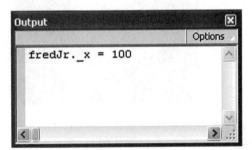

You should notice that the `_x` position of `fredJr` is equal to 100, since `fredJr` inherited this `_x` value from the same property in the `Fred` class.

4. Save this movie as `fred3.fla`.

Prototypes

One of the last concepts we'll look at when working with objects is setting the inheritance chain using the prototype and __proto__ properties. These are used to define the top level of any class. In our case the object Object uses prototypes to define its class. These prototypes therefore define the MovieClip object, and finally they define Fred too.

It is possible to create a prototype for a class, which will then hold true for any instance of that class. We can see this in action by setting up a prototype for the MovieClip class and then watching how it affects Fred.

Remake, remodel

1. To begin, open up a new movie. Add the following ActionScript to the first frame of the default layer to recreate Fred:

    ```
    fred = new MovieClip();
    ```

2. Below this line, add the following prototype to the MovieClip class:

    ```
    MovieClip.prototype.pickupLine = function() {
        trace("Would you like my objects in your Timeline?");
    };
    ```

    The pickupLine method should now be inherited from the MovieClip object and readily available for Fred to use.

3. To check whether or not this has occurred, we now need to add the following line immediately beneath all the previous ActionScript:

    ```
    fred.pickupLine();
    ```

4. Test the movie (CTRL+ENTER) and watch as Fred works his magic in the Output window:

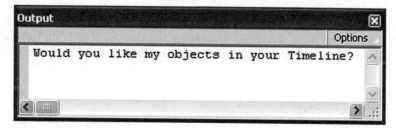

Don't tell Fred, but this pickupLine is now available for any instance of the MovieClip object. So, if:

```
bob = new MovieClip();
```

then:

```
bob.pickupLine();
```

would be the same as Fred's.

5.   Save your movie as `fred4.fla`.

Scope

The last key concept we'll look at for working with objects is **scope**. Scope is essentially the location (i.e. the timeline) where an object is declared. It is always possible to refer to an object within its own 'location' as `this`. Earlier on in the Rotating Fred exercise, you might have noticed the reference to `this` when declaring the new `rotate` method for Fred. In that particular piece of ActionScript was this line:

```
this._rotation += n;
```

Since we were already inside of the function `fred.rotate`, we knew we were referring to `fred`. We could therefore simply refer to him as `this`. This concept is used heavily in Flash's timeline structure. Since most timelines are found within movie clips it is possible to refer to that movie clip as `this`.

The main timeline, in addition to being able to be referred to as `this`, has its own unique identifier of **_root**. So, it doesn't matter how far down the hierarchy of nested objects you are, because in Flash you can always refer to the main timeline as `_root`. This concept is much like using an absolute path when accessing files on a server. It doesn't matter how many folders deep you are, you can always refer to the root directory with `http://www.WhateverDomainName.com/`.

> Macromedia Flash MX now includes a new **_global** identifier that can be used to set a variable or function so that it can be accessed from **any** timeline.

Finally, the last unique identifier to handle scope is that of **_parent**. Whenever you refer to `_parent` in a target path, it always refers to the object containing the current object. So, for example, if we placed `newMovieclip` within `existingMovieClip`, the `newMovieClip` would refer to `existingMovieClip` as `_parent`.

Determining the scope of objects

The Movie Explorer and the Insert a target path button (in the Actions panel) are two very useful features for determining the scope or target paths of objects.

As well as helping you to organize and locate all the media within a Flash movie, the Movie Explorer (Window > Movie Explorer) can display all of the ActionScript in the movie, and also displays the locations of objects that reside within other objects.

You can also search for specific terms within these objects using the search field:

The second tool, the Insert a Target Path button, lets you find any path relative to the current movie clip or lets you choose a path to an object starting from the root timeline. In order to control movie clips, loaded movies, or buttons, you need to be able to specify the target path in your ActionScript. If you're unsure of the path, then this tool is perfect for locating your objects and the relative paths between them:

Insert a target path button

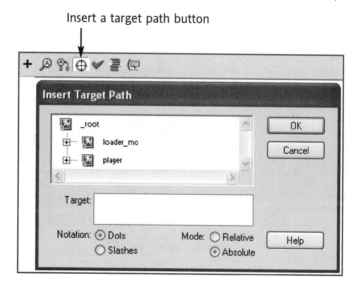

Components

A new addition in Macromedia Flash MX is the inclusion of a new object called the **component**. Components are complex movie clips that have defined parameters, and a unique set of ActionScript methods that allow you to set parameters and additional options at runtime.

Flash MX comes with several pre-built components in the **Components** panel (Window > Components):

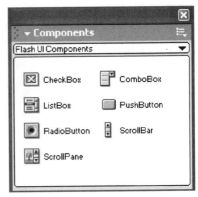

There is now a trend developing of creating completely object-oriented components such as those included with Flash MX. You can also customize the appearance of the components to fit in with your overall web site design. Components allow the user to enter variable values via the Property inspector, or through a custom-made interface.

The ListBox component

We've talked about components; so let's take a look at one. The **ListBox** component comes pre-built in Flash MX and enables you to add scrollable single and multiple selection list boxes to your Flash movies.

If you feel confident after spending some time on object-oriented programming, have a dig through the source ActionScript – it is well organized and can help to reveal a lot about creating classes and organizing code.

For now, let's just take a look at a few of the features including: the customizable skin elements; the separation between public and private classes; and the **Component Definition** panel.

1. Start a new movie. Open up both the Library (F11) and Components (CTRL+F7) panels if they're not already open.

2. Next, drag an instance of the ListBox component out onto the stage.

3. Notice that a Flash UI Components folder has now been added to your Library. Open up this folder and you'll see both the ListBox and ScrollBar components in there:

4. Now open the Component Skins folder and then, within here, go into the FScrollBar Skins folder.

5. Double-click on the fsb_downArrow movie clip icon to go into Edit Symbols mode. If you select the first frame of the **README** layer and open your Actions panel (F9) you'll see the following code:

```
component.registerSkinElement(arrow_mc, "arrow");
component.registerSkinElement(face_mc, "face");
component.registerSkinElement(shadow_mc, "shadow");
component.registerSkinElement(darkshadow_mc, "darkshadow");
component.registerSkinElement(highlight_mc, "highlight");
component.registerSkinElement(highlight3D_mc, "highlight3D");
```

registerSkinElement is a method that allows the component to listen to properties set for the **globalStyleFormat** object. By changing properties in this global object, you can set different properties that *all* components will display (for example, color as in the screenshot):

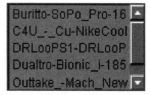

One of the biggest plus points about components is the Component Definition panel. You access this by first selecting your component movie clip in the Library and then choosing Component Definition... from the Library menu. This is where you can add values for variables or allow the user to select from an array of options, so that each instance of the component can be customized effortlessly:

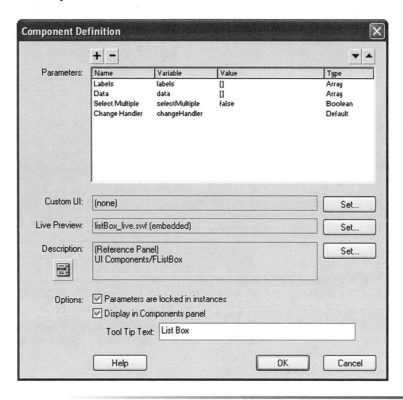

Our sound & video player component

This is what you've been waiting for: in the remainder of this chapter, we're going to build a sound and video player component. It's a kind of multimedia jukebox that'll dynamically load in video clips and MP3 sound files. In the central viewer window the user will be able to watch a video and, in the case of a playing sound file, a visual representation of the sound on a graphic equalizer:

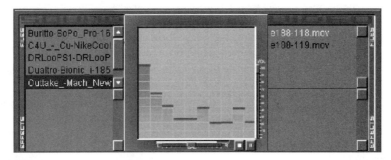

The construction of this player component is organized using objects. These objects have been arranged so that they illustrate the *visual* as well as *programmatic* conceptualization of objects and how we practically start object-oriented programming our player:

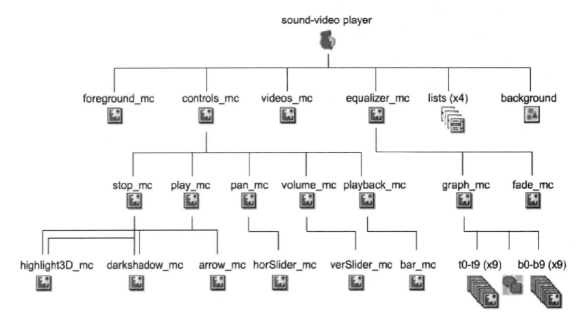

In the following exercise, when each new object is introduced, you can refer back to the diagram above to help visualize the relationship between the objects and how each separate object fits in to the overall player. For each of the objects we're going to build there is an image to act as a guide to the graphics used in the object (which you can adapt to suit your own designs). All the original code and source files for this chapter are available to download from www.friendsofed.com in the usual way.

One difficulty with object-orientated design is that quite often the objects will do very little on their own without interacting with the objects further up the tree. Here we'll have to plough through and create almost all of our movie clips without being able to see any great results. Being individual components though, they can be re-used in other projects - as long as we keep a note of how they interact.

We'll begin by constructing the 'smaller' objects including the **stop** and **play** buttons, the **pan** and **volume** sliders, the **playback** indicator, and the **graph** and **fader**. We will then combine these smaller objects to form the **controls** and **equalizer**. Finally, these two objects will combine to form our **sound-video player**.

Stop button movie clip

Without further delay, let's begin.

1. Open a fresh new movie and create a new movie clip named stop.

2. Rename the default layer graphics and, in the first frame, draw a graphic directly on the stage to represent your button in its default Up state. You can copy our graphic or design your own. Make sure that the graphic's top left corner is at (0,0)

3. Insert a keyframe in frame 2 of the graphics layer and alter your button graphic slightly so that it appears to be depressed (as it would in its Down state):

4. Insert a new layer called actions, insert a keyframe in frame 2, and add a stop action to it.

   The stop button is one of the most basic objects in the sound and video player. Surprisingly however, there are more objects within the stop button itself. These are the movie clips that form the button's appearance. Conveniently, these movie clips are automatically added to your Library if you drag a ListBox component on the stage. These movie clips will listen to any color value you set using the **globalStyleFormat** object as briefly discussed earlier.

5. Open the Components panel (CTRL+F7) and drag a copy of the ListBox component on to your stage. Now select it, and delete it. The movie clips we need for the button are now stored in the Library.

6. Add the following functions to frame 1 of the actions layer:

```
function pressActions() {
    this.gotoAndStop(2);
}
function releaseActions() {
    _parent._parent.stopS();
    this.gotoAndStop(1);
    _parent.play_mc.gotoAndStop(1);
}
```

The pressActions function tells the playhead to go to the second frame of the movie clip to display the selected button graphic. Then, the releaseActions function tells the stop movie clip's

timeline to go back to the first frame, as well as the timeline of its parent movie clip. The line
`_parent.stopS();` triggers the method in the sound-video player that will make the current
sound or video cease playing.

> *In Flash MX that you no longer need to use the Button object to*
> *capture user's mouse clicks. Movie clips themselves can now register*
> *these events, which is precisely what we've just enabled in our* stop
> *movie clip.*

7.   Still in frame 1 of the actions layer, add the following ActionScript:

```
this.onPress = pressActions;
this.onRelease = releaseActions;
this.onReleaseOutside = releaseActions;
stop();
```

This will set the onPress mouse event to trigger the pressActions function while both the
onRelease and onReleaseOutside events trigger off the releaseActions function.

That's it, you've built the first object in the sound-video player. Before we go any further, check
that your timeline matches ours:

Play button movie clip

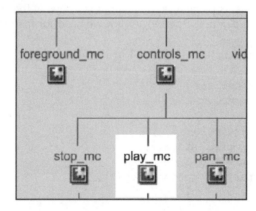

Here we're going to build the play button that will control the playback of files in the sound-video player.
This button's purpose is doubled as it will also form the pause button in our controller. If a file is playing,

the user will be able to click on the play button to temporarily pause playback of the file; pressing it again will continue playback as on a regular audio CD or DVD player.

Constructing the play movie clip is very similar to the stop movie clip except that will also contain a pause button. When the play button is released, the playhead will move to the pause button graphic.

Since the play movie clip will also contain the pause button, there is now an **if** statement to determine if the button is currently in play button or pause button frames.

1.   Create a new movie clip called play, and add a new layer to the timeline. Just as we did in the stop movie clip, name the two layers actions and graphics.

2.   In frame 1 of the graphics layer draw a play button, again making sure that its registration point (0,0) is at the top left corner.

3.   Insert another three keyframes (F6) in both layers. In frame 2 of the graphics layer, alter the play button graphic to make it appear as if it's been selected.

4.   In frame 3 of this same layer, change the play button graphic so it looks like a pause button in its default, Up, state.

5.   Then, in frame 4, make the pause button appear selected.

Here are our buttons and the corresponding timelines if you need a guide at this point:

play button   selected play button   pause button   selected pause button

6.   In frame 1 of the actions layer add the following code for the pressActions and releaseActions functions:

```
function pressActions() {
    if (this._currentframe == 1) {
        this.gotoAndStop(2);
    } else if (this._currentframe == 3) {
        this.gotoAndStop(4);
    }
}
function releaseActions() {
    if (this._currentframe == 2) {
        _parent._parent.playS();
        this.gotoAndStop(3);
    } else if (this._currentframe == 4) {
```

continues overleaf

```
                    _parent._parent.pauseS();
                    this.gotoAndStop(1);
            }
        }
        this.onPress = pressActions;
        this.onRelease = releaseActions;
        this.onReleaseOutside = releaseActions;
        stop();
```

7. Insert a stop action in each of the remaining three keyframes in the actions layer.

    Your play movie clip's timeline should now look like this:

Pan movie clip

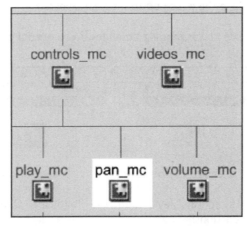

We're now going to move on and add a **pan** controller that will enable the user to control the balance of sound between left and right audio channels:

1. Start by creating a new movie clip and calling it pan.

2. Rename the default layer graphics and draw a thin rectangle shape on the stage without any fill, approximately 80 pixels wide. This graphic will form the horizontal path for the pan slider control.

3. Add another new layer called text and use the Text tool to add the appropriate 'L' and 'R' letters to either end of the slider path as we've done in the screenshot. Feel free to customize your slider path – add some level marks, for example.

4. Insert a new layer called slider and draw a shape in the first frame to represent the slider control button that the user will drag along the path:

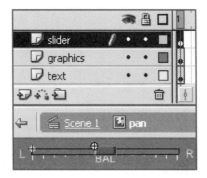

5. Next, select the slider graphic and convert it into a movie clip (Insert > Convert to Symbol), naming it horSlider (short for horizontal slider, as opposed to the volume control which will have a vertical slider), and making sure that its top left registration point is at (0,0).

6. Still in the pan movie clip's timeline, select the horSlider movie clip on the stage and give it an instance name of horSlider_mc using the Property inspector:

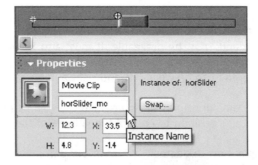

If you give a movie clip an instance names that ends in _mc in Flash MX, this will force a pop-up to appear with the properties of the MovieClip object as soon as you type the period after the instance name in the Actions panel.

Now we're going to add the ActionScript to make this slider control work.

7. Create a new layer called actions. In frame 1 add the following functions:

```
function getPan() {
    var x = horSlider_mc._x;
        if (x>=35) {
    (pan=(x-35)/35);
    } else {
    (pan=-(35-x)/35);
    }return pan;
}
function pressActions() {
    horSlider_mc.startDrag(false, 0, horSlider_mc._y, 69,
    ➥horSlider_mc._y);
    this.onEnterFrame = function() {
            _parent._parent.adjPan(getPan()*100);
    };
}

function releaseActions() {
    horSlider_mc.stopDrag();
}
this.onPress = pressActions;
this.onRelease = releaseActions;
this.onReleaseOutside = releaseActions;
```

You may notice that the pan movie clip has a similar ActionScript structure to both the stop and play movie clips. The main functional difference is that the slider bar, the horSlider movie clip which will control panning of the sound, must be draggable. It must also be able to calculate what percentage of the distance it is along the slider's path from left to right so that it can report this information back to the Sound object, altering the pan between left and right audio channels accordingly.

We're going to use these same principles when we build the volume movie clip later in the chapter, using information about the slider's position to control the volume of the Sound object.

Let's look in more detail at how this actually works in our pan movie clip.

In the ActionScript you just added to the actions layer of the pan movie clip, look at this line in the pressActions function:

```
horSlider_mc.startDrag(false, 0, horSlider_mc._y, 69, horSlider_mc._y);
```

The parameters that define the limits of how far the user can drag the movie clip to the left or right have been set to 0 and 69. This allows the user to drag the instance of the horSlider movie clip between 0 and 69 on the x-axis. As the pan control takes the form of a horizontal slider, the draggable slider button needs to be prevented from moving at all along the y-axis. This is achieved by setting both the top and bottom parameters to horSlider_mc._y.

Immediately beneath this, there is the following function:

```
this.onEnterFrame = function() {
    parent._parent.adjPan(getPan()*100);
};
```

This sets the `enterFrame` handler to pass the current percentage of the horizontal distance across the slider's path to its `_parent._parent` movie clip – remember this is the sound & video player movie clip (you can refresh your memory with the diagram illustrating the scope of the sound-video player at the start of this exercise). The next `getPan` function actually calculates this percentage value and returns it.

> In Flash MX you can now set movie clip event handlers from **any** timeline, such as the `onEnterframe` handler above.

Volume movie clip

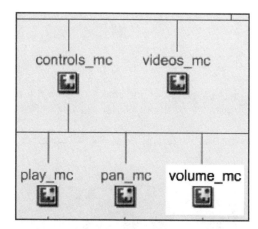

We're now going to move on and build another slider object that will form part of the sound and video player's user interface. This is very similar to the pan movie clip we've just made, only this time it'll be a vertical slider and will enable the user to control the **volume** of the sound being played:

Constructing the volume movie clip is very similar to the pan movie clip we made in the previous section.

1. Make a new movie clip symbol with a top left registration point at (0,0) and call it volume.

2. Rename the default layer graphics and draw a thin vertical rectangle with no fill to represent the slider path. Make the height of the rectangle 91 pixels and position it so that its top left corner has a y coordinate of 21.

    This graphic representing the path for the volume slider does not start at (0,0) like the pan slider in order to leave a little bit of room to add the word 'VOL' at the top.

3. Add a new layer, call it text, and use the Text tool to type in 'VOL' at the top of the slider path.

4. Still on the text layer, add in some markings along the side of the slider path, such as numbers at intervals between 0 and 100, to represent the scale of the volume:

5. Next, insert a new layer called slider and make sure it's the top layer in your timeline. In frame 1 of this layer drag an instance of the horSlider movie clip from your Library onto the stage.

6. Select the horSlider on the stage and press F8 to convert it into a movie clip symbol, naming it verSlider:

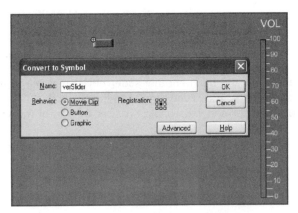

7. Double-click on the verSlider movie clip on the stage to go into Edit Symbols mode. Use CTRL+SHIFT+9 to rotate it clockwise through 90 degrees so that now looks like a vertical slider, and position it so it has a top left registration point and is aligned to (0,0).

8. Go back into the edit mode for the volume movie clip and position the verSlider at the top of the slider path:

9. With verSlider still selected, go into the Property inspector and give it an instance name of verSlider_mc:

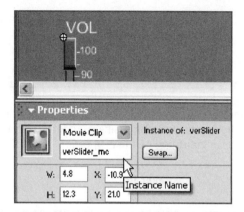

That's all of the graphics taken care of. Let's go ahead and give verSlider the ActionScript it needs to control the sound volume.

10. Insert a new layer and called actions. With the Actions panel open (F9) and frame 1 of the actions layer selected, type the following function into the Script pane:

```
function getVol() {
    return ((112-verSlider_mc._y)/91)*100;
}
```

For this volume movie clip we've used the getVol function as opposed to the getPan function. In the second line of the above script we're calculating a percentage value that is based on the _y property of verSlider_mc.

11. Now add the following code directly beneath:

```
function pressActions() {
    verSlider_mc.startDrag(false, verSlider_mc._x, 21, verSlider_mc._x, 112);
    this.onEnterFrame = function() {
        _parent._parent.adjVol(getVol());
    };
}
```

The startDrag function sets up the dimension constraints for a draggable object that limits where the user can drag the object. In the case above, the values constrain the movement of verSlider_mc along its x-axis, but allow it to move anywhere between 21 and 112 on the y-axis.

12. Finally, add the following code underneath the previous sections to complete this section:

```
function releaseActions() {
    verSlider_mc.stopDrag();
}
this.onPress = pressActions;
this.onRelease = releaseActions;
this.onReleaseOutside = releaseActions;
```

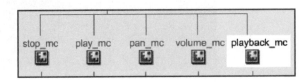

There is one small object left to build before we combine all our control objects together, and that is the **indicator bar**. This is a horizontal bar progressing from left to right across the screen as the sound or video file plays, giving the user an indication of the proportion of the file already played (and still left to play):

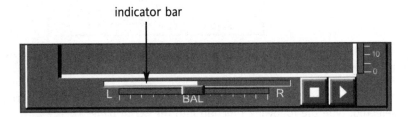

indicator bar

The indicator bar

1. Create a new movie clip symbol called soundLength with a top left registration point.

2. Rename the default layer 'actions' and insert two new layers called 'edges' and 'length'.

3. In frame 1 of the edges layer draw a thin rectangle with no fill to represent the outline of a 'window' through which we'll see the moving indicator bar. Make it 100 pixels wide and 3 pixels high, and position it so that its top left corner is at (0,0).

4. In frame 1 of the length layer draw a small, stroke-less, rectangle just inside the left-hand edge of the indicator 'window' shape you've just drawn. Scale this rectangle so that it is 2.3 pixels high and has a width of 1 pixel.

5. With this small rectangle still selected, use F8 to convert it to a movie clip symbol called 'length'. Make sure that its top left corner is at (0,0).

6. Go back into the soundLength movie clip and open the Property inspector (CTRL+F3). Give this length movie clip an instance name of bar_mc.

7. Finally, add a stop action to frame 1 of the actions layer.

You may be wondering why the indicator bar (the length movie clip) has a tiny width: it's invisible, right? The bar will be invisible when there no files playing, but if a sound or video *is* playing Flash is going to change the _width property of the bar_mc instance of length to equal the percentage played of the sound or video file. Therefore the width of the rectangle, the length movie clip, will change to directly represent how much of the currently playing file has elapsed.

We'll add the appropriate ActionScript to make the length movie clip act accordingly when we piece together the final sound-video movie clip a little later on in this chapter. For now, we're going to put together all the objects we've built so far to form the user interface.

Building the controls movie clip

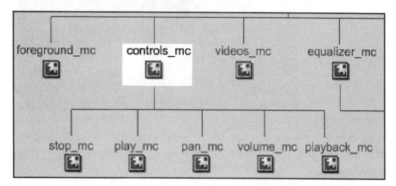

In this section, the beauty of object-oriented development will become even clearer. We're going to assimilate all the individual objects we've built so far in this chapter into one complete **controls** movie clip that will form the user interface for the sound-video player component:

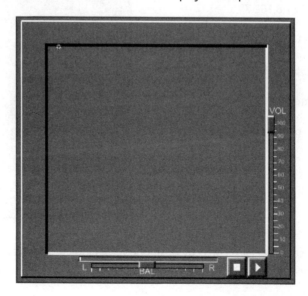

▶▶

1. Begin by creating a new symbol and call it 'controls'.

2. Inside of this controls movie clip add five layers, so that there are six layers in total, and name them 'actions', 'play_stop', 'pan', 'volume', 'indicator bar', and 'viewer' from the top downwards.

   Before we can position our objects on the stage itself we need to know the size and shape of the overall player component so we can accurately place them. We'll set this up by drawing the viewer window for the player component.

3. In frame 1 of the viewer layer, draw a graphic to represent the window outline that our video will be displayed inside. You can design any shape you like for the viewing area but here's our source file example (with dimensions and position) as a guide:

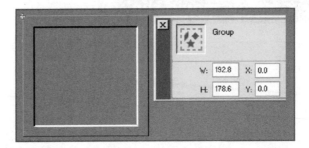

4. Next, drag out an instance of each of the play, stop, pan, volume, and soundLength movie clips from the Library and place them on frame 1 of their correspondingly named layers (with soundLength going on the indicator bar layer).

5. Now position the objects within this viewer area. In the source file these controls sit at:

   ● **play** (157.8,162.7)

   ● **stop** (142.2,162.7)

   ● **pan** (36.0,166.7)

   ● **volume** (176.2,57.1)

   ● **indicator bar** (36.5,163.7)

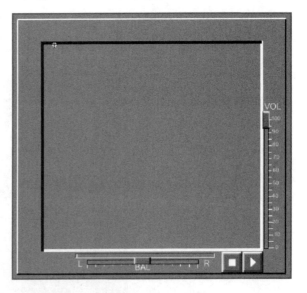

Now that these objects are correctly positioned, let's look at the ActionScript that'll link them with the sound-video player component.

As each of these movie clips will be called from the sound-video player movie clip (their _parent._parent movie clip) we need to assign instance names to all of them.

6. Use the Property inspector to give the objects instance names of 'play_mc', 'stop_mc', 'pan_mc', 'volume_mc', and give the soundLength movie clip an instance name of 'playback_mc.'

7. Finally, in frame 1 of the actions layer add the following code:

```
stop_mc._visible = false;
play_mc._visible = false;
stop();
```

This will make the stop and play buttons invisible at the start of the movie. They'll become visible once the first sound or video file has been loaded and is ready to play. The ActionScript that causes this to happen will be added later when we build the final component.

Now that we've created our controls movie clip, we'll move on to create the next object in our sound-video player, the **graphic equalizer**.

The equalizer

The equalizer (often referred to as a graphic equalizer) is a visual representation of the range of frequencies of a sound file currently playing. In our player component here, it's not going to be an exact accurate representation of what you'd see on your own typical home audio system, but it's a cool-looking effect when we construct it using ActionScript. This is what the finished equalizer will look like:

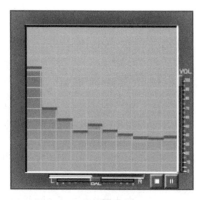

At the core of the equalizer is a set of 20 movie clips. There are 10 movie clips representing the bottom of the bars in the graph and another 10 representing the top. On the stage in the authoring file they are very small, as you can see in the screenshot below, but their height properties will be controlled by the ActionScript in the background making them move in tandem with the music.

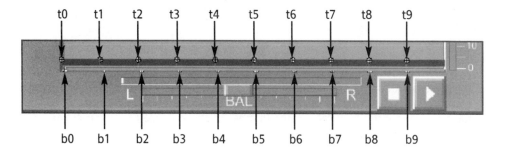

Objects for the equalizer

We're going to begin by creating the individual **top** and **bar movie clips**, and in the next section duplicate them across the bottom of the parent **bar graph** object. Here's how they'll all fit into the object hierarchy.

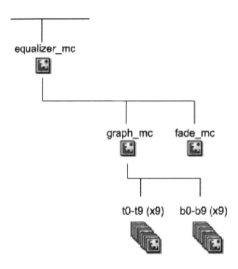

Let's begin.

1.   Create a new movie clip called 'top' with a top left registration point.

2.   In frame 1 of the default layer draw a rectangle with no stroke. Make it 15 pixels wide and 2.5 pixels high, with its top left corner aligned to (0,0).

3.   Create another movie clip and call it bar. Again, make sure it has a top left registration point.

4.   On the default layer create a simple graphic for the bar – draw a rectangle, again with no stroke, and make it 15 pixels wide and 1.1 pixels high.

5.   Open the Color Mixer panel (SHIFT+F9) and change its Alpha value to 60%.

6.   Insert a new layer called 'actions' and, in frame 1, add the following function:

```
function getNum(n) {
    return n._name.substr(1, 1)
}
```

As we said earlier, this bar movie clip is going to be duplicated so that there are ten of them across the whole width of the equalizer. When we come to actually do this later in the exercise, we'll give each one an instance name of b0, b1, b2 and so on, all the way through to b9. The getNum(n) function we've just added returns the number of the instance of the bar movie clip by taking the second character from its instance name, i.e. its number.

7. Now add this function directly beneath the previous lines of code:

```
function inv(n) {
    var x = int(getNum(n));
    return (_parent.maxHeight/2)*(1-(1/(x+1)));
}
```

This function actually computes the _y value for the height of the bar movie clip and the _y position of the corresponding top movie clip. When a sound file is played the height of the movie clips will form a nice curve from the left-most bar down to the right-most bar, to symbolize a typical stereo system that has the bass turned up louder than the treble.

8. Add the following lines of code:

```
function adjBar() {
    //adjust bottoms
    var startY = this._y;
    var dis = -startY-_parent.amplitude+adj;
    (!_parent.stopPlay) ? (this._y += dis*_parent.frc+random(11)-5) :
➡this._y--;
```

The function and variables above do all the dirty work in making the height of the bar movie clip change in proportion to the amplitude (volume) of the sound that is currently playing. If you select the bar graphic on the stage and increase the value in the height field of the Property inspector you'll notice that it adds length to the bottom of the image.

The adjBar function first computes the new height of the bar, and then it determines how to position it so that the bottom of the graphic is still aligned to the bottom of the graph. This adds the value of the variable dis (distance) to the height of the bar if it is below the current amplitude, or subtracts 1 if it is above the current amplitude.

You may be wondering why we are also calculating the value of random(11)-5 as part of the height calculation. This allows the bar to move to any _y position within 5 pixels of its original target _y position, giving the bars a more realistic effect during playback.

9. Add these next lines beneath the previous ActionScript:

```
if (_parent.stopPlay || (this._y>0)) {
    this._y=0;
}
    this._height = -this._y;
```

This code checks whether the sound is still playing and also that the height of the bar movie clip has not moved below the bottom of the graph (it passes below the bottom of the graph when its height, _y, is greater than 0).

The if statement is true if either of these two events are true. Therefore, the _y position of the bar will be set to 0 in either of these cases, making the movie clip invisible. If neither of these events are true, the last line of code simply sets the `_height` of the bar movie clip equal to the opposite of its `_y` position, making the bar graphic visible on the bar graph.

10. Add this final section of code to complete the actions for the bar movie clip:

```
//adjust tops
if (this._y< _parent["t"+num]._y){
    _parent["t"+num]._y=this._y;
    step=0;
} else {
    _parent["t"+num]._y+=step;
    step+=.90;
}
}
adj = inv(this);
num = getNum(this);
this.onEnterFrame = adjBar;
```

This simply makes the value of bar's corresponding top movie clip change to be equal to the top of the bar when the bar's height is greater than top's height. It also makes the top movie clip fall down towards the bar movie clip when the height of the bar is less then the top's height.

The falling motion is created by having top move a greater distance towards bar for each execution of the code. The final line, `this.onEnterFrame = adjBar` forces the `adjBar` function to execute every frame.

The bar graph

graph_mc

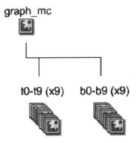

t0-t9 (x9)   b0-b9 (x9)

We're now going to take the bar and top movie clips we've just made and combine them on a grid-like background in a new movie clip object, to simulate the 'bar graph' look of a traditional graphic equalizer.

1. Begin by creating a new movie clip symbol. Call it 'bar graph', and check it has a top left registration point.

2. Add three new layers so that there are four in total. From the top down, label them 'actions', 'tops', 'bottoms', and 'grid'.

3. Draw a simple grid graphic on frame 1 of the grid layer to act as the background for our moving equalizer bars. If you're following along with the source file the dimensions are included in the screenshot.

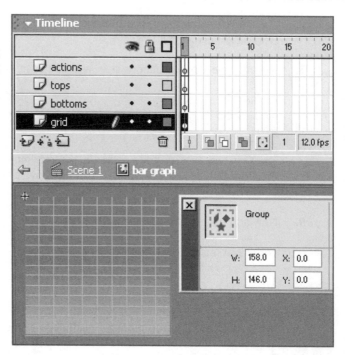

4. Select frame 1 of the bottoms layer and drag out ten copies of the bar movie clip from the Library. Use the Align panel (CTRL+K) to align them in a row on the bottom edge of the bar graph, with each instance of bar fitting snugly in its own section of the grid:

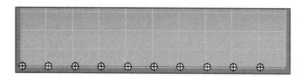

Earlier in this exercise we said that the sound-video player component was going to control these bars according to the amplitude of the sound playing. We therefore need to give each of the bars an instance name.

5. Working across the stage from left to right, use the Property inspector to give each bar movie clip an instance name, starting with b0, b1, b2, ... all the way through to b9 on the far right-hand side.

6. Select frame 1 of the tops layer, and repeat the same process – drag ten copies of the top movie clip from the Library and align them in a row directly above the bar movie clips:

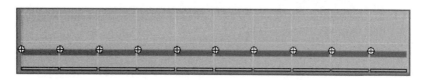

7. Then, give the top movie clips instance names of `t0`, `t1`, `t2`, ... through to `t9`, again working from left to right across the stage.

8. Select frame 1 of the actions layer and open the Actions panel. Add the following code:

```
maxHeight = 140;
minHeight = 5;
frc=.10;
```

The first two lines of code establish the maximum and minimum height values for our moving equalizer bars so that they cannot stretch above or beneath the actual grid background. The third line sets the value for friction.

9. Now add this function beneath the previous lines:

```
function stopPlaying() {
    this.stopPlay=true;
}
```

The `stopPlaying` function triggers the bar graph movie clip to set the amplitude to 0 whenever the graph is told to stop playing. This function is accessed from outside of the bar graph symbol.

10. Type in the following lines of code:

```
function startPlaying() {
    stopPlay=false;
    n=0;
    this.onEnterFrame=getAmp;
}
```

The `startPlaying` function is similar to the `stopPlaying` function in that it is a public method, but differs as it sets the `stopPlay` variable equal to false and sets the `onEnterFrame` event equal to `getAmp`.

11. Add this section of ActionScript:

```
function getAmp() {
    if (!(n%4) && !stopPlay) {
        amplitude = random(maxHeight-minHeight)+minHeight;
    } else if (!stopPlay){
        amplitude—;
    } else {
        amplitude=0;
        delete this.onEnterFrame;
        this.gotoAndStop(1);
    }
    n++;
}
this.onEnterFrame = getAmp;
```

The getAmp function *randomly* creates the amplitude and frequency for the sound files. Firstly, for every execution of the ActionScript the value of n is incremented while the sound is still playing, and then reset to 0 when the sound stops. Then, the getAmp function checks to see if the modulus of n is not equal to 0, and that the value of stopPlay is equal to false.

> *Modulus is the value of the remainder after one number is divided by another, and is represented by the % character.*

By checking to see what the remainder is after dividing two numbers, you can time an event to occur every other frame, every third frame, every fourth, and so on. In the case above, we've made Flash calculate the new amplitude value every fourth frame.

Fade-in

We're now going to make a movie clip to form a quick transitional effect when the user switches between playing back a video or sound file. To give you a clearer picture of how this'll work, imagine the user currently playing a sound file. As they listen to the sound, the graphic equalizer will be active, visually representing the sound file's attributes. Now imagine the user wants to watch a video instead.

We'll use the fade movie clip as a visual transition, making the graphic equalizer appear to fade out revealing the video screen underneath. This will also work in reverse when the user switches from video to sound playback. Here's where it sits in our overall structure:

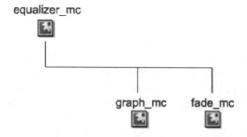

1. Create a new movie clip symbol with a top left registration point and call it 'fade'.

2. In frame 1 of the default layer draw a rectangle with a black fill and no stroke. Make it 158 pixels wide and 146 pixels high (the same size as the bar graph movie clip). Align it so that its top left corner is at (0,0).

3. Insert a new layer called 'actions'. Open up the Actions panel and add the following code to frame 1:

```
function fadeOut() {
    (this._alpha>0) ? (this._alpha -= 5) : (delete this.onEnterFrame);
}
```

continues overleaf

```
function fadeIn() {
    this.onEnterFrame = function() {
            if (this._alpha<100) {
                this._alpha += 5;
            } else {
                _parent.gotoAndStop(1);
                delete this.onEnterFrame;
            }
    };
}
this.onEnterFrame = fadeOut;
```

That's it for the fade movie clip. Let's move on to the equalizer movie clip where we'll deploy this little fade effect.

The equalizer movie clip

Remember that this is what the final equalizer movie clip will look like when it's running:

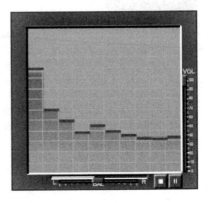

However, we don't always want the equalizer bar graph visualization to display during runtime as we'll be using this space to view our video clips. Therefore we'll make this equalizer movie clip two frames long so that the parent movie clip, the actual sound-video player component, can choose to go to either of these frames (based on user input) depending on the type of file being played: sound or video.

1.   Create a new movie clip symbol called 'equalizer' and, as always, make sure it has a top left registration point.

2.   Insert two new layers so that there are three in total and, from the top down, call them 'actions', 'graph', and 'fade'.

3.   On frame 1 of the fade layer, draw a top left-aligned black rectangle that is 158 pixels wide and 146 pixels high.

4.   Still on this layer, insert a keyframe in frame 2 and delete the black rectangle you've just drawn.

5.   With frame 2 still selected, go into your Library and drag out a copy of the fade movie clip onto the stage. Align its top left corner to (0,0) and give it an instance name of fade_mc.

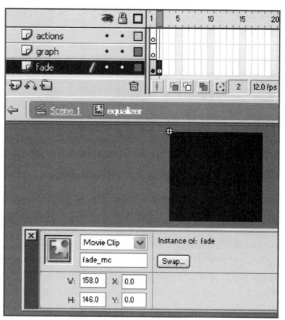

6. Insert a keyframe (F6) in frame 2 of the graph layer and drag out a copy of the bar graph movie clip from your Library. Align its top left corner to (0,0).

7. Go into the Property inspector and give the bar graph an instance name of graph_mc.

The actions for the equalizer movie clip are fortunately very simple. The parent movie clip is going to use a gotoAndStop action to determine which frame is played in the equalizer movie clip, depending on whether a sound or a video file is being played. So, all we need to do is keep the frame visible once the command from the parent movie clip has been made.

8. Insert a keyframe (F6) in frame 2 of the actions layer. Open the Actions panel (F9) and attach a stop action to both keyframes.

We're almost there now but there's something very important that's missing: where's the video?

The video files

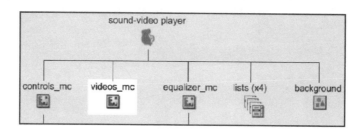

The videos movie clip acts as a kind of holding clip for all of the video content we want to use. Within this there are individual movie clips named sequentially video1, video2, and so on – one individual movie clip for each video file we want to use.

Bringing in the video

In this exercise we're going to place two video files in the in the videos movie clip to illustrate the process but you can keep adding more and more if you like. Feel free to experiment with your own video material, but if you want to stick with our example, we've included two MOV files in the download files for this chapter.

1.   Create a new movie clip symbol called 'video1'.

2.   Insert two new layers, and from the top down name these layers 'actions', 'mask', and 'video1'.

3.   Double-clicking on each layer's icon to open the Layer Properties dialog box, make the mask layer a (surprise!) Mask layer and set the video1 layer to Masked. Your timeline should now look like the one shown.

4.   In frame 1 of the actions layer add a stop action. In frame 2 insert a keyframe.

5.   Insert another keyframe in frame 2 of the video1 layer – this is where we are going to place our video file.

6.   With frame 2 still selected, go to Insert > Import... and locate a suitable video file on your hard drive. If you're following our example, import the e188-118.mov file (located in a folder called assets in the download files for this chapter).

7.   When the Import Video dialog appears, check Embed Video in Macromedia Flash document and adjust the settings in the Import Video Settings window to suit your own particular video file. In our example here, we've decreased the Quality to 80% as the source is a retro grainy piece anyway.

8. One you're happy with your settings click on OK to import the video:

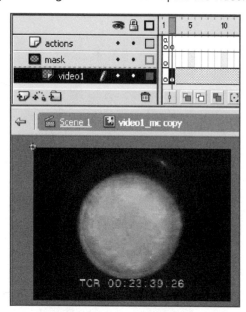

At the moment, our video is 240 pixels wide and 180 pixels high, which means the video is too large to display fully in our sound-video player. To ensure that our video fits snugly and doesn't overlap the controls movie clip or something equally disastrous, we're going to place a mask over the video that is the same dimensions as the viewing area itself. You should only really do this to tidy up any edges – any video material that is there and not showing is a potentially big waste of file-size in Flash.

> If you're using a video that you want to see all of in the viewing area, then you'll have to rescale the video while in editing Mode for video1 so that it matches the dimensions of the viewing area.

9. Insert a keyframe in frame 2 of the mask layer.

10. With frame 2 still selected, draw out a rectangle that is 156 pixels wide and 144 pixels high. Of course, it's easier to draw one roughly the right size and use the Property inspector to make sure that it's exactly right.

All through this exercise we've been aligning our movie clip objects to their top left corners. However in this case we need to think a little more carefully about aligning the mask and the video. We want the top left part of the viewable section of the video to be aligned to (0,0) so that it lines up smoothly inside the viewing area. Therefore, we need to align the *mask* shape's top left corner to (0,0) *not the video*.

11. Select your mask shape on the stage and use the Property inspector to align its top left corner to (0,0).

12. Next, select the video in frame 2 of the video1 layer and move it on the stage so that it is centrally positioned behind the mask, irrespective of its coordinates (you may find it useful to temporarily view the mask layer in outline mode).

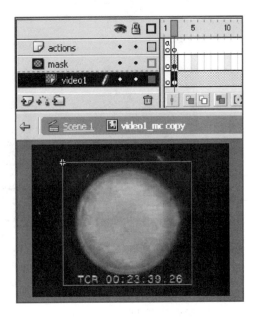

After the user has played this video we want video1 to reset itself to frame 1, ready to begin playing again if the user wants.

13. Find the last frame of your video in the timeline (frame 90 in our example). At the same frame number in the actions layer, insert a keyframe and add the following:

```
this.gotoAndStop(1);
```

14. Finally, insert blank frames (F5) in the mask layer so that it is exactly the same length as the other two layers (90 in our example). Remember to lock your layers so that the mask will function.

And that's it for the video1 movie clip. It's sitting there in the Library waiting to be built into the final sound-video player component.

We're now going to make another one of these movie clips for a different piece of video but we're going to reuse the video1 moviecip we've just made, so it won't take long.

15. Select the video1 movie clip in the Library and then use the Library menu to duplicate it. In the resulting dialog call it 'video2'.

16. Rename the video1 layer video2 and delete the existing video content from it.

Now it's just a matter of selecting frame 2 and importing a new piece of video, so let's do just that.

17. Click on frame 2, go to File > Import, and import your chosen video file. Our example file here is e188-119.mov (in the same assets folder as the previous video).

18. As a final check, make sure that all layers are extended or shortened as appropriate to match the length of your imported video. In our example, check that all frames extend to frame 122.

Our two video movie clips are now built. You can keep on repeating this same process to create more video clips, incrementing the movie clip symbol name by 1 each time, but now we've got some video content already there we'll combine it in the **videos** movie clip:

19. Create a new movie clip symbol called 'videos'.

This movie clip has a very basic structure. Each individual video clip we've made sits on frame 1 of its own individual layer with the same instance name as its movie clip, only with '_mc' appended. There are no actions involved, as they will be called directly from the sound-video player component.

20. Rename the default layer 'video1' and place a copy of the video1 movie clip in frame 1.

21. Use the Property inspector to align its top left corner to (0,0) and give it an instance name of 'video1_mc'.

Repeat these steps on a new layer for each and every video clip that you want to use.

22. In our example there is only one other video movie clip, so make a new layer called 'video2', and place a copy of video2 at (0,0). Don't forget to give it an instance name of 'video2_mc'.

That's it for our video content. To conclude this chapter we're going to move on and build the final sound-video player component

Putting everything together

This is a large section with some pretty advanced ActionScript involved but it's the final leg, and by the end of it all you'll have produced a fully-functioning sound and video player component that can be reused time and time again in your web site designs.

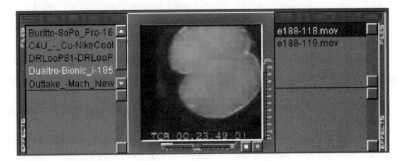

1. Begin by creating a new movie clip symbol called 'sound-video player'.

2. Add 5 new layers to the timeline. From the top downwards, label our layers 'actions', 'controls', 'videos', 'equalizer', 'scroll components', and 'background'.

3. In frame 1 of the controls layer drag a copy of the controls movie clip out of the Library. Position it at (9.2,1.5) and give it an instance name of 'controls_mc'.

4. In frame 1 of the equalizer layer, drag out a copy of the equalizer movie clip and position it at (27.5, 18.0). Give it an instance name of 'equalizer_mc'.

5. Select frame 1 of the videos layer and drag a copy of the videos movie clip out onto the stage. Position it at (27.5, 18.0) and give it an instance name of 'videos_mc'.

Now, we're going to use a built-in Flash component, the **ListBox**. There'll be four of these in our sound-video interface: two to display the sound and video files and another pair to display sound and video effects. In this chapter we are only going to use the sound and video files in the top two ListBoxes but we'll add the functionality to the effects ListBoxes so that you can simply add in your own effects if you want to take this further. The two we're using here though, are going to display a list of the sound and video files available for the user to select and play.

6. You should already have a ListBox component in your Library. With frame 1 of the scroll components layer selected, drag out four copies onto the stage. Position them on either side of the central interface, like so:

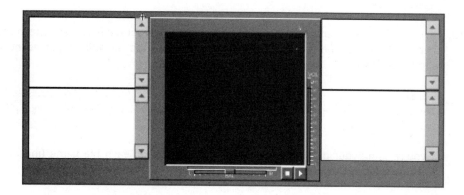

7. Use the Property inspector to make to make each ListBox 136 pixels wide and 86 pixels high.

8. Select each ListBox in turn and give them the following instance names: 'soundList (top left), 'sound_effects' (bottom left), 'videoList' (top right), and 'video_effects' (bottom right).

9. Still in the Property inspector, select each instance of the ListBox component in turn, and type 'onChange' in the Change Handler field (located under the Parameters tab).

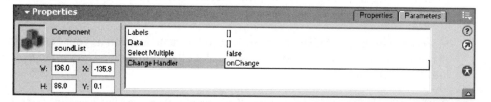

10. With the videoList instance selected on the stage, go into the Property inspector and double-click in the Labels field. In the resulting Values window use the plus button to add two fields and label them according to the names of your video files:

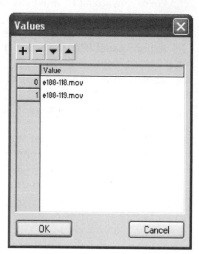

These labels appear in the ListBox component and are selectable so that the user can choose which video file is played.

For the soundList ListBox we're now going to do something a little different. We're going to dynamically call in the sound file names from a text file, where Flash will parse this and display the information within the component.

11. Open up your default text editor program, such as Notepad or SimpleText, and type in the following:

```
&soundFiles=
```

12. If you're following our example and using the download source files then type in the following lines immediately after the previous text. Due to the way the file will be parsed no carriage returns should be used.

```
Buritto-SoPo_Pro-1627.mp3|C4U_-_Cu-NikeCool-1689.mp3|DRLooPS1-DRLooPS-
1552.mp3|Dualtro-Bionic_i-1855.mp3|Outtake_-Mach_New-4417.mp3|Oddgroov-
OakLeY-1350.mp3
```

If you're using your own MP3 sound files, simply type in each file name (including its extension) that you want to use, separating each file with a '|'.

13. Once you've included all of the files you want, type in this text (again, with no carriage returns):

```
&done=true&
```

14. Save your file as list.txt and close it.

It's important at this point to think about the organization of your files for this exercise. Flash is going to look for list.txt and all of the sound and video files in a folder called assets at runtime so you need to arrange your files accordingly. If you've downloaded our source files you'll notice that they're already in a folder called assets.

15. Make sure you have a folder called assets in the same location as your FLA for this sound-video player. If you haven't already done so, move all of the source sound and video files, and list.txt into the assets folder.

We're now going to move on and tie all of our object movie clips together using ActionScript.

16. Go back into your Flash movie, and the editing mode for the sound-video player. Open up the Actions panel (F9) and select frame 1 of the actions layer. Type in the following:

```
location = "assets/list.txt";
```

This first variable is simply the location of the text file we just made, which stores the MP3 file names.

We'll now move on to set the overall 'look' of our components using ActionScript. We discussed globalStyleFormat property settings earlier in the chapter. These property settings are being listened to by the registerSkinElement that will make all of the components' background, selection, buttons, and so on, match the color settings described on the next page.

> *The next few steps involve quite a few lines of code. Obviously, it's a good idea to look at them and get an idea of what they do, but you may like to save your fingers, and cut and paste the code for steps 16 to 23 from* `Chapter_11_code.txt` *in the downloads section for the book.*

17. Add the following underneath the previous line:

```
function setStyleFormat() {
    //This function sets the skin colors of the ListBox and playback
➥buttons
    //You can optionally set the font and font size below. Note: the
➥Listbox
    //will adjust to fit an exact row based on the font and font size
➥chosen
        //
        //globalStyleFormat.textFont = "hooge 05_54"; //www.miniml.com
        //globalStyleFormat.textSize = 8;
        //
        globalStyleFormat.textColor = 0x000000;
        globalStyleFormat.background = 0x88894B0;
        globalStyleFormat.backgroundDisabled = 0xC0C0C0;
        globalStyleFormat.selection = 0x010EA3;
        globalStyleFormat.selectionDisabled = 0xC0C0C0;
        globalStyleFormat.selectionUnfocused = 0x88894B0;
        //
        globalStyleFormat.arrow = 0xFFFFFF;
        globalStyleFormat.face = 0x7080A0;
        globalStyleFormat.shadow = 0x000000;
        globalStyleFormat.darkshadow = 0x373F59;
        globalStyleFormat.highlight = 0xFFFFFF;
        globalStyleFormat.highlight3D = 0xA8B0C8;
        globalStyleFormat.foregroundDisabled = 0x7080A0;
        globalStyleFormat.scrollTrack = 0x7080A0;
        //
    globalStyleFormat.applyChanges();
}
```

18. Add the following functions:

```
function adjVol(v) {
    soundIns.setVolume(v);
}
function adjPan(p) {
    soundIns.setPan(p);
}
function resetPlayButton() {
```

```
                controls_mc.play_mc.gotoAndStop(1);
        }
        function buttonsVisible() {
                controls_mc.stop_mc._visible = true;
                controls_mc.play_mc._visible = true;

        }
```

The functions above are acting as the middlemen between the user's selection and what gets passed on to the other objects we've created so far. There is one new object introduced here, the soundIns, which is the sound Object for the player.

19. Now add this next set of functions:

```
function playS() {
    switch (kind) {
      case "sound" :
          if (soundLoaded) {
                stopSound = false;
                equalizer_mc.gotoAndStop(2);
                soundIns.setVolume(controls_mc.vol_mc.getVol());
                soundIns.setPan(controls_mc.pan_mc.getPan());
                if (pauseSound) {
                    startTime = pauseTime/1000;
                    soundIns.start(startTime);
                    pauseSound = false;
                } else {
                    soundIns.start();
                }
                equalizer_mc.gotoAndStop(2);
                equalizer_mc.graph_mc.startPlaying();
          } else {
          trace("no sound loaded");
          }
          break;
      case "video" :
          if (pauseVideo) {
                this.videoInitialize(numVideo, pauseFrame);
                pauseVideo = false;
          } else {
                equalizer_mc.gotoAndStop(1);
                this.videoInitialize(numVideo);
          }
          break;
      default :
          break;
      }
      this.onEnterFrame = run;
  }
  function stopS() {
```

```
    resetPlayButton();
    controls_mc.playback_mc.bar_mc._width = 0;
    switch (kind) {
    case "sound" :
        stopSound = true;
        pauseSound = false;
        equalizer_mc.graph_mc.stopPlaying();
        soundIns.stop();
        break;
    case "video" :
        stopVideo = true;
        pauseVideo = false;
        this["videos_mc"]["video"+numVideo+"_mc"].gotoAndStop(1);
        break;
    default :
    break;
    }
    delete this.onEnterFrame;
}
function pauseS() {
    switch (kind) {
    case "sound" :
        pauseSound = true;
        pauseTime = soundIns.position;
        equalizer_mc.graph_mc.stopPlaying();
        soundIns.stop();
        break;
    case "video" :
        pauseVideo = true;
        this["videos_mc"]["video"+numVideo+"_mc"].stop();
        pauseFrame = this["videos_mc"]
                ➥["video"+numVideo+"_mc"]._currentframe;
        break;
    default :
        break;
    }
}
```

The playS, stopS, and pauseS functions entered above are being triggered when a user clicks on either the play, pause, or stop buttons. These functions then determine whether they need to process a sound or a video clip, and what settings need to be changed.

Each instance of ListBox placed in the sound-video player movie clip earlier in this section, had their Change Handler defined as onChange in the Properties inspector. The ActionScript on the next page is set up to detect the onChange function when the user selects one of the items in the ListBox, and then perform the appropriate action:

20. Add these lines of code:

```
function onChange(component) {
    if (component._name == "soundList") {
        kind = "sound";
        var num = component.getSelectedIndex();
        _root.loader_mc.initLoad("_level0", "SOUND", "loading
➥"+soundArr[num]);
        this.soundInitialize("assets/"+soundArr[num]);
    } else if (component._name == "videoList") {
        stopS();
        kind = "video";
        equalizer_mc.fade_mc.fadeIn();
        numVideo = component.getSelectedIndex()+1;
        numOfVideos = component.getLength();
        buttonsVisible();
    }
}
```

21. We'll now add two new functions, soundInitialize and videoInitialize, that are called by the onChange handler whenever the user selects a new file and then presses the play button. Add the following:

```
function videoInitialize(n, m) {
    var x = numOfVideos+1;
    if (m == null) {
        m = 2;
    }
    while (x--) {
        if (x == n) {
            this["videos_mc"]["video"+x+"_mc"].gotoAndPlay(m);
        } else {
            this["videos_mc"]["video"+x+"_mc"].gotoAndStop(1);
        }
    }
}
function soundInitialize(path) {
    stopS();
    videoInitialize(null)
    soundIns = new Sound(this);
    soundIns.onLoad = function(success) {
        if (success) {
            resetPlayButton();
            buttonsVisible();
            soundLoaded = true;
        } else {
            trace("Download of MP3 file failed!");
        }
```

```
    };
        soundIns.loadSound(path, false);
}
```

22. Next, we'll introduce a new function called `percent` that gathers the percentage of either the sound or video file being played, so that the file can be temporarily paused by the user and Flash knows where in the file this occurred. It can then start playing the file from the correct point when the user triggers this. Add the following lines of code:

```
function percent() {
    switch (kind) {
    case "sound" :
        var num = soundIns.position;
        var denom = soundIns.duration;
        break;
    case "video" :
        var num = this["videos_mc"]["video"+numVideo+"_mc"]._currentframe;
        var denom = this["videos_mc"]["video"+numVideo+"_mc"]._totalframes;
        break;
    default :
        break;
    }
    return num/denom;
}
function indicatePlaying(p) {
    controls_mc.playback_mc.bar_mc._width = p*100;
}
```

23. The next function, `sortAssets`, splits the array that is passed in from the file `list.txt` and stores the values in `soundArr`. Add the following:

```
function sortAssets() {
    soundArr = soundFiles.split("|");
    var i = soundArr.length;
    soundList.removeAll();
    for (var x = 0; x<i; x++) {
        soundList.addItem(soundArr[x]);
    }
}
function loadAssetList(l) {
    var startTime = getTimer();
    var wait = 3000;
    loadVariables(l, "");
    this.onEnterFrame = function() {
        currTime = getTimer();
        var n = currTime-startTime;
        if (done == "true") {
```

continues overleaf

```
                    sortAssets();
                    delete this.onEnterFrame;
              } else if (n>=wait) {
                    trace("could not find asset list");
                    delete this.onEnterFrame;
              }
        };
   }
   function run() {
        per = percent();
        (per<.99) ? indicatePlaying(per) : stopS();
   }
   setStyleFormat();
   loadAssetList(location);
```

Phew! That's all of the ActionScript done now for the sound-video player movie clip. All that remains now is to finish off the graphics and we'll be ready to test our movie.

24. On the background layer, draw a rectangle around the whole player to finish off the graphic elements.

25. Go into the main timeline of your movie. Rename the default layer 'player' and drag out the sound-video player movie clip onto the stage.

26. Finally, insert another layer called 'actions' and add a stop action to frame 1. Now test your movie with CTRL+ENTER to see your full sound and video component:

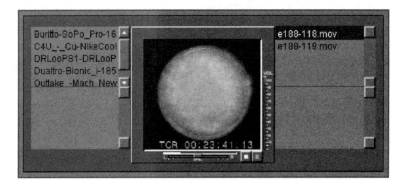

27. Save your movie and close it.

Summary

Macromedia Flash began as an animation tool with very little scripting ability. Over the course of just a few years Flash has absorbed an object-oriented programming language allowing it to become a robust web application development tool. Now users can not only reuse and customize drag and drop objects, but they can create their own objects and package them as Flash MX components.

In this chapter, you've looked at the fundamental concepts and theory behind object-oriented programming, how to adopt an object-oriented approach in Flash design, and built a full sound and video player component using objects. Not bad, eh?

If ActionScripting is your thing and you're eager to experiment even further with this component, take a look at the sound and video sequencer in the downloads section at the friends of ED web site. The player object can be adapted even further, transforming it into a sound and video sequencer where the user can simultaneously play both sound and video clips, and arrange them on a Flash-like timeline to control the order of playback.

All of this involves some quite advanced ActionScripting but we hope we've given you an insight into the amazing creative possibilities open to us when we apply ActionScript and OOP techniques to our video projects, and that you're inspired to take this even further in your Flash designs. Go forth and create.

Outro

Congratulations on making it to the end of Flash MX Video. You're now fully prepared to go out and make some cutting-edge Flash MX presentations.

You don't have to stop here, though. This book has introduced you to a number of exciting new areas, and friends of ED (www.friendsofED.com) are here to help you, whichever path you take through the world of web design.

From this book, there are two main routes that you can choose to travel down. That's not to say that you have to choose between them, though – you can always take both!

The first option is to take a closer look at the world of digital video that we introduced in Chapters 2 and 3. The shooting and preparation of digital video is a complete art in itself and **DVision**, friends of ED's own digital video imprint, is the place to explore further.

Go and take a look at www.DVision.info, and you'll see titles on all the main digital video editing packages – Premiere, Final Cut Pro, After Effects, iMovie, QuickTime Pro – as well as books like *Transitions (Voices on the Craft of Digital Editing)*.

Alternatively, you could explore the Flash MX landscape further, as we started to do in our last chapter. www.flashmxlibrary.com features the friends of ED line up for this new and exciting version. Whether you want a beginners guide such as *Foundation ActionScript*, more advanced applications of Flash as in *Macromedia Flash MX Studio*, or more, it's all there.

We don't want you to disappear at the end of this book – please tell us what you thought of the book, what we can do to improve it, and what books you'd like to see from us in future. We listen closely to feedback, and often produce books when people ask for them often enough. Mail us at feedback@friendsofed.com, or just pop around to the forums and say hi.

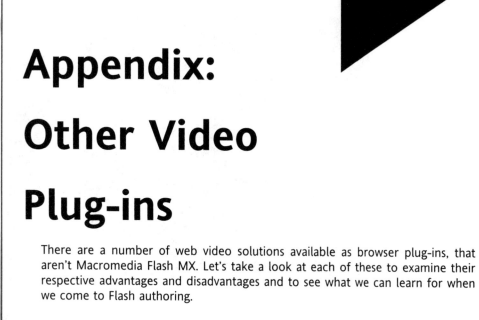

Appendix:

Other Video

Plug-ins

There are a number of web video solutions available as browser plug-ins, that aren't Macromedia Flash MX. Let's take a look at each of these to examine their respective advantages and disadvantages and to see what we can learn for when we come to Flash authoring.

QuickTime

QuickTime is a movie and sound player from Apple, which comes as a plug-in and application in one installation. When QuickTime content is displayed on the web, the QuickTime plug-in uses the application to display it:

Distribution

If you're a Mac user, you'll be fully aware of the power of QuickTime because it is an integral part of the Macintosh operating system (both OS X and Classic). If you're a PC user but don't have this plug-in, then you are likely to have seen the QuickTime logo on an enhanced music CD. The reason for this is because the choice multimedia application for producing CD-ROMs, Macromedia Director, has extensive support for QuickTime movies, enabling pop videos and other QuickTime content to be embedded within an interface. You may also have seen the logo when watching a movie trailer at www.QuickTime.com.

QuickTime comes pre-installed on all Macs and can be downloaded, or very often directly installed, from enhanced CDs for Windows or Mac.

Supported file formats

QuickTime supports a number of video file formats including **MOV** (the QuickTime standard), **MPG** or **MPEG**, and **DV**. It also supports Interactive QuickTime elements and Flash 5 **SWF** content (in QuickTime version 6 only).

Streaming

The QuickTime Streaming Server is free to run on Apple servers. An equivalent PC version, called Darwin Streaming Server, is available for free for Linux, Windows, and other servers. The QuickTime Streaming Server has been used to stream various live events including the Glastonbury Festival and the infamous Eminem chainsaw tour!

Interface

The QuickTime application interface is pretty unobtrusive, but one of the best things about QuickTime content embedded in HTML web pages is that it is virtually undetectable. You can choose whether to embed QuickTime content with or without a controller:

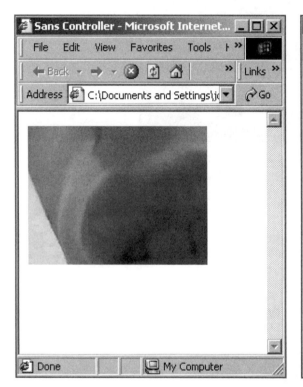
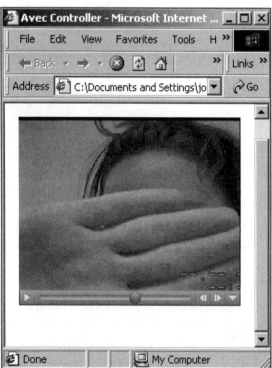

This is a very useful feature as it enables video to be seamlessly embedded within web pages and presentations. We'll soon learn that Flash MX will enable us to work in the same way, giving us the ability to enhance the user's experience into a flowing one.

Other information

You might not be aware of this, but installing the basic QuickTime application simultaneously installs the QuickTime Pro application onto your system. QuickTime Pro is unlocked by purchasing a registration key from Apple, and enables you to edit and manipulate various formats of video and sound.

RealOne Player

RealOne Player is the media player from Real Networks. A basic installation includes the RealOne Player plug-in and also the browser plug-in.

Distribution

RealOne Player is attainable by download only and the basic version is available for free. Paid for versions offer more flexibility and an end to a number of annoying pop-ups.

Supported file formats

RealOne Player has some exclusive formats such as **RAM**, **RV** (video), and **RA** (audio), as well as the ability to play all the standard web formats like MOV and MPEG. The current version has the ability to play Flash 4 SWF content.

Streaming

The sever for RealMedia can be run on PC servers for a price. The price is calculated according to the number of streams allowed at any one time. A number of BBC television programs are available to view through RealMedia streams.

Interface

The interface for RealOne Player is its major drawback. The interface is clunky and has way too many adverts and off-putting features. Also, there is the problem that it does not allow content to be easily integrated into a web site or web page. When a RealOne Player movie is launched from a web site, the RealOne Player application is opened and the movie is played back in this separate window, taking a great deal away from the user's experience.

Windows Media Player

Windows Media Player is the Windows equivalent of QuickTime.

Distribution

Windows users will be wholly familiar with this application as it is used to play everything from video files to audio CDs. As with QuickTime on Macs, Windows Media Player comes pre-installed on Windows machines and a stripped down version (for playing certain exclusive file types) can be downloaded for the Mac.

Supported file formats

Windows Media Player has a number of exclusive file formats such as **WMV**, **ASF,** and certain additions for the **AVI** format. It also supports most of the standard formats like MPEG and MOV files.

Streaming

Streaming Windows Media Player movies is free on Windows servers only, and is not available for Linux, Unix, or Mac OS X.

Interface

The application interface is unobtrusive and well categorized into different, easily navigated, areas. Unfortunately however, content embedded within a HTML page is opened up separately in the application, as with RealOne Player.

Index

The index is arranged hierarchically, in alphabetical order, with symbols preceding the letter A. Many second-level entries also occur as first-level entries. This is to ensure that users will find the information they require however they choose to search for it.

Notes

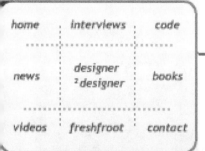

home · interviews · code

news · designer ² designer · books

videos · freshfroot · contact

friendsof ED

DESIGNER TO DESIGNER™

You've read the book, now enter the community.

friendsofed.com is the online heart of the designer to designer neighbourhood.

As you'd expect the site offers the latest news and support for all our current and forthcoming titles – but it doesn't stop there.

For fresh exclusive interviews and videos every month with our authors – the new and future masters like Josh Davis, Yugo Nakamura, James Paterson and many other friends of ED – enter the world of D2D.

Stuck with a design problem? Need technical assistance? Our support doesn't end on the last page of the book. Just post your query on our message board and one of our moderators or authors will make sure you get the answers you need – fast.

Welcome to friendsofed.com. This place is the place of friends of ED – designer to designer. Practical deep fast content delivered by working web designers.

Straight to your head.

www.friendsofed.com

Who this book is for

- Anyone wishing to use Final Cut Pro 3 to edit digital video material to a professional competence
- Aspiring and independent filmmakers
- All who require expertize in post production in the filmmaking process

What this book covers

Revolutionary Final Cut Pro 3 Digital Post Production takes readers from the digitizing of footage through to the outputting of enhanced digital video. Focussing on how Final Cut Pro 3 can be utilized with other technologies to add SFX and titling, this book imparts knowledge acquired over many years from real-world filmmakers and editors and how that applies to the color correction, real-time, and other groundbreaking functionality that Apple have included in the latest release. There is an equal emphasis on output with serious consideration given to how choice of output – broadcast, DVD, Web, film – affect workflow decisions in the edit bay.

If you're serious about making movies, for whatever reason, then you need this book.

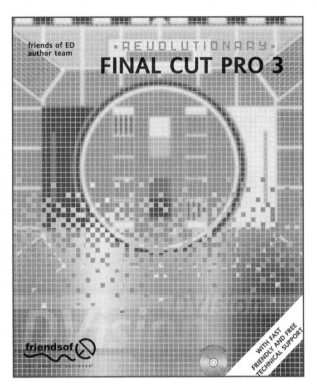

"I would like to thank you for doing this book because of the light it will shed on the editorial process."
Tina Hirsch A.C.E., President of American Cinema Editors

These words sum up much of what Transitions is about. It's a shedding of light; it's an empowerment of digital editors with the lessons and wisdom of the old ways. It speaks of the art of editing and the experience and even lifestyle of editing – showing digital editors that however shrouded in (and often obscured by) tradition and convention, this art is theirs. And it's now on the desktop – the technology has strengthened not diluted the art.

There is a great deal to being an editor. From the tricky decision of which cut to make first and the intricacies of building narrative, to the specifics of editing in genres, Transitions aims to capture the life and art of the editor, showing their overlap, indulging their differences, engaging in every author's unique experience and tapping into their hard-gotten wisdom.

Transitions is the ultimate resource for anyone who has learned the tool and wants to learn the technique, the art and the craft from the best.

Featuring an interview with Paul Hirsch – Oscar-winner for Star Wars!

www.DVisionaries.com

Foundation Flash MX

What's Covered?

This book focuses relentlessly on the core skills that you need to get you started on your journey: understanding the interface; familiarizing yourself with the creative tools and their capabilities; grasping the relationships between a Flash movie's graphical, multimedia, text, and code ingredients; gaining insight into how to put all the pieces together and hook them up with ActionScript; and using ActionScript to articulate your movies and make them truly dynamic and interactive. All these aspects (and much more) are covered in detailed tutorials and exercises, reinforced with a case study that runs throughout the book and builds into a fully functional personal web site.

Who's it for?
Anybody who has never used any version of Flash before.

Foundation Action Script for Macromedia Flash MX

One of the biggest compliments paid to a friends of ED book last year was Amazon.com's judgment that "Foundation Actionscript is perhaps one of the finest introductory programming books ever written".

With the release of Flash MX, scripting in Flash has moved from being a desirable asset to an essential skill in the world of web design. It's also become a whole lot more difficult, and the major advances with Flash MX are code based. If you're scared of the idea of code, but even more scared of missing out, this is the book for you.

This is no simple re-write - with the help of friends of ED Flash guru Sham Bhangal, Foundation ActionScript has been re-written from beginning to end, with the addition of substantial new material to reflect the major changes bought about with Flash MX.

If you've never coded in Flash, you're going to want to very soon. This book will make that desire reality, with fully worked examples and a chapter-by-chapter case study that turns into a fully fledged top ActionScript site by the end of the book.